THE OATMAN MASSACRE

The Oatman Massacre

A TALE OF DESERT CAPTIVITY
AND SURVIVAL

BRIAN McGINTY

University of Oklahoma Press : Norman

Also by Brian McGinty

Strong Wine: The Life and Legend of Agoston Haraszthy (Palo Alto, Calif., 1998)

Library of Congress Cataloging-in-Publication Data

McGinty, Brian.
　　The Oatman massacre : a tale of desert captivity and survival
　Brian McGinty.
　　　p.　cm.
　　Includes bibliographical references and index.
　　ISBN 978-0-8061-3667-7 (cloth)
　　ISBN 978-0-8061-3770-4 (paper)
　　1. Oatman, Olive Anne—Captivity, 1851.　2. Oatman, Mary
　Ann, d. 1852—Captivity, 1851.　3. Indian captivities—Southwest,
　New.　4. Apache Indians—History.　5. Mohave Indians—History.
　I. Title.

E87.O63M34　2004
979.004'9725—dc22

2004058018

This book is published with the generous assistance of the Wallace C. Thompson Endowment Fund, University of Oklahoma Foundation.

The paper in this book meets the guidelines for permanence and durability of the Committee on Production Guidelines for Book Longevity of the Council on Library Resources, Inc. ∞

To Jim Barnett
Without his help this book would not be what it is, or half as good.

"*Much of that dreadful period is unwritten, and will remain forever unwritten.*"

ROYAL B. STRATTON
Captivity of the Oatman Girls (1857)

"*We met as friends giving the left* hand *in friendship, which is held as a sacred pledge, among some tribes. I conversed with him in his own language, making many enquiries about the tribe.*"

OLIVE OATMAN
"A Narative [*sic*]" (1864)

"*She said: 'This is the last I shall see of you. I will tell all about the Mohave and how I lived with them. Good bye.' We shook hands and I saw her go off.*"

TOKWATHA ("MUSK MELON")
to Alfred L. Kroeber (1903)

Contents

Illustrations

FIGURES

MAPS

Acknowledgments

It would be impossible to name all those who helped in the research and writing of this book. I would be remiss, however, if I did not mention Ed and Dorothy Abbott of Morrison, Illinois; Camilla A. Berger of the Pomona Public Library in Pomona, California; Arba Blodgett of Redding, California; Elda Butler of the Ahamakav Cultural Society in Mohave Valley, Arizona; Walt and Dorothy Fields of Fulton, Illinois; Amelia Flores, Director of the Library and Archive of the Colorado River Indian Tribes in Parker, Arizona; Helen Matthew, Director of the Webster County Historical Museum in Red Cloud, Nebraska; Helen McMinn of the Red River Historical Museum in Sherman, Texas; and Paula Jabonler, Archivist of the History Museums of San Jose in San Jose, California.

I also received help and advice from Michael N. Landon and William W. Slaughter of the Archives Division of the Historical Department, Church of Jesus Christ of Latter-day Saints in Salt Lake City; Doris Clark of Mountlake Terrace, Washington, and Las Vegas, Nevada; Ron Romig of the Archives of the Community of Christ (formerly the Reorganized Church of Jesus Christ of Latter Day Saints) in Independence, Missouri; Steve Charter of the Department of Special Collections at the Library of Bowling Green State University in Bowling Green, Ohio; Professor Charles W. Stockton of the

Laboratory of Tree-Ring Research at the University of Arizona in Tucson; the Reverend Steven Yale, Archivist at the Graduate Theological Union in Berkeley, California; the Reverend David Samuelson of the Yreka United Methodist Church in Yreka, California; and the Reverend Andrew C. Burr, pastor, and Russ Stanhope, moderator, of the First Congregational Church in Worcester, Massachusetts.

Help in tracking research leads was provided by Linda Milligan Oatman of Hansen, Idaho; DeAnne Blanton of the National Archives in Washington, D.C.; Don Walker, University Archivist at the University of the Pacific in Stockton, California; and the librarians and staffs of the Arizona Historical Foundation in Tempe; the Arizona Historical Society in Tucson; the Arizona State Library and Archives in Phoenix; the Bancroft Library of the University of California at Berkeley; the Beinecke Rare Book and Manuscript Library at Yale University; the California State Library and Archives in Sacramento; the Hayden Library of Arizona State University in Tempe; the Huntington Library in San Marino, California; the New York State Library and Archives in Albany; the Cline Library at Northern Arizona University in Flagstaff; the Newberry Library in Chicago; the Rensselaer County Historical Society in Troy, New York; the Rochester Public Library in Rochester, New York; the Sharlot Hall Museum Library/Archives in Prescott, Arizona; the Sophia Smith Collection at Sarah Smith College in Northampton, Massachusetts; the Sutro Library in San Francisco; the University of Arizona Library in Tucson; and the Worcester Public Library in Worcester, Massachusetts.

Sincere thanks to them all.

THE OATMAN MASSACRE

Introduction

It is early February 1851. An emigrant wagon covered with a weathered canopy of canvas and drawn by two teams of malnourished oxen has just left Maricopa Wells in the northern reaches of the Mexican state of Sonora. Driven by a forty-two-year-old farmer from Illinois named Roys Oatman,[1] the wagon heads west onto a desert plateau covered with rough gravel, thickets of mesquite and paloverde, and occasional stands of saguaro cactus. In the wagon with Oatman are his thirty-eight-year-old wife, Mary Ann, and their seven children, ranging in age from two years to seventeen. Mary Ann Oatman is expecting the birth of an eighth child within a few days, so she keeps to her seat, shading her eyes from the sun and attempting to conserve her strength for the ordeal that lies ahead.

For eight days the Oatmans travel alone. All of their former companions—men, women, and children in wagons like their own who were with them when they set out from Independence, Missouri, six months earlier—have abandoned the journey, unwilling to go on with them into the forbidding desert. By February 15 the Oatmans reach the southern bank of the Gila River, the sandy waterway that then marks the border between Mexico and the United States. Three days later they find themselves atop a rocky cliff above the river, pausing to share a late afternoon meal before pushing on to their ultimate destination, the confluence of the Gila and Colorado rivers, 120 miles to the west.

As the family is finishing its meal on that fateful February 18, a band of Indians approaches on foot. After some discussion with Roys Oatman, the Indians attack the family with clubs, killing Roys, Mary Ann, and four of their children. One boy, fourteen-year-old Lorenzo, is badly bloodied and left for dead. He manages to return to Maricopa Wells and tell the white people there what has happened. Meanwhile, two of his sisters, thirteen-year-old Olive and eight-year-old Mary Ann, are taken captive and led away into the nearby mountains.

Olive and Mary Ann are held by the Indians—probably Tolke-payas, or Western Yavapais[2]—for about a year and then traded by them to the Mohaves. For four years the girls live with the Mohaves in the Mohave Valley, which straddles the Colorado River at the place where the states of California, Arizona, and Nevada later intersect. In 1855 a famine falls across the valley, and Mary Ann Oatman, then twelve years old, dies, along with many members of the Mohave tribe. Olive survives, and early in 1856 U.S. Army officers at Fort Yuma learn that she is living among the Mohaves. In February the officers bring her to the fort, where she is united with her brother Lorenzo.

The story of the "Oatman Massacre," and the capture of Olive and Mary Ann Oatman, is widely covered in the newspapers of the 1850s, and the year after Olive's arrival at Fort Yuma, it becomes the subject of a sensational book written by a Methodist minister named Royal B. Stratton. First published in San Francisco in 1857 but reissued in New York in 1858, Stratton's *Captivity of the Oatman Girls* becomes a best seller throughout the United States. After Olive and Lorenzo Oatman leave the West for New York in 1858, Olive goes on the lecture circuit, telling audiences from New York to Illinois the story of her experiences. Her lectures help to keep Stratton's book on the best-seller list and make her a celebrity.

This, in barest outline, is the story of the "Oatman Massacre," one of many tragic dramas in the history of the American West but one that has reverberated in the southwestern desert for more than a century and a half. Since the day Royal Stratton's *Captivity of the Oatman Girls* appeared in 1857, a good part of the American reading public has been fascinated with the Oatmans' story. The book was one in a long series of "Indian captivity narratives" that, from the late seventeenth century on, enthralled readers with tales of white Americans (usually young, sexually vulnerable females) snatched from their homes and families to endure unimaginable horrors at the hands of the "savages."[3] Like many other such narratives, *Captivity of the Oatman Girls* was a curious mixture of fact and fantasy, written by a minister of the gospel to demonstrate the superiority of the Christian religion over the "superstitions" of "pagans" and thus permeated with a glaring anti-Indian bias. Unlike its predecessors, the story appeared at a time when newspapers were reaching the reading public from one end of the country to the other with an efficiency and rapidity unimaginable only a few years earlier. Communities of enterprising news gatherers had, in the early 1850s, established themselves in San Francisco and Los Angeles, where reports from all over the West were collected and packaged for prompt distribution; mail shipments from the Pacific to the Atlantic Coast (carried by oceangoing steamships and Panamanian mule trains) quickly disseminated western news, including reports of confrontations between whites and American Indians, to all parts of the country. Further, the venue of the Oatman story—the vast, still largely unknown southwestern desert—was just beginning to capture American imaginations in the older and more settled regions. It is hardly surprising that after news of the attack on the Oatmans first broke, Americans throughout the country were anxious to know more about the perpetrators of the massacre and the captors of Olive and little Mary Ann, impatient to hear every grisly detail of the family's bloody encounter with the southwestern Indians.

For almost ten years *Captivity of the Oatman Girls* enjoyed brisk sales, and even after it lost popularity with the general public, it was still widely read by students of western history. Beginning in the twentieth century, a succession of reprint editions appeared, each differing a little from the original but following the basic outlines of the text that Royal Stratton delivered to his first pubisher in San Francisco. It mattered little that the book was never very good—that the author's ponderous writing style made it difficult for most readers to get through the text without annoyance, that the book's anti-Indian bias was almost suffocating, or that it strayed repeatedly from the factual record of the Oatman tragedy as it could be determined from diaries, letters, and contemporary news reports. *Captivity of the Oatman Girls* told a very good story, even if it did not tell it well, and the appeal of the story itself accounted for its persistent popularity. Nearly 150 years after the first copy was sold in a San Francisco bookstore, the book was still in print and still attracting readers from one end of the country to the other.

But at the dawn of the twenty-first century, it is impossible for an intelligent reader to examine Stratton's book without asking a whole host of questions. How would the Oatman story read if it was stripped of its heavy baggage of prejudice and supplemented with modern research into the historical record? How did Stratton's obvious contempt for the Indians twist his narrative? Did the Mohaves, as the minister insisted, respect Olive Oatman's virginity during the four years she lived among them, refusing to subject her to the least "unchaste abuse"? Or did she, according to rumors that circulated in and out of the Mohave Valley before and after she left there, take a Mohave husband and give birth to a half-Mohave child, or (by some reports) children, whom she was forced to leave behind when she left the valley to return to the world of white Americans?

I began research for this book in the hope that the true facts of the Oatman story could be discovered beneath the accumulated misinformation of a century and a half. A handful of writers—some scholarly, some more driven by the imperatives of a "good story" than a respect for historical facts—have attempted over the years to recast the narrative in a format and style that would convincingly answer the questions raised by Stratton's book. None has been very successful. This is not surprising, for many of the factual leads have grown cold or completely disappeared. Some of the most prominent characters in the story have seemingly vanished altogether from the historical record. Tracking down the Oatmans has been much like detective work, hunting for bits of evidence and, when they are found, pursuing them wherever they may lead.

In pursuing the evidence, I have not forgotten that the existing historical record was written almost exclusively by whites. There is no doubt that Indians who lived along the Gila and Colorado rivers in the 1850s knew much about the attack on the Oatman family and the subsequent fates of Olive and Mary Ann Oatman; that they (or at least some of them) knew of the circumstances that led up to the massacre and how, where, and by whom the girls were taken captive; that they knew what happened to the girls during the time they lived in the Mohave Valley and why Olive ultimately left the valley and returned to the world of the whites. But, except for a few Indian statements passed on, hearsay fashion, by whites, the Indian side of the story has largely been lost.

Notwithstanding this, a good deal is known of the history of the southwestern Indians in the mid-nineteenth century, and some Indian statements that might help explain what happened to the Oatmans have survived. I have incorporated this history and these statements (or so much of them as are relevant to the Oatmans) in the following pages so that the story I tell will fairly reflect not just the experiences of the Oatman family but also those of the Indians who came in contact with them while they were in the southwestern desert.

This book also tells a part of the Oatman story that Royal Stratton chose to ignore and that subsequent writers have dealt with only tentatively, if at all. *Captivity of the Oatman Girls* contains not even a hint that Roys Oatman and his family were Mormons and that the westward journey that brought them to the banks of the Gila River in February 1851 was motivated by a quest for the "Land of Zion" proclaimed in Mormon revelation. The Oatmans had been Mormons since the days of the prophet Joseph Smith, Jr.; after Smith was assassinated, they rejected Brigham Young's bid to succeed him as president of the Church of Jesus Christ of Latter-day Saints. Setting out on a restless search for other leadership, the family moved from a prairie farm in Hancock County, Illinois, to the Cumberland Valley of Pennsylvania, back again to Illinois, and finally to Independence, Missouri, where they joined a company of coreligionists led by James Colin Brewster, the self-appointed prophet of the "Church of Christ of Latter Day Saints, or Saints of the Last Days."[4] A "seer and revelator" in the tradition of Joseph Smith, Brewster claimed that he had discovered, in "lost books" of the Old Testament prophet Esdras, directions to the Mormons' true "gathering place." He said that the Saints would build their "Zion" at the confluence of the Gila and Colorado rivers, at a place Esdras referred to variously as the "Land of Bashan," "Cedonia," the "Land of Peace," and "California."[5] (Before September 9, 1850, when California was admitted to the Union as the thirty-first state, its eastern half overlapped the western section of New Mexico—no boundary having yet been established—and included most of what later became Nevada and Arizona.) In this book I refer to Brewster's "gathering place" as "Bashan" to follow what seems to have been his preference and to avoid confusion.

The main body of Mormons under Brigham Young had found their own Zion in the Valley of the Great Salt Lake almost four years before Brewster's followers left Independence in search of Bashan. The "Salt Lake Mormons," as some called them, had rejected Brewster's bid for Mormon leadership (they dismissed his followers as "Brewsterites," while the latter, in turn, rejected Young's flock as "Brighamites"). Some Mormon historians would later attempt to create the illusion that near unanimity reigned in the "Latter-day Saint" movement in the wake of Joseph Smith's assassination. In fact many Mormons were unsure of their future at that troubled juncture of their church's history. Their faith in the *Book of Mormon* unshaken, they were nevertheless unconvinced that Young was Smith's rightful successor and anxious, almost desperate, to find some other leader. To a small number of Mormons, including Roys Oatman and his family, Brewster was the answer to their prayers.

I briefly recount some of the early history of Joseph Smith's Latter-day Saints and, in greater detail, some of the history of James Colin Brewster's Saints of the Last Days because both histories are basic to the tragedy that befell the Oatmans. Smith's life story has been told and retold countless times, and although parts of it remain controversial, readers familiar with it will find no new revelations here. Brewster's peculiar story is more obscure and more in need of telling here. Both histories are intimately tied to the Oatman story in at least two important ways.

First, Smith's life paralleled Roys Oatman's in several notable particulars. Both men were born on farms in south-central Vermont in the early nineteenth century; both moved with their large families to western New York when they were still boys; both lived for a time in Ohio and Illinois; and the lives of both men eventually became intertwined with a new, quintessentially American religious movement, Smith as its prophet and Oatman as one of its priests. In western Illinois in the early 1840s, Oatman lived not more than thirty miles from Smith and his growing flock of Saints. James Colin Brewster was first a follower of Smith, then an imitator, and finally a pretender to the mantle of his church's leadership. Second, the religious pilgrimage that brought the Oatman family to the southwestern desert in 1851 was a direct product of Smith's and Brewster's leadership. Without their prophecies the Oatmans would never have set out on their chimerical, and ultimately fatal, quest for Bashan. If they had not been Mormons, they would not have believed implicitly in the promise of a "gathering place" in a remote and desolate corner of North America. If they had not been Brewsterites, they would not have found themselves in a covered wagon on the banks of the Gila River on February 18, 1851, vulnerable to attack by Indians. I am not the first to note the close ties between the Oatmans and early Mormon history. More than half a century ago Dale L. Morgan, an eminent historian of the American West (and one born and raised in the Mormon tradition), identified this link: "The history of Brewster's church cannot be written without taking account of what befell the Oatmans."[6] Conversely, the history of the Oatmans cannot be written without taking account of Brewster's church.

I have also included brief descriptions of the Indian peoples who inhabited the Gila country in the mid-nineteenth century, including the territories they occupied and the lifestyles they followed. These peoples—Apaches, Yavapais, Akimel O'odham (or Pimas), Tohono O'odham (or Papagos), Maricopas, Quechans (also called Yumas), and Mohaves—lived along and near the Gila in a kind of uneasy peace, interrupted periodically by bloody conflicts, for hundreds of years before the Spanish arrived in the region in the sixteenth and seventeenth centuries. The arrival of large numbers of Americans in the nineteenth century added a new and unpredictable component to the region's already volatile ethnic mix. The Indians the Oatmans encountered when they traveled along the Gila, the tribal territories they crossed, and the Native cultures they observed are all keys to understanding what happened to the family on that tragic afternoon in February 1851. Since the attacking Indians were never incontrovertibly identified (it is likely but by no means certain that they were Tolkepayas), it is useful to pay some attention to the native communities in the vicinity in order to determine how they interacted with other peoples, including intruders, and what motivations they might have had to attack an emigrant family traveling along the river.

The history of the American West is long and, to its students, ceaselessly fascinating. For nearly two centuries white Americans have delighted in telling and retelling this history, which seems to so many of them to demonstrate the best qualities of their people— their boldness, determination, resourcefulness, persistence, courage. For these people, the history has been heroic. For the Indians of the region, the history has inevitably been less so. For them, the theme of the history was not the "winning of the West" but the "loss of our homelands." The Indian history of the West, no less than the white history, was marked by boldness, determination, resourcefulness, persistence, and courage. But these qualities were not enough for the Indians to prevail. The positive aspects of the Indian history were obscured by countless defeats, innumerable humiliations, and in the end, the harsh fact of white domination. But for all the peoples of the region—Europeans and Native Americans, whites and Indians— the history has been punctuated with missteps, disappointments, defeats. The story of the Oatman family is one of the tragedies of the American West. It is neither the least nor the greatest in the region's history, but for those who experienced it firsthand—the Oatmans, their loved ones, the whites and Indians who tried to help them, and the Native people who were ultimately blamed for the calamity—it was tragic beyond dimension.

This book is a narrative history. It tells the story of the Oatman family from their origins in New England through their years in New York and Illinois, their experiences with the Mormons, and their fateful encounter with southwestern Indians. It traces the lives of Olive and Lorenzo Oatman to their deaths and concludes with a discussion of the deep marks the Oatmans and their desert experiences made on the history of the Southwest and of the United States. In telling the Oatman story, I have chosen those facts that best delineate the experiences of the family and the Indians they clashed with. In many cases, my choices have been limited by the paucity of available evidence. In no case, however, have I taken liberties with the facts: no anecdote has been manufactured, no incident imagined, no word of dialogue invented to make the story more dramatic. This is history, not historical fiction, however strange it may at times seem.[7]

Geographically, the story of the Oatmans ranges widely over the United States—from the nation's northeastern corner to its southwestern extremity, from the plains of the upper Midwest to the hills and valleys of Texas, from the Pacific to the Atlantic. But much of it focuses on the narrow corner of the great desert that lies along the Gila and Colorado rivers. The story unfolds on the banks of those rivers, in the Mohave Valley, and in the mountains that wall the rivers and the valley off from the surrounding desert. Here a family of dissident Mormons clashed with American Indians in the middle of the nineteenth century. And here we must look for answers to the questions the tragic story raises.

CHAPTER 1

The Family

The story of the Oatmans begins far from the southwestern desert—nearly a continent away, in the southwestern corner of Vermont, in a wooded valley where white settlers had, late in the eighteenth century, begun to clear timber and put up fences on land wrested from the Western Abenakis, a fishing and hunting people of the northeastern woods. There were a good number of Oatmans in Vermont's Rutland County when Roys Oatman was born in the first decade of the nineteenth century—enough to give his mother and father a sense that their home, though far from the population centers of New England, was secure and that their newborn would grow to manhood unmolested by "marauding Indians."

The Oatmans were descended from Dutch emigrants who had arrived in New York from Holland at the end of the seventeenth century. Their first American ancestor was a gold- and silversmith named Johannes Outman [sic] who with his wife, Femmetje Koch, worshipped in New York's Dutch Reformed Church. In the early eighteenth century, Johannes Outman's descendants began to migrate into neighboring colonies, first Connecticut, then, sometime after 1749, Vermont. The first Outman to make his home in Vermont was Johannes's grandson George, who settled in the town of Arlington about 1760. George and his son George Jr. (who Americanized the spelling of the family name to "Oatman") both fought in the American Revolution on the side of the colonists. After the war, the son moved to the Rutland County village of Middletown, where he cleared a plot of forest that became known as the Oatman Farm. George Jr.'s son Lyman married Lucy Hartland of Middletown on November 27, 1801, then set about raising a large family that eventually included twelve boys and five girls. Roys, the fourth child and the third son of Lyman and Lucy Hartland Oatman, was born on or near the Oatman Farm on an unrecorded date in 1809.[1]

The Oatmans had apparently abandoned the Dutch Reformed Church of their ancestors sometime before they moved to Vermont, for George Sr. was a practicing Anglican by 1747. But the communion of the English kings and queens proved no more durable an association for the Oatmans than the Dutch faith, and sometime around the turn of the nineteenth century, they were caught up in a new religious fervor that swept over the hills and valleys of Vermont. This was the "rule and method" developed in England by the brothers John and Charles Wesley and planted in the United States when the first "Methodist" bishop in North America was installed at Baltimore in 1784. The first Methodist minister appeared in Middletown in 1801, and though a permanent Methodist church was not built for many years (the town's two oldest churches were the Congregational and the Baptist), there was a flurry of Methodist activity early in the new century—study classes, sermons given by itinerant ministers, and camp meetings. Much of the local enthusiasm for Methodism was inspired by a compelling if eccentric preacher named Lorenzo Dow, who traveled widely along the Atlantic seaboard. Dow spoke outdoors, sometimes for as long as three hours at a time and always held his audiences rapt. He often closed his perorations with a parting promise: "One year from this day, at 2:00 P.M., I will preach here again." The people laughed at his audacity in setting an appointment so far in advance and dismissed him as "Crazy Dow"; but a year later to the day, who should appear in town at the appointed hour but Lorenzo Dow? As the expected crowd gathered round him, the preacher shouted with evident pleasure, "Crazy Dow is with you once again."[2]

Roys Oatman's grandfather George Jr. converted to Methodism, and Roys's uncle Eli Oatman was one of the founders of the Methodist Episcopal Society in Middletown. Roys was also a Methodist, and when his oldest son was born in 1836, he named him Lorenzo Dow Oatman, in honor of the itinerant minister who had preached in Middletown during his youth.[3]

Though the mountains and valleys of Vermont were often breathtakingly beautiful, much of the soil was far from fertile. To farm previously untilled land, Vermonters had to clear it of its dense tree cover and haul away the rocks that choked the ground. Settlers also found that the weather in Vermont could be harsh. The summer of 1816, when Roys Oatman was seven, was particularly cold, with snow in June and a hard frost in July that wiped out crops across the state (for years after, Vermonters called this year "eighteen hundred and froze to death"). The Oatman family left Vermont not long after this disaster to settle on a new farm near the town of Locke in western New York.

Locke was eight miles south of Lake Owasco, one of the long, narrow Finger Lakes of western New York. The family that Lyman and Lucy Hartland Oatman brought to Locke was large, though, judged by the standards of the time, not extraordinarily so. When the United States census taker visited their home in Locke in 1820, he found ten Oatmans in residence, eight of whom were minor children and two who were adults.[4]

Roys Oatman probably did not stand out from his siblings in this ample brood. Like his brothers, he worked on his father's farm, rising early in the morning, retiring early at night, perhaps stealing a few hours at the end of the day to read a book by candlelight. He attended school, at least for a while, and acquired a fairly good education.

During the spring and summer, he spent most of the daylight hours working in the fields, following the directions of his older brothers and father. It is unlikely, however, that he did this with much joy. Years later, his children remembered him as a cheerful man with an optimistic outlook on life. But men and women who traveled with him on the western trail knew he could be difficult: he did not like to follow orders; he had an obstinate turn of mind; and once he had set his mind on a course of action, it seemed that he would rather suffer some calamity than back down.

Life in Locke was not much different from that in any small northeastern town during Roys Oatman's boyhood. If the routine of farmwork was dull, it was enlivened by an exciting, at times even frightening, religious life. In western New York, Congregationalists, Baptists, Methodists, and Presbyterians vigorously contended for members. On Sundays preachers lectured their congregations about the virtues of Bible study, and on hot summer evenings they retreated to tents at the edges of the towns and urged their audiences to repentance. Revivals swept across western New York with such regularity that the region came to be called the "Burned-Over District," a place where the fires of faith and devotion burned hot and repeatedly. The evangelical fervor of western New York was reflected in other parts of the United States, as traveling preachers exhorted the population to piety, laying the foundations for new denominations (among them the "Millerites," later renamed the Seventh-Day Adventists, and the "Campbellites," or Disciples of Christ) and raising existing sects to new prominence (Methodism exploded from just over a thousand members in 1773 to one million in 1844, making it the largest denomination in the United States). Religious feeling reached a pitch not seen since the "Great Awakening" of the 1730s and 1740s, prompting historians to describe the period as America's "Second Great Awakening."

The Oatmans were not immune to the religious ferment of the time. If they were already committed to Methodism, the tent revivals of the itinerant Methodist ministers no doubt stimulated their faith, while meetings conducted by other preachers hinted at the wider world outside the revival tents.

The Oatmans remained in Locke for a dozen or more years. Although western New York must have seemed a vast improvement over the rocky hills and valleys of Vermont, it was hardly an earthly paradise. The completion in 1825 of the Erie Canal (which crossed the Finger Lakes region just thirty miles north of Locke) gave western New Yorkers hope of new prosperity, but when towns and cities along the canal did not grow as rapidly as expected, settlers began to talk of moving farther west. A steady stream of settlers left New York in the 1820s and 1830s for the Ohio River Valley. The Oatmans joined this throng, leaving Locke probably in the early 1830s. They may have lived for a short time in Ohio but soon moved across Ohio and Indiana to Illinois.

They found a tract of land in the western part of Illinois, on a prairie between the Illinois and Mississippi rivers. There, in the town of Franklin—later renamed La Harpe, after an early French trapper—in Hancock County, about fifteen miles from the Mississippi and twenty-five miles northeast of Keokuk, Iowa, Lyman and Lucy Oatman built a one-and-a-half-story log cabin and fitted it up as a public inn. The business prospered, and by 1836 they were able to buy two lots across the road and put up a larger building that they called the Tremont Hotel.

It is not clear whether Roys was with his parents when they first arrived in Illinois or he came on a little later. He was by this time an adult, capable of choosing his own home and the woman he wanted to share it with. In 1832, the year he turned twenty-three, he married Mary Ann Sperry, the eighteen-year-old daughter of Joy and Mary Ann Lamont Sperry of Trumbull County, Ohio. The marriage took place in the Sperry's home in Mecca, Ohio.[5]

Like the Oatmans, the Sperrys had pursued a steady westward course in the early years of the nineteenth century. Mary Ann's mother was born in New York and her father in Massachusetts, but they had all moved into northeastern Ohio sometime before 1820. Roys Oatman did not cut a very impressive figure: though no pictures have survived, his children recalled that he was not much above five feet tall and had a round face and black hair. But the Sperrys were probably satisfied with the match, for in the same year that Roys and Mary Ann were married, Roys's sisters Florella and Lorania both married Sperry boys. Bound by three marriages, the Oatman and Sperry families would follow closely parallel paths in the years that followed.

If Roys had not moved to Illinois before his marriage, he arrived soon thereafter, settling in the same Hancock County township as his parents. He bought land on the prairie and set about farming it but, after a couple of years, opened a store in La Harpe. Mary Ann presented him with children almost with the regularity of prairie corn crops. A daughter, Lucy, was born in August 1834, and a son named Lorenzo Dow in July 1836. A second daughter, Olive Ann, was born on September 7, 1837. Mary Ann, named for her mother, followed in 1843, Roys Jr. in 1846, Charity Ann in 1848, and Roland in 1849. Before they left Illinois, Roys and Mary Ann Oatman were the parents of seven children.[6]

Meanwhile the prairies of western Illinois were filling with settlers. Wagons heavy with grain raised clouds of dust as they rolled along country roads cut through fields of corn and wheat. Steamboats from the delta country of Louisiana docked along the shore of the Mississippi to discharge traders, speculators, and freight and receive cargos of grain. In Hancock County, as elsewhere in western Illinois, towns were growing rapidly. Joy and Mary Ann Sperry, Mary Ann Oatman's parents, moved from Ohio in 1836, settling on a farm in Adams County, just south of Hancock. Within the year, however, they moved on to La Harpe, where Joy built a house and took up a small farm. While his unmarried sons, William,

Aaron, Charles, and Harrison, helped with the farmwork, Joy worked in and around La Harpe as a carpenter and millwright.[7]

The character of western Illinois changed dramatically in April 1839, when a charismatic former Vermonter named Joseph Smith, Jr., settled at the western edge of Hancock County, about thirty miles from La Harpe. Smith was well-known to the Oatmans and Sperrys before he came to Illinois, for he had achieved an astonishing celebrity (some called it notoriety) as the self-proclaimed prophet of a religious sect officially designated the "Latter-day Saints" (or "Saints of the Latter Days") but informally known to most Americans as Mormons.

Like Roys Oatman, Smith was a native of Vermont (he was born in 1805 in Sharon, about forty miles northeast of Oatman's birthplace in Middletown). Like the Oatmans, the Smiths were farmers who had struggled year after year to extract a living, first from Vermont's rocky soil and then, after 1816, from land near Palmyra in western New York, less than fifty miles from the Oatman farm at Locke. From western New York the Smiths had moved farther west, to Ohio, then to Missouri, and finally to western Illinois. But beyond those superficial resemblances, the story of Joseph Smith's life could hardly have been more different than Roys Oatman's—or that of almost any other young American of his generation.

From an early age, Smith evinced an extraordinary gift for spiritual (some might say magical) insights. He used "seer stones" (polished rocks with some of the same properties as crystal balls) to see "ghosts, infernal spirits, [and] mountains of gold and silver" buried in the ground. When only twenty-five years old, he published his celebrated *Book of Mormon,* a "volume of holy scripture" that he had "translated" from golden plates he found buried in the side of a hill near his father's farm. The *Book of Mormon* purported to be a history of ancient peoples who fled Jerusalem about 600 B.C. and later settled in North America, where Jesus visited them after his resurrection. Two of these peoples, the Nephites ("a white and delightsome people") and the Lamanites ("a dark, a filthy and a loathsome people"), engaged in a long series of wars concluding in the Lamanites' defeat of the Nephites. Smith was secretive about his golden plates, concealing them in a locked box so skeptics could not examine them, hanging a curtain across the room in which he worked at his translation so no one could see the process by which he transformed the "reformed Egyptian" characters on the plates into something that resembled the English style of the King James Bible. His New York neighbors were first amused, then puzzled, and finally out-raged by the *Book of Mormon*. While some were willing to dismiss it as a piece of harmless fiction, others branded it an "impudent fraud" and "blasphemy."

The scorn heaped on the *Book of Mormon* did not seem to bother Smith's own family, who embraced it as "the word of God," or the family members and friends who, in April 1830, helped him found his "Church of Christ"—later renamed the "Church of Jesus Christ of Latter-day Saints"—at Fayette, New York, about twenty-five miles from the Oatman farm at Locke. Now calling himself a "Seer, a Translator, a Prophet, an Apostle of Jesus Christ," Smith took the headquarters of his church to Kirtland, Ohio, about thirty miles east of Cleveland, where he and his followers built a handsome stone temple. At the same time, however, he sent a colony of the faithful to western Missouri, where, according to one of the many revelations he received directly from the Almighty, they were to build their "New Jerusalem" or "City of Zion"—the "place of gathering" that would be the center of the "kingdom of God on earth."[8]

But Smith's "Saints"—or as other Americans now habitually referred to them, Mormons—aroused opposition wherever they went. In Ohio in 1838 Smith and several of his followers were tarred and feathered and then run out of the state. In Missouri differences between Mormons and "gentiles" (as Smith called all those who did not accept his leadership) led to angry arguments, battles, and finally a "war" that did not end until the Prophet and about five thousand of his followers fled into Illinois in April 1839.

Most Illinoisans welcomed the Mormons to their midst, believing that they had been treated shamefully in Missouri. Still determined to build a "New Jerusalem" on the western frontier, Smith acquired a tract of land on the Mississippi about thirty miles west of La Harpe, named it Nauvoo, and began to transform it into another "City of Zion." As the foundations of an imposing temple were dedicated, Mormons from all over the country began to "gather" to the place. When the population topped eleven thousand, with a third more in the outlying areas of Hancock County, Smith's followers boasted that their "New Jerusalem" in Nauvoo was the largest city in Illinois.[9]

No one now knows precisely when or under what circumstances Roys Oatman and his family became Mormons. Years later Mary Ann Oatman's brother Charles Sperry recalled that their father, Joy, joined the church in the summer of 1839, shortly after Joseph Smith's arrival in Hancock County and that "part of the family" followed him at about the same time. The Oatmans, however, may not have joined the Latter-day Saints until about a year and a half later, when Mormon elder Z. H. Gurley spent several weeks in La Harpe proselytizing for "Zion." In March 1841 the church's official newspaper in Nauvoo, the *Times and Seasons,* reported that, in only six days, Gurley had the "unspeakable privilege" of baptizing fifty-two residents of La Harpe (all by the prescribed Mormon ritual of total immersion) and that there was "a prospect of great accessions to their number."[10] That the Oatmans were attracted to Mormonism is not surprising, given the enthusiasm with which they had embraced Methodism when it was new (Joseph Smith himself had once attended Methodist camp meetings). After a branch of Smith's church was organized in La Harpe, the town quickly took on the character of a Mormon village. There was almost constant contact between La Harpe and Nauvoo, and inhabitants eagerly read Mormon tracts and newspapers.

Though Mormonism was thriving in Hancock County, the same could not be said of all the Mormons themselves. Life on the western frontier could be hard, and wresting a living from a country where the winters were harsh and economic conditions unpredictable was a challenge. There were periodic financial crises, some precipitated by local conditions, others linked to events in distant parts of the United States. The financial panic that struck New York and other eastern cities in 1837 was the most frightening that the young republic had yet experienced, and its effects were soon felt throughout the country. On the western frontier, paper money became worthless and mortgage foreclosures were rife. An economic depression ensued that lasted for several years. Olive and Lorenzo Oatman later remembered that the hard times of 1842 and 1843 bore down heavily on their father. Unable to pay his debts, he tried to sell his land but found no market for it. Eventually his creditors resorted to legal process against him. Admitting financial failure, Oatman gathered his family and headed out of Hancock County to seek a new home in some other part of the country.[11]

His destination was an infant city near the southern tip of Lake Michigan called Chicago. Though not yet as large as Nauvoo, the city was strategically situated astride a major east-west trade route. Roys taught school, but he was not happy in Chicago and, after about a year, moved his family back to western Illinois.

The Oatmans may have returned to La Harpe, at least for a while. Their Oatman and Sperry relatives still lived in the town and could have helped them reestablish their home; and in La Harpe they could have renewed their commitment to Mormonism. The population of Latter-day Saints was still growing rapidly in Hancock County, though gentile opposition was also increasing. The Mormons in and around Nauvoo as a whole impressed their non-Mormon neighbors as hardworking people, and even their detractors confessed admiration for their religious devotion. Yet there was something about the Mormons that aroused resentment. It was not just that they held unconventional religious beliefs: radical religious sects were legion in the nineteenth-century United States, but none aroused as much opposition as the Latter-day Saints. Perhaps it was their stubborn insistence that they alone were God's "chosen people"; perhaps it was the suspicion that Smith was laying plans to seize political as well as religious power and unite church and state in a "kingdom" with himself as its head. More than anything else, it may have been the growing awareness that Smith and some of his closest followers were engaging in sexual practices that not only offended prevailing moral principles but also violated Illinois law. Smith never publicly defended polygamy (or what he preferred to call the "principle of plural marriage"), but he received a revelation (disclosed only to his family and closest associates) that not only sanctioned the practice but also threatened divine destruction for anyone who opposed it. After his death no one was surprised to learn that he had taken many wives, but the total number—more than thirty, perhaps even as many as fifty—was shocking even to many Mormons.[12] And it soon became known that other Mormon leaders had also embraced "the principle" with what detractors regarded as unseemly enthusiasm.

Fair-minded "gentiles" in Illinois wanted to ensure the Mormons the kind of religious freedom they had been denied in Missouri. But as they saw the walls of Smith's temple rising above the Mississippi, as they watched the prophet parading with his "Nauvoo Legion" (a private army of which he was the "lieutenant general"), and as they learned more about the sexual "indiscretions" practiced in Nauvoo, they began to wonder if they could live in peace with "such people." To more and more gentiles in Hancock County, Mormonism seemed not just harmless humbug but a menace to the community.

Disaffection with Smith's leadership was also growing among the Mormons themselves. Some of his advisers grumbled about his political activities, others about his reckless financial practices; yet others expressed outrage at his sexual profligacy. By mid-1844 opposition to Smith among Mormons was so strong that a newspaper was launched to publicize it. On June 7 the first (and also the last) issue of the *Nauvoo Expositor* rebuked Smith for his concupiscence and his efforts to unite church and state under the leadership of a "king" ("[C]hrist is our only king and lawgiver," the *Expositor* declared). Outraged, Smith ordered the Nauvoo Legion to smash the newspaper's press. As non-Mormons raged against the Prophet's assault on freedom of the press, Hancock County authorities procured a warrant for his arrest. He fled across the Mississippi into Iowa, but on assurances of safety from Illinois governor Thomas Ford, he returned to await trial in the Hancock County seat at Carthage. There, on June 27, two hundred state militiamen, transformed by anti-Mormon rage into a lawless mob, fired a barrage of rifle shots into the cell Smith occupied with his brother Hyrum and two other Mormons, almost instantly killing the two brothers.

Smith's death left an eerie emptiness in Nauvoo. Only thirty-eight years old when he was murdered, the Prophet had made no preparations for succession to the highest church leadership. Sidney Rigdon, the sole surviving member of the church's three-member First Presidency, quickly claimed the right to be the church's "guardian." James Jesse Strang, a recent convert to Mormonism from Voree, Wisconsin, produced a letter from Smith purporting to confer the mantle of leadership on him. But Rigdon and Strang were both challenged by Brigham Young, a one-time carpenter from Vermont who, as president of the Quorum of the Twelve Apostles, had demonstrated not only an unswerving devotion to the principles of Mormonism but also an exceptional administrative ability. Holding no personal claim to Smith's authority, Young argued simply that the Quorum held the "keys of the kingdom of God in all the world," and a general conference of Saints promptly agreed. Thus Brigham Young, as president of the Quorum of Twelve, acceded to the highest leadership of Joseph Smith's church.

Rigdon remained for a while in Nauvoo, but after Young brought charges against him for "fomenting dissension," he was "cut off"

from the church and delivered over to the "buffetings of Satan."
Rigdon left Nauvoo in the fall of 1844 for his home state of Pennsylvania, where he established his own "Church of Christ," reaffirming
his faith in the *Book of Mormon* but condemning the "debasing and
demoralizing" doctrine of plural marriage.[13]

While dissension racked the church's highest ranks, Mormons in
Hancock County pondered their futures. In La Harpe and neighboring towns, priests and elders met to debate whether Young,
Strang, or Rigdon (or perhaps some other person entirely) was
entitled to Smith's mantle. While Joy Sperry and his family were
confident that the Quorum of the Twelve Apostles was the church's
lawful governing body, Roys Oatman was not so sure. In September
1845 he met one of Rigdon's missionaries traveling along the Mississippi, and the man quickly won him over to Rigdon's cause.
Oatman soon offered himself as a priest in Rigdon's church. Sometime in late 1845 or early 1846, he, Mary Ann, and their children
headed eastward to Rigdon's "Adventure Farm," near the town of
Greencastle in south-central Pennsylvania. Blessed with fertile soil
and ample timber, Adventure Farm seemed well suited to become
"the glory of the whole earth" that Rigdon promised it would be. But
the Oatmans found Rigdon's leadership difficult to follow. Sick and
ill tempered, he delivered angry sermons, made frightening predictions
about the imminent destruction of the world, and quickly alienated
almost all of his followers.[14]

Convinced that Rigdon was not the right man to lead Smith's
church, the Oatmans returned to Illinois, this time to Whiteside
County in northwestern Illinois, where they found a tract of rolling
prairie just east of the Mississippi River town of Fulton, about 120
miles northeast of Nauvoo. The land there was fertile. Old-timers in
the area said the Sauk and Fox Indians, known to be skilled agricul-
turalists, had once farmed it, and the wooded bluffs it backed up to
promised a ready source of timber. For their first year in Whiteside
County the Oatmans lived in a cellar carved out of the prairie soil,

but then Roys erected a log cabin and furnished it as a farmhouse. While Mary Ann busied herself in the kitchen, Roys began to plow, and his children took their lessons in a one-room school at nearby Cottonwood Corners.[15]

Meanwhile the Mormon community in Hancock County was in turmoil. After Joseph Smith's death, Brigham Young seemed to believe that the Saints could remain in Illinois for the foreseeable future. But a rising chorus of gentile newspapers cried out for their expulsion. It was not an easy matter to move the whole population of the state's largest city, particularly when nobody had a clear idea of where they might go. More important, Young and the other Mormons wanted desperately to finish the temple that Smith had begun, for it was only within its walls that they could conduct the "endowment" rituals that Smith had told them were essential to "exaltation in the celestial kingdom."[16] And so while Young assured the gentiles that the Saints would soon be leaving, Mormons worked feverishly to complete the temple. As the temple continued to rise above Nauvoo, the non-Mormons' patience grew short. The two groups skirmished more than once; guns were fired, houses burned, and even some murders committed. Finally, Young bowed to the inevitable, promising that the Saints would leave for a new Zion in the West in the spring of 1846. He kept his word, sending the first party of Saints across the Mississippi in February of that year.

Joy Sperry and his wife, Mary Ann, made preparations to leave Hancock County with Brigham Young in the spring of 1846. Roys and Mary Ann Oatman came down from Whiteside County to see them off. They wanted, no doubt, to wish Mary Ann's parents well on their journey westward: they were going to a "New Jerusalem" somewhere in the West, but exactly where not even Brigham Young knew for sure. But the visit quickly took on a disagreeable tone. Sperry, an ardent Young supporter, may well have tried to persuade the Oatmans to join them on the trek. But Roys wanted none of Young's leadership. The two Mormons argued their respective positions for about a week, until the day the Oatmans were to start back to Whiteside County. Joy's son Charles later remembered that the two men "got to arguing at the breakfast table and they both got quite warm and in earnest in their argument." Finally Roys said to his father-in-law, "I see, Father Sperry, it is no use to talk with you. I prophesy in the name of the Lord that if you go west with your family, your children will go hungry and some will starve to death and your throats will be cut from ear to ear by the Indians." A more reasonable man would have regretted the words as soon as they parted his lips, but Roys Oatman apparently never did so. Joy Sperry was older, perhaps wiser, but no less firm in his convictions. His only reply to Roys was "Be careful how you prophesy in the name of the Lord."[17]

The Sperry family crossed the Mississippi into Iowa soon after the Oatmans said their final good-bye in La Harpe in May or June of 1846.

The exodus from Nauvoo was one of the greatest organized migrations in U.S. history. More than ten thousand Saints left Hancock County between 1846 and 1850, crossing the Mississippi on ferries and leading their wagons onto rutted roads that led through the rolling hills of Iowa. From a place the Mormons called "Winter Quarters" on the west bank of the Missouri River, the trail led along the Platte and Sweetwater rivers to South Pass in the Rocky Mountains, thence toward the southwest, through the Wasatch Range and into the Valley of the Great Salt Lake. Brigham Young himself left Nauvoo in February 1846; he crossed the Wasatch and proclaimed the famous words "This is the place" on July 24, 1847, almost a year and a half after the trek had begun. His followers, stretched out over the whole length of the trail, took many more months to complete the journey.

Hardships on the trail tested the determination of both Young and his loyal Saints. At a place they called "Mount Pisgah" in Iowa, Joy Sperry and his family stopped long enough to build a shanty and lay out a little garden. They knew they could not make it all the way

to the new Zion without resting their animals and replenishing their
dwindling supplies of food. While sixty-four-year-old Joy and his fifty-
six-year-old wife, Mary Ann, rested, their three sons went back to
gather provisions, Aaron and Charles to the Des Moines River and
William all the way to La Harpe. When the brothers returned to
Mount Pisgah, they learned that their mother had fallen victim to
"chills and fever" and died. When, about a month later, a train of
Saints from La Harpe came through Mount Pisgah, the grieving
Sperrys accepted an invitation to join them on the next leg of the
journey. By the time they arrived at a camp called Highland Grove,
Aaron was suffering from great sores on his feet and legs (his brothers
said he had the "black leg," caused by a lack of fresh vegetables).
After Charles and William and even father Joy came down with the
"ague" (malaria), the family was nearly immobilized. In mid-December,
Aaron died, and on January 1, 1847, Joy Sperry followed his son.[18]

When word of the deaths of Joy, Mary Ann, and Aaron Sperry
reached Whiteside County, Mary Ann Oatman was crushed. Although
there is no record of Roys Oatman's reaction to the news, he should
not have felt any vindication. Although he had predicted an awful
fate for the Sperrys if they followed Brigham Young westward, he
had told them they would die of starvation and Indian attacks, not
"black leg" or the "ague." Yet even he must have realized that the hardships of the western trail were not of Young's making. The surviving
Sperrys, at least, were convinced of that, for after they buried their
dead, they continued their journey, finally arriving at the Great Salt
Lake in October 1847.[19]

While the Sperrys struggled on toward the Great Salt Lake, Roys
and Mary Ann Oatman remained on their Whiteside County farm.
They increased their holdings from a small tract to two hundred
acres. Anxious to advertise their success, they invited Mary Ann's
younger sister, Sarah, and her new husband, Asa Abbott, to take up
land near theirs. The Abbotts had been married less than a year
when they accepted the Oatmans' invitation. In July 1847 Asa and

Sarah purchased 120 acres adjoining the Oatman farm and began building a cabin. Soon they invited Asa's parents, Benjamin and Dorcas, to join them. By 1848, when the elder Abbotts settled at Whiteside, the area around the Oatman farm had come to resemble a little village.[20]

But the Abbotts did not share the Oatmans' enthusiasm for Mormonism. Sarah was a Baptist and Asa a trustee of the local Methodist church. The Oatmans were still Mormons, but it was difficult for them to follow their faith without a leader to direct them. By 1848 the community of Mormons who had gathered around Sidney Rigdon after Joseph Smith's death had scattered through several states, and only a handful still looked to him for leadership. James Jesse Strang was a more compelling leader, but most Mormons regarded the letter naming him as Smith's successor a palpable forgery. And many were troubled by Strang's obvious enthusiasm for plural marriage. Of course, Brigham Young embraced "the principle," but many Mormons still found it profoundly offensive (Rigdon condemned it as "ruinous to society").[21]

Saints like the Oatmans who rejected Young, Strang, and Rigdon but still maintained their faith in the *Book of Mormon* were constantly looking for signs that a new leader would appear to them. They had no idea how or when that leader might be revealed. They were confident, however, that it would be through the intercession of the Holy Spirit, the same divine "personage" who had inspired Joseph Smith in the early years of Mormonism.

CHAPTER 2

The Vision

Not long after Brigham Young arrived at the Great Salt Lake, a bid for leadership of the Mormons came from a very unlikely source: a young man scarcely past adolescence who still lived with his mother and father in Springfield, Illinois, but claimed to have some of the same powers as Joseph Smith. His name was James Colin Brewster (though his family and friends always called him "Colin"), and he was born near Buffalo, New York, in 1826. Colin Brewster's parents, Zephaniah and Jane, joined the Mormons in the early 1830s and, with their son, moved to Kirtland, where Zephaniah, a carpenter, helped other Mormons build Smith's first temple.

If Brewster's own recollections are any guide, he came to Joseph Smith's attention while the latter was still in Kirtland, probably when Colin was only ten years old. Some Mormons in the town had noted his gift for "seeing in vision distant objects not seen by the natural eye" and heard him describe a "vision" in which he was shown a large round table on which was a "vast quantity of writing." He inquired as to the meaning of the vision and was told that the round table denoted equality and that the writings were "ancient records that are to be written."[1] The boy was soon summoned to a meeting in the temple, where he met Smith's father, Joseph, Sr., and two elders. "We went in," Brewster later recalled, "and the door was locked." One of the elders called on the Lord. Then the three men proceeded to lay their hands on the boy's head and bless him as "a prophet, a seer, a revelator and translator."[2]

When Joseph Smith, Jr., left Kirtland in 1838, the Brewsters traveled with him as far as Dayton, Ohio, where Colin had another vision: he saw a large number of books in the English language and was told that they were the "lost books" of Esdras (an ancient Israelite prophet). In September 1838 the Brewsters continued on to Springfield, Illinois, where an angel appeared before Colin and said, "It is the will of the Lord that you should commence and write those books of Esdras."[3]

In obedience to the angel, the boy began writing in December 1838, but as he was still too young (only twelve) to do so intelligibly, he asked his father to take his dictation. Zephaniah obliged, but he too was nearly illiterate, so two scribes were employed to finish the work. As the writing progressed, a curious message was received. It was that a new gathering place had been appointed for the Saints. The revelation did not disclose its exact location, but it was to be far beyond Missouri, beyond Texas even, in a remote corner of North America that Esdras described variously as "Cedonia," the "Land of Bashan," the "Land of California," and the "Land of Peace."[4]

By this time it was common knowledge among the Mormons in Springfield that the Brewsters claimed to have the writings of Esdras. Zephaniah went to Nauvoo to show the writings to Smith, but the Prophet was too busy to look at them. In the fall of 1840, Smith's brother Hyrum happened to visit Springfield and stopped at the Brewster house to examine the writings. Hyrum was unsure of their import and advised the Brewsters to take them back to Joseph.

When Zephaniah returned to Nauvoo the following June, Joseph took the writings and promised to read them. But after six days he returned them. Colin Brewster later recalled Smith saying, "I have inquired of the Lord concerning this, and have not received an answer." Back in Springfield the Brewsters continued to record the words of Esdras, and Mormons came to their house for readings.

Uncertain whether they had a duty to publish the words of Esdras, the Brewsters prayed for guidance, and on March 29, 1842, Colin received a revelation commanding them to publish "small portions" of the Books of Esdras and reveal the "place of safety" described in them.[5]

In compliance with the heavenly command, the Brewsters arranged for the printing of a pamphlet entitled *The Words of Righteousness to All Men.* Composed, like the *Book of Mormon* itself, in a style that vaguely resembled the King James Bible, this extract from the lost Books of Esdras combined pious declarations of God's glory with warnings of things that had gone awry in the church of Joseph Smith:

> And it shall come to pass in the last days that great destruction shall come upon the face of all the earth, so that the earth shall be covered with blood and the bodies of dead men[;] even those who have been slain in battle, shall be heaped up in heaps, upon all the face of the earth.[6]

According to Smith's newspaper, the *Times and Seasons,* Brewster's pamphlet was "assiduously circulated, in several branches of the church."[7] But recognizing that its message was critical of the Prophet, the newspaper denounced the pamphlet as "a perfect humbug" and repeated an old but still resonant revelation received by Smith in 1830: "No one shall be appointed to receive commandments and revelations in this church excepting my servant Joseph Smith, Jun., for he receiveth them even as Moses."[8]

Two weeks after the *Times and Seasons* condemned Colin Brewster's writings, a Mormon named John Darby came to visit Smith. Darby had been reading *The Words of Righteousness to All Men* and told Smith that he was "going to California." Joseph's response was quick and searing: "I will say as the prophet said to Hezekiah go and prosper, but ye shall not return in peace. Brewster may set out for California but he will not get there unless some body shall pick him up by the way and feed him &c." Smith told Darby that Brewster had shown him his manuscripts. "I enquired of the Lord," Smith now said, "and the Lord told me the book was not true," thus contradicting Brewster's recollection of the same incident. "It was not of him. If God ever cal[l]ed me, or spoke by my mouth, or gave me a revelation, he never gave revelations to that Brewster Boy or any of the Brewster race."[9]

Smith's rebuke did not chasten Brewster. He returned to Springfield, where he continued to "translate" the Books of Esdras. By 1845, after Smith's death elevated Brigham Young to leadership of the main body of Saints, Brewster was ready to publish another portion of the books. *A Warning to the Latter Day Saints,* published at Springfield in July 1845, inveighed against "works of darkness" in Nauvoo and set forth the first clear reference to the new "place of gathering" appointed for the Saints:

> They who fear God shall escape through the wilderness, and go beyond the river Amli unto the land of their inheritance, a land of hills, of vallies, of plains and pleasant places, which brings forth in abundance, that they who go there shall prosper. The land of Bashan shall be given to the saints."[10]

While Mormons pondered these words, Brewster investigated the men who claimed the leadership of Joseph Smith's church. He was confident that Young and the Quorum of Twelve had no right to lead, but he was still unsure who did. He wrote to Strang, hoping to learn more about his claims. Soon, however, he announced that in a vision, he himself had received divine authority to take the mantle of Smith's leadership. "Therefore," God had told him in the vision, "fear not the power of man or Satan, neither secret combinations of wicked men, but go forth and build up the kingdom, and you shall be prospered in all works of righteousness."[11]

In the spring of 1848, Brewster published *An Address to the Church of Christ, and Latter Day Saints,* a pamphlet including the eleventh Book of Esdras and a more precise description of the Saints' new "place of gathering":

The country designated for the commencement of this great work, is Eastern California, or the valley of the Colorado and Gila rivers, where the Saints are to gather from all the countries of the earth, and establish and build up the Kingdom of Righteousness, which shall never be left to other people, but shall stand forever.[12]

Brewster said that, pending the new gathering, those who accepted his revelations were to reestablish the church on the foundations laid by Joseph Smith in 1830. Heeding the "Boy Prophet's" command (Brewster was only twenty-one), a small group of prominent Mormons traveled to Kirtland in June 1848 to organize what they called the "Church of Christ of Latter Day Saints, or Saints of the Last Days."[13] There were only nine organizers, including Brewster himself, but they could take solace in the knowledge that Smith had begun his own church with only six members in 1830 and that in the years since, it had grown to many thousands.

The president of the new church was not Brewster but a veteran Saint named Hazen Aldrich. Converted to Mormonism in 1835, Aldrich had moved to Nauvoo in 1840 and become a member of the Nauvoo High Council. When Sidney Rigdon organized his Pennsylvania church in 1845, Aldrich became Rigdon's second in command. But he soon gave up on Rigdon and joined Strang in Wisconsin. By 1848 he had also lost faith in the Wisconsinite and announced his belief that the Boy Prophet held the real key to the future for Mormons. Soon a sprinkling of eastern and midwestern Saints were sending their names and tithes to Kirtland and claiming allegiance to Aldrich and the Boy Prophet.[14]

The new church affirmed its faith in the *Book of Mormon* and recognized Smith as a prophet of God, but it charged that Joseph had become a "fallen prophet" when he introduced new rituals into the church and began in earnest to practice plural marriage. "This was the time," Brewster wrote, "when many fell into darkness." Adamant in their opposition to "the principle," Brewster and his followers thought it ironic that Brigham Young and the other apostles branded all who did not follow them "apostates," while their own polygamy constituted the worst apostasy of all.[15]

Despite his condemnation of plural marriage, Brewster was a firm supporter of the role of prophecy in the church, though he viewed it differently than either Smith or Young. While Smith lived, he had jealously guarded his prophetic authority, repeatedly reminding his followers that only he could speak for the Lord. Brewster, in contrast, believed that the church could have many prophets but that not all prophecies were equally true. Some were inspired by God, while others were the "devil's work," and it was the mission of pious Saints to distinguish one from the other. The fact that an event that had been prophesied came to pass might be taken as proof of the prophecy's truth; if the event did not occur, the opposite conclusion could be drawn. Similarly, if God conferred his blessings on Saints who embraced a particular prophecy, it might be taken as evidence that God approved it. But if calamity befell them, it would prove that the prophecy was false.[16]

When Young and Strang heard of Brewster's church, they condemned it as "apostasy." But Brewster and his followers were not discouraged. Two months after they organized their church, Aldrich and a former high priest in Nauvoo named Austin Cowles began to publish a monthly newspaper dedicated to Brewster's cause. Designed to disseminate the young prophet's revelations and spread knowledge of his church, the *Olive Branch*, or *Herald of Peace and Truth to all Saints*, was directed to "the saints scattered abroad, in all Lands; to those that are afar off, and those that are nigh."

The January 1849 issue of the *Olive Branch* announced that, although Brewster was not yet sure when the first party of Saints would leave for the Land of Bashan, he believed they would "arrive at the place appointed before the close of the year 1851." While Brewster insisted that he had learned of Bashan by translating the Books of Esdras, skeptics might have suspected him of first reading some of the western travel journals published in the secular press. One of the most popular of those travelogues was Rufus B. Sage's *Scenes in the Rocky Mountains, and in Oregon, California, New Mexico, Texas, and the Grand Prairies,* published in Philadelphia in 1846. A newspaper compositor from Ohio, Sage had traveled widely over the Great Plains and Rocky Mountains from 1841 to 1844, gathering material for his book. But he never traveled any farther southwest than Taos, New Mexico, so his descriptions of most of the southwestern desert— including the land around the confluence of the Gila and Colorado rivers—were based on second- or third-hand reports he had gathered along the trail and, after his return to Ohio, embroidered with flights of speculation. Sage's book presented a rosy picture of the region that Brewster called "Bashan," and the Boy Prophet was eager to share the picture with his followers. Thus the January 1849 issue of the *Olive Branch* copied a long passage from Sage, including the following:

> The bottoms of the Colorado and Gila, with their tributaries, are broad, rich and well timbered. Everything in the shape of vegetation attains a lusty size, amply evincing the exuberant fecundity of the soil producing it. There are many sweet spots in the vicinity of both these streams, well deserving the name of earthly Eden. . . . The natives, for the most part, may be considered friendly, or, at least not dangerous.[17]

It was a rosy, and dangerously misleading, picture of the south-western desert, as events would later demonstrate.

When or where Roys Oatman joined the church of James Colin Brewster is unknown, but he did so with enthusiasm. In December 1849, the same month Brewster called on his followers to begin preparations for their journey to Bashan, Oatman firmly decided to join the first company of "Brewsterites" on the western trail. He sold his Whiteside County farm for $1,000 and his personal property for an additional $500. The following month, the *Olive Branch* published instructions for those who were going to Bashan, urging them to take along cows and young cattle, farm implements, heavy wagons, and provisions for at least six months' travel ("although a year would be better"). Mechanics were counseled to bring the tools of their trades. The newspaper also expressed hope that some of those who went in the first company would be able to take a portable gristmill and sawmill and a printing press and type. Even in the wilderness, the printed word would be critical to the success of Brewster's kingdom.

In February Oatman began traveling around Illinois, spreading word of the *Book of Mormon* and Colin Brewster's Books of Esdras. He was a Mormon priest now and a zealous missionary for what he called the "Word of Life." The imminent departure for Bashan seemed to be exciting Saints all over the Midwest. There were reports of converts in Illinois and Iowa and Wisconsin, even some drawn from the ranks of the "Brighamites." In March Oatman reported that he had brought four former Mormons into the Brewster fold at Fulton and baptized one gentile.[18]

On Monday, May 6, the Oatman family left Whiteside County on the first leg of their journey to Bashan.[19] There were a total of nine persons in the party, including Roys and Mary Ann and their seven children (the youngest, Roland, was still a babe in arms). They headed west from northwestern Illinois, crossed the Mississippi by ferry, then pointed their wagons south. On the outskirts of a village called West Buffalo, they were joined by a family of Brewsterites named Meteer. George Meteer, the family's head, had been one of the organizers of Brewster's church in Springfield, Illinois, and later became presiding elder of a branch in West Buffalo. In the town of Moscow, the Oatmans and Meteers joined another Brewsterite family named Thompson. The head of this clan was Ira W. Thompson, a native Vermonter who had moved westward through New York, Ohio, Indiana, Illinois, and finally Iowa in an episodic quest for prosperity and religious peace. Eight years older than Roys Oatman, Thompson was still a vigorous man and determined to lead his wife and four children to a new Zion

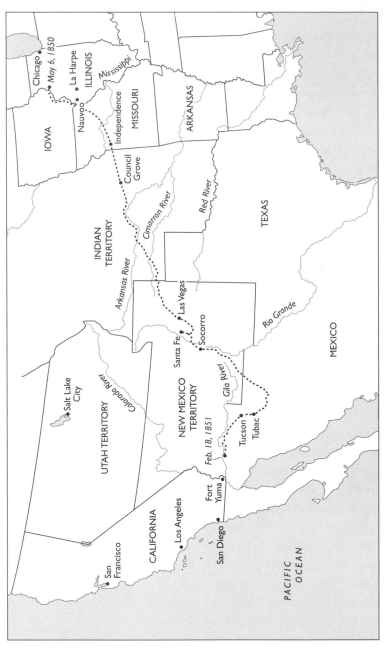

The Oatman Trail from Illinois into the heart of the Southwestern Desert, 1850–1851. New Mexico Territory then included land that later formed parts of Colorado, Arizona, and Nevada. All territory south of the Gila River belonged to Mexico before the Gadsden Purchase was made in 1853.

in the West. During the two days the Oatmans and Meteers spent with the Thompsons in Moscow, the families became good friends. Lucy Oatman, in particular, struck up a close friendship with Ira Thompson's daughter Susan.

The Oatmans, Meteers, and Thompsons pulled their wagons into a little train on June 8 and headed south. At the end of their first day on the trail, they made camp, and Roys baptized another new Mormon. As they continued into Missouri, they settled into an easy, predictable routine. They arrived in Independence, the traditional starting place for journeys across the southern plains, on June 29, and were surprised to find that they were the first Brewsterites in town. While they waited for the others to arrive, Oatman, Meteer, and Thompson checked over their wagons and rested their animals for the strenuous journey ahead. Always zealous, Roys spent much of the time preaching, holding meetings, and receiving new converts into Brewster's church. "The Lord is truly with us," he declared in a cheerful letter sent back to Kirtland.[20]

Other families straggled into Independence in the first two weeks of July. The Brewsters themselves were the last to arrive, on the 13th. Old Zephaniah Brewster headed up the clan, while the Boy Prophet rode in one of the wagons. The other travelers were more than a little annoyed by the Brewsters' lackadaisical attitude. They had set out from Springfield with an old cat in one of their wagons, and not long after their arrival in Independence discovered that the cat had been left some miles behind. So Zephaniah hitched up a wagon and slowly went back to get it. A while later, he and Colin announced that they had also left one of their wagons behind and had to go back to retrieve it. This second delay sent a wave of anger through the camp.

When all of the Brewsterites who were expected to travel with the first party had arrived in camp, they tallied their combined resources. Jackson Goodale, a recent convert to Brewsterism, was unpleasantly surprised to learn that, even if they pooled all of their resources, they did not have enough cash or supplies to carry them through to Bashan and that they would probably have to stop in New Mexico for additional food. They bought what they could in Independence stores, then set about the job of repairing wagons that needed work.[21]

On Monday, July 15, the travelers organized themselves into an "emigrant company" and elected Goodale as captain. He seemed a competent man, but Colin Brewster was disturbed by signs of unrest in the group. On July 22 the wagons moved to a new camp about twenty miles west of Independence. Here some of the travelers said they wanted to withdraw from the emigrant company, though they still believed in the Books of Esdras and intended to travel with the others to Bashan. One family, headed by Andrew Patching, not only held themselves aloof from the company but refused to share their extra supplies with needier travelers. The situation was aggravated when a mysterious Mormon camped near the main body of travelers and spent the better part of ten days huddled with the Patchings. He claimed to believe in the writings of Esdras, but Brewster suspected he was "sent by the Salt Lake Mormons" to sow dissension among them. A quiet struggle for the Patchings' allegiance continued until the evening of July 27, when, according to Brewster, the "secret agent manifested his true character and feelings." Brewster was heartened when the family agreed to join the company, but only temporarily, for after reconsidering, the Patchings finally decided to turn back. Brewster wrote Aldrich on July 30 that "all that the power of Satan and the iniquity of the ungodly could accomplish, has been done to produce discord and division among us."[22]

Surviving records do not reveal the exact number of men, women, and children who made up the final company. Although Brewster compiled a list of seventeen families comprising ninety persons, his list was made before the company was complete. Mary Ann Oatman wrote her sister Sarah Abbott back in Whiteside County that there were ninety-three persons in the company, but she did not specify names or families. A few months later, Ira Thompson reported to the

Olive Branch that there were eighty-two persons in the train, but, like Mary Ann Oatman, he did not list names. By adding the numbers given for all of the families in Brewster's list to the names of persons known to have joined the company but not listed by Brewster, it can be determined that the company as finally constituted included at least eighty-five and possibly as many as ninety-three persons.[23]

With nine members the Oatmans ranked as one of the three largest families (the Brewsters and the Meteers numbered ten each). Jackson Goodale's and J. B. Wheeling's families included seven each. A. W. Lane's family numbered five, while that of his father, William W. Lane, numbered three. Willard O. Wilder's family included four, as did that of John Richardson, while William J. Conner's family numbered three. There were four bachelors in the company: O. F. Beckwith, Neville Stuart, and two brothers, Robert and John Kelly. No record of the number of persons in Norman Brimhall's or Robert Cheeseborough's families has been found. These fifteen or sixteen families had between them over twenty-five wagons, about two hundred head of cattle, and what Brewster called "a few horses." Roys Oatman himself had two fine horses that made such an impression one of the pioneers offered him $250 for the pair. Colin Brewster urged him to accept the offer (horses were not nearly as effective in pulling wagons as oxen), but Oatman refused it, preferring to keep the animals for use after he got to Bashan. The travelers seemed well supplied for the journey, but at the last minute, Oatman, Colin Brewster, Jackson Goodale, and a few others returned to Independence to buy more supplies. Back in camp on August 4, they were ready to begin the journey. On the morning of August 5, more than a month after the initial departure date set by Colin Brewster, the wagons finally headed out onto the open prairie.[24]

They had decided to follow the Santa Fe Trail across the plains and into the mountains of New Mexico. American traders had begun to follow the eight-hundred-mile-long track from western Missouri to the city of Santa Fe soon after Mexico won its independence from

Spain in the early 1820s, and in the ensuing years it had become an important trade route between the United States and its southern neighbor. During the Mexican War, the trail became a military road over which U.S. Army troops marched to and through the Mexican territories of New Mexico and California. During that war, too, five hundred Mormons loyal to Brigham Young marched over the trail under the command of Philip St. George Cooke, a lieutenant colonel in the U.S. Army dragoons. Called the "Mormon Battalion," these Saints had volunteered to aid the United States in its war with Mexico after Young had determined that the enlistees (and his church) would derive substantial benefits from their service—good army pay, arms and outfits that they could keep when their enlistments ended, and an opportunity to move West at government expense.[25] While the Mexican War raged on and especially, after its conclusion, when the Santa Fe Trail became one of the principal travel routes for California-bound gold seekers, the Indians of the plains (Kiowas, Comanches, Pawnees, Arapahos, Utes, and other tribes) raged in disbelief at the thousands of mule trains, wagon caravans, and military columns that snaked across their lands, cutting deep ruts in the prairie grass and killing many thousands of the buffalo on which they depended for food, clothing, fuel, and lodging.

None of the men and women who followed Brewster into the Indian country in the late summer of 1850 had much personal experience with its Native occupants. During the Mormon ascendancy in Nauvoo, some Indians had come into town to trade with the Mormon shopkeepers, but only infrequently. Roys Oatman had had a few fleeting contacts with the Indians in Illinois and Iowa. Despite limited experience with Indians, however, Mormons had definite ideas about them—ideas deeply rooted in Mormon scripture.

Central to the *Book of Mormon* is a long and involved history of "wars and contentions" among the ancient inhabitants of America. The book identifies the principal warring peoples as the "Nephites" and the "Lamanites," both of whom descended from an Israelite named Lehi who emigrated to America about 600 B.C. The Nephites were a "white, and exceedingly fair and delightsome," people who were obedient to God's commands. The Lamanites were unruly and disobedient, in consequence of which God "cursed" them: they became a "dark, and loathsome," people, "full of idolatry and filthiness; feeding upon beasts of prey; dwelling in tents, and wandering about in the wilderness with a short skin girdle about their loins and their heads shaven." To defend themselves against the Lamanites, the Nephites erected "small forts, or places of resort; throwing up banks of earth round about" them. But the Lamanites proved their military superiority, and around 421 A.D. completely defeated the Nephites. To preserve their history, the last surviving Nephites—a prophet named Mormon and his son, Moroni—abridged their written records, recorded the abridgment on golden plates, and buried the plates in the New York hill where Joseph Smith, Jr., unearthed them in the 1820s.[26]

It was clear to any nineteenth-century American reader of the *Book of Mormon* that the Lamanites were supposed to be ancestors of the American Indians and also that Mormon doctrine regarded the Indians as a "loathsome" race whose dark skins and "wicked" ways contrasted sharply with the "white" and "delightsome" Nephites. If there had been no more to the *Book of Mormon*'s concept of the Lamanites, however, the testament could have been dismissed as just another ill-informed, racist white diatribe against the "savage" peoples of North America. In fact the book offered a more complicated theory, envisioning that the Lamanites (Indians) would play an important role in the restoration of God's church. The *Book of Mormon* itself stated that it was written in part for "the benefit of our brethren, the Lamanites," and in an early revelation, Joseph Smith was told that the golden plates had been preserved so that the Lamanites "might know the promises of the Lord." Mormon scripture predicted that the Lamanites would one day accept the gospel, whereupon "their scales of darkness shall begin to fall from their eyes; and many generations shall not pass away among them, save they shall be a white and a delightsome people."[27] The book also predicted that when the Lamanites repented of their sins, they would take the lead in building up the "New Jerusalem." Underscoring the Lamanites' role in the *Book of Mormon*'s scheme, Smith had sent missionaries to preach to Indians in the first year of his church's existence. But when the missions had little success, he decided to postpone serious efforts to convert the Indians.[28]

In its explanation of the origins of the American Indians, the *Book of Mormon* was not original. The theory that the Indians were descendants of ancient Israelites (perhaps even the "Ten Lost Tribes" that mysteriously disappeared from Israel in the eighth century B.C.) had been discussed in books, newspapers, and religious tracts for a century or more before Joseph Smith incorporated it into his history of the Nephites and Lamanites in 1830. Smith was alone, however, in sanctioning the speculation with holy writ. Learned men in America had already proposed that the Native Americans more likely came from Asia by way of Siberia and Alaska than from the biblical Holy Land and that they arrived in America thousands of years before 600 B.C. But scientific evidence of the Asian connection was not yet as persuasive as it would later become. Not surprisingly, Colin Brewster enthusiastically supported the doctrine of the Lamanites, claiming that the prophet Esdras had echoed the *Book of Mormon*'s prediction that when the Lamanites received the Mormon gospel, they would "become a pure and delightsome people" like the Nephites.[29]

If Goodale, Brewster, Oatman, or any other members of the party had any definite expectations about the Indians they would encounter, they did not record them. What they did expect, however, were challenges posed by the land they would be traveling through. Grass was needed almost daily to feed the animals that pulled the wagons. Reliable sources of water were also essential: while small stores of the precious liquid could be carried in kegs or barrels, the containers would be rapidly drained when the weather turned hot, and the animals would need frequent access to rivers and streams if they were to avoid a life-threatening thirst. The first week of August was very late in the year for an emigrant train to leave the Missouri frontier. More prudent travelers, mindful of the huge distances that separated Independence from California, tried to leave in April, May, or at the latest, early June. The Brewsterites had not traveled far beyond Independence when they discovered just how late in the year it was, for grass along the trail was already brown and water was scarce. The realization of the lateness of the departure added to the undercurrent of resentment running through the train.

The wagons passed a place called Lone Elm, crossed 110 Mile Creek and the Osage River, and after another twelve days of hard travel, arrived at Council Grove, where a forest nearly half a mile wide straddled the trail and the Neosho River. While the Brewsterites welcomed the opportunity to rest their animals and replenish their supplies of water and wood, they still seethed with discontent. Olive and Lorenzo Oatman later remembered that the discord in Council Grove arose out of "the religious notions and prejudices of a few restless spirits" and became so heated that some of the company threatened to return to Independence. But others persuaded them to stay with the train. In all, the Brewster wagons remained in Council Grove about a week.[30]

If they had not done so previously, at least some of the travelers may have wondered at this point why they had given up their homes and lives in settled parts of the country to follow the "Boy Prophet" to the "Land of Bashan." What persuaded them that this young man, barely beyond his teens, could lead them to a "Zion" in the wilderness? As they got to know him better, they saw that he had none of the charisma of Joseph Smith, none of the administrative genius of Brigham Young, none even of the sly salesmanship of James Jesse Strang. He was an earnest young man, zealous in his pursuit of the prophetic message of Esdras. But he was also disagreeable, quick to take issue, seemingly more anxious to win arguments than hearts.

His message was always more intriguing than compelling. Perhaps, after all, they had chosen to follow Brewster only because he was not Young or Strang.

From Council Grove the trail led to the southwest. As the migrants crossed a broad plain, barren of trees and nearly of grass, the wagons passed Diamond Spring and Lost Spring, then came to the Little Arkansas River. Fording that stream, they entered a broad plain devoid of any water course. Two days later they arrived at the Arkansas River. With headwaters in the distant Rocky Mountains, the Arkansas was an important, life-sustaining stream for all Santa Fe–bound wagon trains, and as they moved westward, the travelers kept close to the river's north bank.

A few more miles brought the wagons to the base of a bluff (perhaps the famous Pawnee Rock, from which Pawnee Indians often surveyed the surrounding prairie). Atop the bluff, amid a profusion of rocks, Colin Brewster found a stone engraved with mysterious characters. "They have the appearance of great antiquity," he told his followers, "but are still distinctly visible." Following the example of Joseph Smith, who claimed to have "translated" documents marked with Egyptian hieroglyphics, Brewster announced that he had unlocked the secrets of the inscription. His translation read: "Kommor, the son of Kish and Lahanto, chief catam of the armies of Kish, king of the people of Gerad, sojourned in this valley in the third year of his reign."[31]

Beyond the bluff, the wagons stopped to make camp at the confluence of the Arkansas and the Pawnee Fork. Here or nearby they encountered a traveler named Max Greene. Greene had been a newspaper printer in Pennsylvania before deciding in the late 1840s to visit the American West. He traveled for months on the prairie, going as far as the Rocky Mountains and making the acquaintance of soldiers, fur trappers, buffalo hunters, and countless trains of emigrants. He was on another of his excursions across the plains when he met the Brewsterites and asked if he might join them for part of their journey. They agreed, and he became the only person to observe the dissident Saints from an outsider's perspective. Greene quickly noticed the rancor that pervaded the company and just as quickly blamed it on Roys Oatman. In a book he later wrote about his western travels, he claimed he had joined the Brewster train only because he was "on the lookout for novelty." Oatman was a good enough fellow in most respects, Greene wrote in *The Kanzas [sic] Region*, "but sinfully reckless" and "always 'in for a muss.' . . . He was, in short, a most dangerous companion on the Grand Prairie, where, being beyond the aid of police, the palladium of government abides in kindly fellowship and the general love of order. Could we, therefore, have exchanged him for the small-pox, the measure would have had a majority vote."[32] According to Greene, Oatman was the center of virtually all the disagreements that racked the company. There were angry arguments, meetings that deteriorated into shouting matches. Some of the travelers sought to quiet the arguments and restore peace, but nothing seemed to mollify Oatman and his supporters. And it was too late in the year to turn back now, for the wagons had gone too far.

From Pawnee Fork the train continued westward, still following the north bank of the Arkansas. It was now approaching one of the great forks in the Santa Fe Trail, where the road divided into a northern, or "mountain," branch that led toward Bent's Fort in what would later become the southeastern corner of Colorado, and a southern, or "desert," branch that crossed to the south side of the Arkansas and pointed toward the southwestern corner of what would later become the state of Kansas. Santa Fe was a hundred miles nearer by the southern than by the northern route, but the latter was better supplied with wood and water, and Bent's Fort offered some protection from Indian attack. The southern branch, though shorter, crossed one of the driest deserts on the whole trail, a sixty-mile-wide expanse of sand and rock without a single river or stream. It ended on the banks of the Cimarron River, an east-flowing tributary of the Arkansas that gave the southern route its popular name—the "Cimarron Cutoff." Mexicans called this country a *jornada,* or desert "journey," sometimes a *jornada del muerto,* or "journey of the dead," and the sight of human bones strewn along the road, together with the broken wheels of abandoned wagons, convinced American travelers that the Mexican name was apt. It was early September when the Brewster train came to the fork. Not surprisingly, they chose the Cimarron Cutoff, for it was late in the year and they were anxious to make up for lost time.

When the wagons crossed the Arkansas, a party of thirty or forty Indians, possibly Comanches, came into the travelers' camp. The Brewsterites were relieved when after about two hours the Indians left, but they were hardly reassured when they later learned that the same Indians had been implicated in a recent attack on a nearby wagon train. On September 12 at Sand Creek, about two-thirds of the way through the jornada, a U.S. government mail train approached the wagons with the unwelcome news that it had made camp a few miles away, but seeing some Indians nearby, had decided that it was unsafe to sleep and that they should move on. The drivers said that the Indians had followed their train to within a mile of the Brewsterite camp.[33]

Later, at Cold Springs, a party of Santa Fe–bound Americans attended by a "strong guard" passed by the Brewster wagons, stopping long enough to report that they had met some Indians just before reaching Sand Creek, that shots had been exchanged, and that several of the Indians had been killed. They had seen Indians within a few miles of Cold Springs and were so concerned about the possibility of attack that they dared not stop. The Americans advised the Brewsterites to leave the place immediately. But they ignored this warning, apparently believing that they were under the special protection of the Almighty. ("Esdras says the ungodly shall perish," Brewster reassured his followers, "after they are separated from the saints, and not while they are with them.")

The first casualty of the Brewster train was not the result of an Indian attack, but a much more prosaic risk of western travel, illness. On September 16 at Middle Springs sixteen-year-old Mary Ann Lane succumbed to the ravages of "consumption."[34] It was little solace to her family to know that her death was attributable as much to chronic illness as the rigors of traveling with a wagon train.

The wagons were on a high prairie now, surrounded by short, fine grass but no trees. Their altitude rose steadily as they passed through the northwestern corner of what is now the panhandle of Oklahoma and into northeastern New Mexico. They passed monuments familiar to a generation of Santa Fe–bound travelers: the lonely mountain called "Rabbit Ears," a second eminence known as "Round Mound," and the dramatic formation named "Wagon Mound" for its resemblance to a covered wagon.

The Brewsterites entered New Mexico on or near October 1. The Spanish and Mexicans had been in the province for more than two hundred years, building towns and churches, extracting the region's natural resources to add to the wealth of older settlements to the south, and after the Santa Fe Trail opened, beginning a tentative trade with their American neighbors. The war between the United States and Mexico had erupted in 1846 over territory claimed by both Texas and Mexico. Although the acquisition of California was the real object of President James K. Polk's Mexican policy, the commander in chief sent Brigadier General Stephen Watts Kearny and his "Army of the West" to Santa Fe soon after the hostilities began. Kearny occupied Santa Fe, organized a military government, and proclaimed New Mexico a U.S. territory. Two years later, the Treaty of Guadalupe Hildalgo ratified Kearny's proclamation.

The village of Mora, just east of the snow-capped Sangre de Cristo Mountains, was the first substantial town the Brewsterites came to in New Mexico. Here they stocked their wagons with fruits, vegetables, and corn—commodities all but unknown on the southern high plains—and obtained generous supplies of mutton, which struck them as a delicacy after nearly two months during which wild birds, jackrabbits, and an occasional buffalo or antelope were their only sources of meat.[35]

South of Mora the trail led to the town of Las Vegas. It was already October 9, but more than half of their journey still lay before them. Santa Fe was still a hundred miles distant, "Bashan" more than a thousand miles. Perhaps it was this realization that occasioned a new outbreak of dissension among the travelers. A handful of veiled references to the arguments that broke out at Las Vegas were later left by various members of the train, but no single, cohesive account of the disagreement. Olive and Lorenzo Oatman remembered only that the company had divided into two parties, one zealously guarding its authority (the Brewsters and Goodales) and the other (the Oatmans, Thompsons, Meteers, Wilders, and Kellys) bridling at that authority. Ira Thompson hinted that the choice of Jackson Goodale to serve as captain of the train had been a mistake from the outset. Max Greene recalled that the dissidents (that is, the Oatmans and their friends), having failed to have Goodale removed as captain, decided to defy his authority. Accordingly, when Goodale ordered the train to stop, the Oatmans and their followers defiantly proceeded on. The two groups of wagons continued to travel within sight of each other for the rest of the day, but when it came time to stop for their nightly camp, Goodale and Brewster refused to bring their wagons into a circle with the others. The circle was valuable more as protection for the animals, who could be herded into the open space in the center, than as a precaution for the occupants of the wagons. Brewster and Goodale's refusal, Greene said, put the animals in jeopardy, and when the travelers awoke the next morning, several of their cows were missing. Greene called this "the first fruit of disobedience."[36]

Brewster's version of the dissension is rife with bitterness. He charged that six members of the party who followed the Oatmans had made the trip only "to increase their chances for making money, and to obtain an office of some kind, either temporal or spiritual." Two others, he said, "had no other object than to get rich, it mattered not how," adding: "It is not possible to describe their extreme selfishness."[37]

But Mrs. Willard Wilder, one of the group that sided with the Oatmans, was equally adamant in blaming Brewster for the disagreement. In her version, the dispute came to the boiling point when the two groups could not agree about whether to go to Santa Fe before heading on to Bashan. Santa Fe was on the western side of the Sangre de Cristos, and going there would be something of a side trip that would further delay the train's progress. Mrs. Wilder said that Brewster was determined "to go to Santa Fe to get letters" and would "go the longest and poorest road," if necessary, to get there. The Oatmans, the Thompsons, and their allies were equally determined to bypass Santa Fe and go directly to the main road.

Stratton suggested that at this point the Oatmans and their allies gave up their quest for Bashan and decided that after passing the gathering place foretold by Esdras, they would continue west into California, there to find some more suitable place to establish a settlement. But there is no evidence in any of the travelers' surviving letters or diaries that they had abandoned their pilgrimage or that, because of their inability to get along with the Brewsters and Goodales, they had given up their dream of establishing their Zion at the confluence of the Gila and the Colorado. To the contrary, their decision to go on without the Brewsters and Goodales rather than tarry in Santa Fe suggests that they were even more zealous in pursuing their original goal than the others, that they were determined to get to Bashan without delay.[38]

On October 9, 1850, the parties divided for the last time, with Brewster and his followers heading over the Sangre de Cristos toward Santa Fe and the Oatmans, Thompsons, Wilders, Meteers, and Kellys heading toward the Rio Grande valley. In a last attempt at reconciliation, the Oatman party offered to divide their provisions with the others if they would travel with them as far as the river; but the offer was declined, and the two caravans went their separate ways.[39]

The Oatmans' party numbered about fifty souls now, including the Thompsons, Meteers, Wilders, Kellys, Lanes, Brimhalls, and Cheeseboroughs. The Brewster party, in contrast, numbered thirty-two. Besides Colin and Zephaniah Brewster and their family, it included the Goodales, Conners, Wheelings, and Richardsons. Whether Greene traveled with the Brewsters as far as Santa Fe or left both parties to travel on his own is unknown, for he is not mentioned in either party's subsequent accounts. The Oatman party lost no time in electing Roys, their leader during the preceding dissension, as captain to guide them over the rest of the trail.

As Oatman led the wagons toward the village of La Joya, the alcalde, or mayor, sent out an armed guard to escort them into the town. "The people here are remarkably kind to us," Ira Thompson wrote in a letter.[40] An incident that occurred before the wagons reached the Rio Grande, however, gave the travelers reason to question the Mexicans' seeming friendliness. The migrants had stopped for the night, unhitched their animals to forage for grass, and then fallen asleep. Upon waking in the morning, they discovered that thieves had made off with Roys Oatman's two horses and two oxen belonging to the Meteers and Kellys. They later heard that the horses had been seen in a Mexican village, but when they asked some Mexicans about the animals, they denied any responsibility for the crime. Horses were sometimes stolen from wagon trains by "unfriendly" Indians, the Mexicans said, and then brought into the villages and offered for sale. The Mexicans thought that responsibility for the crime almost certainly rested with these Indians.[41]

Although New Mexico was home to a large population of so-called Pueblo Indians—settled agricultural peoples thought to be descended from ancient inhabitants of the southwestern deserts—there was also a small but widely feared population of Apaches. The Apaches were expert horsemen who ranged widely over the valleys, mesas, and mountain crags of New Mexico, the rugged eastern mountains of what would later become Arizona, and the northern reaches of old Mexico. They often challenged wagon trains that trespassed on their territory; less frequently they attacked the Pueblo Indians in their adobe-walled villages or in their fields. Although either Mexicans or Apaches could have taken Oatman's horses and the Meteers' and Kellys' oxen, Oatman himself shared some responsibility for their loss. As captain of the train, he had failed to properly protect the animals. Mrs. Wilder said as much when she attributed the theft to "poor guarding."[42] If Oatman learned anything from the loss of his horses, it should have been that the peoples of the region—Mexicans and Indians alike—were potentially dangerous adversaries and that travelers in their midst should invariably respect them.

On October 19 the Oatman wagons crossed the Rio Grande. Rankled perhaps by Oatman's failure to guard the company's animals, the travelers immediately elected Norman G. Brimhall as their new captain, and Brimhall appointed Ira Thompson as company secretary. They were emotionally drained now and their animals weakened from their long climb through the mountains, so they decided to pause for a rest. But when they contemplated their position, and the herculean journey that still lay before them, they realized they could not rest long.

They were now in the "Land of Peace," as Colin Brewster called everything west of the Rio Grande. But there was no peace in the company. And they were still far from the juncture of the Gila and Colorado and their real destination, the Land of Bashan.

CHAPTER 3

The Quest

After resting three days on the banks of the Rio Grande, the Oatman party once again moved south.[1] The road hugged the river for a while, then climbed to the top of some high bluffs. It was a very old road, followed by the Indians for centuries before the Spanish arrived in the late 1500s and made it a part of the road system that bound together their far-flung colonial American empire. Grass along the trail was good, and the wagons set a leisurely pace, allowing time for the animals to pause now and then to graze.

After following the river for about a hundred miles, the travelers came to the village of Socorro, one of the oldest settlements in the valley. Nestled between the river and a range of rocky cliffs, Socorro was a typical Mexican town, with a plaza surrounded by adobe houses and a mission church. The Catholic community would have been of little interest to the dissident Mormons were it not for its open-air market—which was well supplied with meat, fruit, vegetables, and grain—and the nearby U.S. Army post, which was offering to buy hay from anyone who would cut and deliver it at Socorro. Learning that inviting fields of uncut grass lay about thirty miles south of town, the travelers hastened to the spot and made camp; then all the able-bodied men went out to cut and gather hay. Army pay for cutting and raking hay was $10 a ton, $50 if the hay was delivered to Socorro;

so during the nine days they stayed at Socorro, the men were able to replenish their depleted pocketbooks with a good supply of government coin.[2]

It was November 10 when the wagons again headed south, following the only route by which wagons could then cross the rugged mountains separating the Rio Grande from the Gila River country to the west. Known as Cooke's Wagon Road, it had been opened by Lieutenant Colonel Cooke and the Mormon Battalion between October 1846 and January 1847. Cooke's Road left the Rio Grande about ninety-five miles south of Socorro, then turned into the mountains, crossed the Mimbres River, and proceeded southwesterly toward Guadalupe Pass, more than five thousand feet above sea level. Much of the route crossed land that was territory of the Mexican Republic and would remain so until 1854, when the Gadsden Purchase added an additional 29,640 square miles of Mexican territory to the United States.

The Oatmans and their companions had been on Cooke's Road only a few days when the train was struck by another death. In letters sent back to Kirtland, A. W. Lane's death was attributed to "mountain fever," though the travelers had no clear idea what his ailment was. The men buried the dead man on one of the adjoining foothills, and the women planted a flower on his grave as a measure of their respect.[3]

It was now November 22, perilously late in the year for a wagon train to be crossing a rugged mountain range in northern Mexico. Any doubts the families may have had about the lateness of the date were erased one morning when they awoke to find their camp mantled with snow. There were about three inches on the ground, but the level soon rose to seven. They might have welcomed a snowfall back in Iowa or Illinois, where they could survey the white fields from snug farmhouses; here, on the exposed southern flank of a great chain of mountains, they were unprotected from the elements, and their fuel supply was dangerously low. While the men scoured the hills for firewood, the women and little children took to their beds, where, covered with blankets and quilts, they tried to insulate themselves from the cold. Within a week, the weather had warmed, the snow had melted, and the wagons were able to move again.[4]

They were now in the territory of the Chiricahua Apaches, one of the southernmost contingents of the widely scattered Apache peoples. The Chiricahua territory was large and rugged, extending westward from the Rio Grande into the Mimbres Mountains and south into the high deserts and mountains of the Mexican state of Sonora. Lorenzo Oatman later remembered that "three large, fierce-looking Apaches" came into their camp one morning early in December. They professed to be friendly, but the men of the train suspected otherwise and asked them to leave. The Indians complied, but that night the dogs of the train barked almost incessantly. The travelers put out their fires, but the men remained on guard until morning. At dawn, they found footprints near the wagons and soon discovered that some of their animals were missing. Lorenzo thought twenty head of stock had been driven away. Mrs. Wilder put the number at eleven head of cattle and one mare. In either case, the loss was so severe that some of the wagons had to be abandoned for lack of animals to pull them. The men followed the tracks of the stolen stock for some distance into the mountains but, soon realizing the danger of further pursuit, returned to the train.[5]

The Apache depredation struck fear into the travelers. Roys Oatman seemed particularly affected by it. No longer willing to rest his animals at regular intervals, he drove them on without stopping, careless of their needs and of the other men's protests. The wagons passed the headwaters of the San Pedro River, where Cooke's Wagon Road turned north to follow the San Pedro Valley. At this time, however, most emigrant wagons continued west toward the headwaters of the Santa Cruz River. After a brief consultation, the Oatmans and the other families decided to follow the latter route. By December 9 the Oatmans were traveling so furiously that the wagons became badly separated. At one point, the Brimhalls and Cheeseboroughs were twelve miles behind them, struggling to keep up.[6]

Such wide separation posed obvious risks for the travelers, but Roys Oatman was driven now by fear as well as stubbornness. It was only through luck that the wagons came back together again by Christmas Day, when they crossed a ridge of hills and entered the Mexican village of Santa Cruz. The villagers were friendly, but they had no food to share. Susan Thompson was told that Apaches had raided the town a short time before, leaving nothing except some pumpkins. She probably did not know that the scarcity of food was aggravated that year by unusual dryness. The winter of 1850–1851 was, in fact, one of the driest on record in the American Southwest, and the drought affected all of its inhabitants, including the Apaches. Realizing there was nothing to keep them in Santa Cruz, the families quickly left.[7]

They were traveling north now along the Santa Cruz River. At Tumacácori they passed a Spanish church, elaborately columned and domed but bereft of any humans (the residents had all fled a little over two years earlier when Apaches had raided along the river). At Tubac the migrants came on the site of an old Spanish fort and, around it, a collection of empty adobe houses (abandoned during the same Apache raid that had sent the residents of Tumacácori fleeing). The river valley here impressed the travelers as fertile, though it too bore signs of the drought that affected the whole region. Some of the families briefly considered stopping long enough to plant and harvest some crops, but their enthusiasm for the idea cooled when they inquired about the Indians. The Mexicans told them that the Apaches posed a constant threat to settled communities in the area. Almost every day they could be seen along the crests of the surrounding hills, peering down into the valley, spurring their horses into displays of speed, awaiting opportunities to ride down into the valley, attack houses, seize animals, and threaten any Mexicans who resisted. The Indians were so bold, the Mexicans said, as to come within a few yards of cattle herdsmen in their fields and taunt them to "take care of those cattle for the Apaches."[8] Even the region's more settled Indians, the Tohono O'odham (called "Papagos" by the Spanish, Mexicans, and Americans) and the Akimel O'odham (called "Pimas" by the same peoples), were almost constantly on the lookout for the Apaches. The travelers' food supplies were perilously low now. Each member of the train was allotted only a biscuit and a half per day, and this was supplemented with bits of meat from birds or coyotes hunted and killed along the road. However hungry they might be, however, the travelers could not offer themselves up as victims to the Apaches by stopping. So they pressed on to Tucson, arriving there on January 8, 1851.[9]

Tucson's history as a Spanish and then Mexican town dated from 1775, when the presidio of San Agustín de Tucson was moved north from Tubac. As an Indian settlement, however, the site was much older, for the Tohono O'odham had lived in villages there for generations, possibly centuries. Following the familiar pattern of Spanish towns in the Southwest, Tucson had a central plaza surrounded by adobe houses arranged along a grid of streets and enclosed by an adobe wall eighteen inches thick and ten or twelve feet high. An almost steady stream of Americans had passed through the town since the end of the Mexican War (the great majority California-bound gold seekers), but few had stopped to settle. The Gadsden Purchase had not yet moved the international boundary south of Tucson, so the town was still a Mexican village, and its three hundred or four hundred Mexican inhabitants spoke Spanish almost exclusively.

The Oatman party had hoped to buy food and supplies in Tucson. But the townspeople had been under an Apache siege for so long, and their fields were so parched by the lack of rain, that their storehouses were nearly empty. If the travelers were too weak to continue on their journey, the townspeople suggested, they should stay for a while and plant some crops. North of Tucson, the country was desolate, and the Apache threat every bit as forbidding as it was around the town.

The families decided to stop in Tucson and ponder their future. They rented some rooms and purchased a small supply of food; then, while the men repaired the wagons and the women mended trail-worn clothes, the children began to explore the town. Years later Susan Thompson remembered that she found an old Mexican who had a large mesquite thorn imbedded in his foot. She made a poultice of soap, sugar, and egg white and used it to remove the spine. The townspeople were impressed by her feat, as well as by her ability to call her father's cattle to her (she said the Mexicans "had never heard of controlling their animals by kindness"). In this way, she managed to win the townspeople's favor. The old man whose foot she healed gratefully rented the Thompsons a house, and his wife insisted on doing their laundry. But Mrs. Thompson had doubts about the Mexican woman's motives and sent Susan down to the river to watch her as she washed.[10]

Susan also recalled a guard who stood on top of the wall that surrounded Tucson and screamed "Apache! Apache!" at "every puff of dust" that appeared in the distance. One morning she was down by the river as her landlord's wife was spreading the family clothes on some bushes when she heard the familiar cry. The Mexican woman was terrified and took her "half-witted brother" and Susan both by the hand and started to run for the safety of the town. But Susan, remembering her mother's concern for the laundry, gathered up the dripping clothes before dashing for the village. The cause of the excitement turned out to be nothing more than a whirlwind. Another day, however, she found herself in real danger as she went into a field near the Thompson house and found two Apaches untying her pet calf. She rushed up to them and screamed, "If you don't let my calf alone, I'll tell the men in the house." The Apaches did not know that Mrs. Thompson was alone in the house, and the girl's boldness frightened them away.[11]

Willard Wilder purchased an ox in Tucson, and Roys Oatman traded one of his wagons for some Mexican cows. The Thompsons,

Meteers, Lanes, Brimhalls, and Cheeseboroughs decided to stay in the town and, following the Mexicans' advice, attempt to raise some food. But the Oatmans and Wilders were impatient to push on. Willard Wilder was willing to go on at least as far as the Pima and Maricopa villages, about ninety miles north of Tucson (the Pimas and Maricopas were skilled farmers, Wilder was told, and often had large supplies of grain and vegetables in their stores); but Roys Oatman was determined to go all the way to Bashan.

Why Robert and John Kelly decided to join the Oatmans and Wilders on the trail north is unclear. As bachelors, they had no families to protect from the Apaches, yet they might still have preferred to remain in the safety of Tucson rather than risk their lives on the trail ahead. Perhaps the Kellys had another reason to push on. One of Robert Kelly's nephews suggested years later that his uncle had fallen in love with Olive Oatman while they were on the trail. Olive was only thirteen when her family left Tucson, but she was a pretty girl, and not too young to return the affection of a handsome young man who had just turned twenty-five. Romances often blossomed on the western trail, and if Olive and Robert Kelly pledged each other their love in 1851, they were neither the first nor the last pioneer couple to do so.

North of Tucson, the emigrant road rejoined the route followed by the Mormon Battalion in 1846. The wagons now crossed the bed of a hard, flat desert studded with cactus and shrubby trees and almost entirely waterless. About forty-five miles north of Tucson they approached a tower of rocks that rose fifteen hundred feet above the roadbed. Called El Picacho ("the Peak"), the mountain had been used for hundreds of years as an observation platform by O'odham, Apaches, and other Indians of the region. Lorenzo Oatman later remembered this country as "the most dismal, desolate, and unfruitful" of the entire journey.[12]

Another forty-five miles brought the wagons to the Pima and Maricopa villages. Scattered along the Gila River, these Indian towns were occupied by about five thousand Pimas (or Akimel O'odham) and four hundred or five hundred Maricopas. The two peoples that comprised these large populations were ethnically unrelated. The Pimas belonged to the large family of Uto-Aztecan-speaking Indians, whose members (including the Tohono O'odham) were widely scattered through northern Sonora and what is now southern Arizona, while the Maricopas belonged to the Yuman-speaking group, whose homeland hugged the banks of the Colorado River north of the Gulf of California. Sometime before the Spanish arrived in the Southwest, the Maricopas migrated east from their Colorado River homeland to the middle Gila, where they entered into a friendly coexistence with the Pimas. Though divided by language and culture, the two peoples shared an agricultural lifestyle and a hatred for the Apaches. When the Oatmans, Wilders, and Kellys encountered them, the Pimas occupied the ten most easterly villages, while the Maricopas resided in two to the west. The settlements were connected by a network of canals that brought water from the Gila to irrigate small but productive fields of wheat, corn, melons, squash, and cotton; but the canals were hardly brimming with water, for the lack of rain had affected the Gila as much as the region's other streams.

The Oatmans, Wilders, and Kellys arrived at the Pima villages on February 5, as Lorenzo later remembered, "wearied, heart-sick, and nearly destitute."[13] The Indians welcomed them but quickly let them know that they could do little to ease their want. Their fields were so badly affected by the drought that they had barely enough food to keep themselves alive. Moreover, they lived under the constant threat of Apache raids. The Pimas fought back bravely whenever the Apaches came down from the mountains to threaten them, but the Apaches usually had the advantage in these confrontations, for they moved so swiftly across the desert on their sleek ponies that they could pilfer storehouses and make off with cattle or sheep almost before their presence had been detected.

Discouraged, the families moved on to the Maricopa villages. About a mile west of these they found a patch of grass and a series of wells that offered fresh water. Called the Maricopa Wells, they were dug by Cooke and the Mormon Battalion on their way to California in 1846, and all subsequent travelers had stopped beside them for rest and recuperation from long treks through the desert. Here the Mormon families made their camp, putting their cattle out to graze. Then, on February 7, behind the worn canopy of the Wilder wagon, Mrs. Wilder gave birth to a baby boy, named "little Willard" for his father.[14]

Not surprisingly, Roys Oatman was impatient to continue the journey to Bashan. They were about 190 miles from the confluence of the Gila and Colorado now, a short enough distance compared to the more than fifteen hundred miles they had already traveled from Independence, Missouri. As there was not enough food in all the Pima and Maricopa villages to sustain the travelers through the winter, remaining might mean starvation. If they pushed on to Bashan, however, Oatman was confident that they would attain the earthly Eden described by Colin Brewster in the prophecies of Esdras.

The Wilders and Kellys did not share Oatman's enthusiasm for continuing the journey. None of them had any clear idea what kind of country they would find between Maricopa Wells and the Colorado River, how many Indians they would encounter along the way, or whether the Indians would welcome them, as the Pimas had, or harass or threaten them, as the Apaches had in the Chiricahua country. Although the Pimas and Maricopas had little food, there was no assurance that any more could be found farther west.

As the families debated their future course, they learned that an American traveler had just arrived in the Pima villages. John Lawrence Le Conte was only twenty-five years old but had already established a reputation as an entomologist and explorer. A graduate of New York's College of Physicians and Surgeons, he had traveled by sea to San Francisco in 1849 in hopes of adding to his already notable collection of coleoptera (beetles). After exploring the area around San Francisco Bay, he traveled by stage coach to San Diego, where he met Brevet Major Samuel P. Heintzelman, commander of the U.S. Army's newly established Camp Yuma at the confluence of the Gila and the Colorado. With Heintzelman Le Conte explored a dry lake bed east of San Diego, then set out with a fellow physician to explore the Colorado River between Yuma and the Gulf of California. Everywhere he went, he added beetles to his collection. He was en route from Camp Yuma to Tucson when he came into the Pima villages in February 1851, traveling on horseback with a Mexican guide known only as Juan the Sonorian. Having followed the Gila all the way from the Colorado to the Pima villages, the two men had had a good opportunity to observe the river. Hastening to meet Le Conte, Roys Oatman asked the scientist about the Gila country and the army post at Yuma. What did Le Conte tell him? The answer to this question vitally affects any attempt to explain the fate that ultimately befell the Oatman family.

Some years after Roys Oatman met Le Conte at the Pima and Maricopa villages, Lorenzo Oatman claimed that the naturalist told his father that in all the country between Yuma and the villages, he "had not witnessed indications of even the neighborhood of Indians." This information, according to Lorenzo, was enough to persuade Roys that it was safe to travel west. Mrs. Wilder wrote that Oatman decided to continue on the journey because he "had heard there was a company of U. S. A[rmy] Soldiers stationed" on the Colorado;[15] this information almost certainly came from Dr. Le Conte. But beyond these two fragmentary recollections, there is little evidence to establish exactly what Le Conte told Oatman. The Pimas and Maricopas knew more about the trail along the Gila River than either Le Conte or Juan, and if asked, they would not have been reluctant to offer their opinions. Whatever Le Conte said, it was apparently not enough to persuade the Wilders and the Kellys to join the Oatmans on this last leg of their journey to Bashan, for they refused to go. The fact that Mrs. Wilder had just given birth would naturally have made her husband reluctant to resume travel so soon; but Mrs. Oatman was also expecting a child, due within three or four weeks at the most,[16] and if

Mrs. Wilder was in no condition to take to the road, Mary Ann Oatman could hardly have been expected to do so. Had the Oatmans
been willing to wait a few weeks for Mrs. Oatman to have her baby and
for both her and Mrs. Wilder to regain their traveling strength, the
Wilders and the Kellys would almost certainly have accompanied them.
Such a wait would not have been too much for a prudent traveler. But
Roys Oatman was not a prudent man, and he was unwilling to wait.

Beyond the Pima and Maricopa villages, the Gila flowed northwest, then west, and then southwest, in an arc-shaped channel that
hugged the base of a knot of mountains called the Sierra Estrella.
This "great bend" of the Gila extended more than a hundred miles
through a rocky desert to come out on a broad plateau about forty-
five miles southwest of Maricopa Wells. To avoid the great bend,
Cooke had followed a route that led in a more or less straight line
southwest from Maricopa Wells to intersect the Gila as it entered the
plateau. This shortcut substantially shortened the westward journey
but subjected travelers to forty-five miles of high, waterless desert. To
prepare for this trek, wagon masters drew as much water from the
Maricopa Wells as all their jugs and barrels would hold. The extra
weight reduced their speed but lowered the risk of running out of
water. The Oatmans' outfit had now been reduced to one wagon and
whatever equipment and supplies it could hold, drawn by two yokes
of cows and one of oxen. Thus accoutred, the family left Maricopa
Wells on February 10.[17]

They headed southwest, following Cooke's Wagon Road as it
crossed the plateau. After a few miles, they entered a large valley
edged by low hills and, beyond it, a range of mountains covered with
brush and magnificent, columnlike cacti (giant saguaros). Viewed
from a distance, the brush and cacti gave the landscape a greenish,
almost grassy appearance; closer up, the desert floor proved hard
and without a trace of grass. For about five days the wagon crept
along the road, the weak animals stumbling painfully.[18] At last the

family came in sight of the Gila as it circled round the mountains from its great bend and emerged on the plateau. To the south, the desert spread out over cactus-studded mesas and valleys to a ridge of jagged mountains. To the north rose another mountain range, which marked the river's bank as far as the eye could see.

In this pre-Gadsden year of 1851, the Gila was the international boundary between the United States and the Republic of Mexico. But no one who knew the region well paid much attention to the boundary, for actual control of the land rested neither in Washington nor Mexico City but in the hands of the Indian peoples who had made it their home for centuries, perhaps even millennia, before the Oatmans first saw it.

To the east and northeast, Apaches occupied the high deserts, mountains, and canyons that separated the Gila basin from the valley of the Rio Grande and the broad plateau that straddled the Grand Canyon of the Colorado. These Apaches—known as Western Apaches—effectively defended a territory of approximately ninety thousand square miles, though without the advantage of large numbers: their total population was about five thousand in 1850. Although the Western Apaches practiced some agriculture, their economy was essentially built on hunting, gathering, and raiding. It was their skill in raiding that permitted them to control an area larger than some eastern U.S. states (more than fifteen times the size of Connecticut and nearly twice that of Pennsylvania). Although the point just below the great bend of the Gila was more than a hundred miles from the nearest Apache camps, informed white travelers were conscious of the Apaches' presence in the region and wary of encounters with them.

North of the great bend and west of the Apache territory was another expanse of approximately twenty thousand square miles occupied by a people loosely grouped under the heading of Yavapai, though that name masked a great diversity of peoples and cultures. The total Yavapai population was not substantially smaller than that

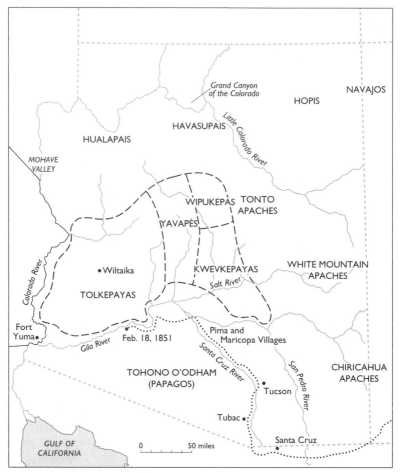

The end of the Oatman Trail in what later became Arizona. This map shows the location of the principal Indian peoples of the region in 1851. The trail ended when the family was attacked by a band of Indians (probably Western Yavapais, or Tolkepayas) on February 18, 1851, on a cliff overlooking the Gila River. Olive Oatman and her sister Mary Ann were caputred and led away into the nearby mountains.

of the Western Apaches (estimates place it between two thousand and three thousand), but the Yavapais were much less visible to white travelers than their eastern neighbors. Perhaps this was because they were not as devoted to raiding as the Apaches (they did conduct raids, but not as frequently or as boldly as the Apaches); perhaps because the major routes followed by early white travelers skirted the edges of their extensive territory rather than plunging into its midst; perhaps because the Yavapais had not yet adopted the use of horses, as many of the Apaches had, and so did not have the speed and mobility to effectively challenge Spanish or American intrusions into their domain. The diffuse character of Yavapai culture undoubtedly contributed to their relative anonymity: they lived in small bands that roamed the deserts and mountains north of the Gila and east of the Colorado River, hunting and gathering, moving their camps as the seasons changed, maintaining a respectful distance from their Indian neighbors and white travelers.

Because their territory was so large the Yavapais had over the generations divided themselves into four groups or peoples. Those who lived in the north-central part of the territory were called Yavapés; in the northeast, Wipukepas; in the southeast, Kwevkepayas; and in the west, Tolkepayas. Although these groups were politically autonomous and economically independent, they shared a mutually understandable language and a common culture and heritage. All of the Yavapais were members of a larger linguistic family, called Yuman, that also embraced the Pai peoples (Hualapais and Havasupais), who lived in and along the Grand Canyon north of Yavapai territory; the Mohaves, Quechans,[19] and Cocopas, who lived along the Colorado River west of the Yavapai territory; and the Maricopas, who were neighbors to the Pimas near Maricopa Wells. These peoples shared a common Yuman heritage, spoke Yuman languages, and followed a lifestyle that combined agriculture with hunting and gathering. The four Yavapai peoples maintained peaceful relations with the Mohaves, Quechans, and Cocopas, though they warred with the Pais

in the northwest and the Maricopas in the southeast. Although the
Maricopas were Yuman speakers, some event or series of events in
their history had earned them the everlasting enmity of the other
Yumans, and before the first Europeans came into the Southwest,
they fled their original homeland on the Colorado River, coming up
the Gila to find safety near the Pima villages. Long after that migra-
tion, the Maricopas remained bitter enemies of the Yavapais, Mohaves,
Quechans, and Cocopas. (The Pimas, as allies of the Maricopas, were
also enemies of those peoples.) The Wipukepas and Kwevkepayas
maintained close and amicable relations with a people whose territories bordered their own: the Tontos, one of the northern subdivi-
sions of the Western Apaches. In fact the Kwevkepayas shared camps
with the Tontos, sometimes joined their raiding parties, and even
permitted marriages between the two groups.[20]

South of the Gila and west of the Pima and Maricopa villages was a
vast, rocky stretch of desert controlled by the Tohono O'odham. The
principal Tohono O'odham villages were far to the south, however,
and it was rare for large numbers of those Indians to venture as far
north as the river.

Though the country surrounding the Gila may have seemed
empty to the Oatmans, it was in fact the locus of a complex community of American Indians and a rich history of commerce and
communication. The Gila had, from time immemorial, guided Indian
travelers across the desert. The first Spanish explorers had followed
the river as they traveled from colonial settlements in Sonora to
distant outposts in California. Early contacts between the Spanish
and the Indians in the region had been amicable, but over time there
were clashes and, almost inevitably, bloodshed. Jesuit missionaries
came north from Mexico in the late seventeenth century, remaining
for almost a hundred years to build a chain of missions among the
O'odham peoples and introduce European methods of agriculture
and animal husbandry. The Jesuits were replaced by the Franciscans

in 1768, and in 1779 and 1780 those clerics, supported by Spanish soldiers and settlers, established two missions at Yuma among the Quechans. Relations between the Quechans and the Spanish, peaceable at first, soon soured. In July 1781 the Quechans attacked the missions, killing all four of the resident priests and more than a hundred soldiers and settlers (including many women and children). Seventy-four captives taken at the same time were later rescued, but the attack effectively ended Spanish attempts to build missions along the Gila.[21]

Although Mohaves and some Yavapais became acquainted with the Franciscans during their brief sojourn at Yuma, Catholic priests never established any missions in Mohave or Yavapai country, and those Indians remained largely untouched by the Spanish presence. The Apaches, similarly, were beyond the reach of the missionaries, for they were too mobile, too defiant, to present an easy target for proselytizers.

More important to the Mohaves, Apaches, and eventually Yavapais were the fur trappers—originally French but later mainly American—who began to come over the mountains from New Mexico in the mid-1820s, intent on exploiting the large beaver population that inhabited the Gila, the Gila's northern and eastern tributaries, the Salt and Verde, and the Colorado River itself. The trappers were reckless adventurers, and when native inhabitants of the region objected to their trespassing on Indian land, they were quick to take offense. In 1826 a large party of French trappers was challenged by Indians on the great bend of the Gila. A battle ensued in which Indians, French, and some nearby American trappers joined. An unknown number of French trappers and more than a hundred Indians perished in the fighting. The surviving trappers moved on to the Mohave Valley, where there was more bloodshed—two trappers and more than sixteen Mohaves killed. One of the Americans ghoulishly boasted that his people left a host of dead Mohaves hanging from trees "as a proof, how we retaliated aggression."[22]

Trappers had virtually disappeared from the Gila by the mid-1840s, not because of Indian challenges but because beaver hats had gone out of fashion in New York, London, and Paris, where silk hats were now all the rage. But the region's Native inhabitants had only a short respite from white intruders, for the discovery of gold in California in 1848 unleashed a sudden and even more furious flood of westward travelers. During 1849 and 1850 the road through the New Mexico mountains was crowded with long caravans of emigrant wagons filled with California-bound gold-seekers. These "forty-niners" followed the same route that the Oatmans would later pursue, through Tucson and the Pima and Maricopa villages and along the Gila west to the Colorado River. From there they crossed the southern California desert to San Diego or Los Angeles. At least twenty thousand gold seekers came along the Gila trail in 1849 and 1850. By 1851 the gold fever had subsided, and the trail once again became quiet. Though many of the California-bound travelers died of thirst, hunger, or disease, diaries of the period are notably silent about "Indian troubles."[23] Helpless to stem the flood of trespassers crossing their lands (it is one thing to challenge a solitary wagon or even a few, quite another to intercept a flood of twenty thousand), the region's Native peoples apparently chose not to resist.

Once they had come within sight of the Gila, the Oatmans struggled to get their wagon down to the riverbed. They quickly found traces of the emigrant road, but the going here was even more difficult than it had been on the plateau above, for the banks were clogged with sand and rocks slowed the wagon's pace to a crawl.

On the sixth day of their trek westward from Maricopa Wells, the family was overtaken by Dr. Le Conte and Juan the Sonorian. In the time the Oatmans had taken to leave Maricopa, Le Conte and his guide had visited Tucson, returned to the Pima and Maricopa villages, then set out again for the Colorado River. They were shocked by the Oatmans' apparent distress: their animals were weak almost to collapsing and their food supplies perilously low. Roys Oatman was delighted to meet a friend and immediately asked Dr. Le Conte to take a letter to Major Heintzelman. The doctor agreed, and Oatman wrote the following (the bracketed dashes indicate holes in the paper, caused by later handling):[24]

> February 15th at camp on the Hela river
> To the honorable commandant of Fort Yumas
> Brevet Major S. P. Heintzelman
> Honorable sir I am under the necessity of calling upon you for assistance. there is my self, wife & seven children and without help sir I am confident we must perrish I can [——]ly give a [——] we have not but [——] [pro]visions sir I wish you to send for [——] [horses][25] with Harness for two I have gear for one [——] will meet your men as near your camp [as pos]ible I am now sir about 1.40 [140] miles from your [c]amp. I have been Robed of my animals. So that I have not sufficient in their Present condition to take me through. I send this by Dr Jno Lecont in haste.
> Yours with Due respect
> Roys Oatman
> Br[evet] Major Heintzelman

Lorenzo later recalled that Le Conte promised to deliver his father's letter at Yuma with dispatch. The knowledge that help might soon be forthcoming from the army post seemed to buoy the family's spirits. Roys was particularly elated because he believed that Le Conte would deliver his letter promptly and that the scientist had some influence with Heintzelman (a mistake, as it turned out).[26]

As Le Conte and Juan the Sonorian disappeared on the trail ahead of them, the family struggled on with their wagon. It had rained recently and the ground was soft. The wagon's progress was made even harder because at intervals the trail climbed up the slopes of cliffs adjoining the river, then soon descended again to the river, only to climb up another cliff a few miles farther on. This repeated ascending and descending was exhausting for both animals and humans, for often all of the wagon's contents had to be removed before it could be pulled up the slope. Sometimes they even had to help the weakened animals by pushing and pulling the vehicle themselves. As they struggled on, the family's mood dragged lower and lower, until the elation generated by Le Conte had disappeared. Had they known the doctor's fate after he left them, they would have been even more discouraged.

On Sunday, February 16, the day after they left the Oatmans, Le Conte and his guide encountered four Indians on the trail. They were traveling on foot but were armed with bows and arrows. From what Juan could understand of their speech, he took them to be "Yumas" (that is, Quechans) and not friendly. He and Le Conte tried to get the Indians to go away, but they insisted on following. After a little while, they seemed to lose interest and disappeared into the hills. That night the two travelers made their camp in a secluded spot, tethering their horses nearby, but they could not get to sleep until dawn. When they awoke, they found the horses were gone. They picked up the animals' tracks, along with the footprints of what they supposed to be four Indians. The conclusion was obvious: the horses had been stolen, almost certainly by the Indians they encountered the previous day.[27]

Now stranded some sixty miles from Camp Yuma without animals,[28] Le Conte sent Juan ahead on foot with Roys Oatman's letter to Heintzelman and a request that the guide return as soon as possible with replacement horses. The doctor himself started walking toward Yuma, his pistol at the ready should the Indians approach him again. Before he got very far, however, he remembered the Oatmans struggling with their wagon farther back on the trail and decided to leave a note advising them of his run-in with the Indians. He attached the paper to a tree beside the road where the travelers would be likely to see it.[29]

Toward evening the following day, the Oatmans led their wagon down another cliff bordering the Gila and onto yet another rock-strewn section of the river bank. Sighting a sandbar in the middle of the stream, they plunged into the water and crossed over to it. Night was falling, so they retreated to high ground in the middle of the bar and made camp for the night.

Lorenzo later remembered that his father was as dejected and forlorn on this night as he had ever seen him. It is unlikely that he had found Dr. Le Conte's note, for the family had probably not yet traveled that far down the trail; if he had seen it, he did not share its contents with his children.[30]

The next morning, Tuesday, February 18, the family crossed the river on the other side of the sandbar, came up on the opposite bank, and saw that the trail climbed yet another cliff.[31] Although the road was cut deep into the cliff's side, it was so steep and the top of the cliff so high (Lorenzo estimated it to be 200 feet, though it was probably closer to 120)[32] that the cows and oxen could not pull the wagon up. Discouraged, Roys ordered his family to set to the familiar ritual of removing everything from the vehicle and then pushing and pulling on the wagon. Once they reached the top of the cliff, they walked back down the road, carried their possessions up to the top, and repacked them in the wagon. The top of the cliff was a long, flat, mesa littered with black rocks, scrub brush, and cacti and edged on either side by deep gorges. To the south and west, the sky was clear and blue. To the north and east, tall mountains loomed over the river.

It was now late in the afternoon. The family decided to travel through the night, using the light of the moon to guide them, so that their animals would be spared the harsh midday sun; but before they got under way, they needed nourishment. There was enough food left for Mary Ann Oatman to prepare a pot of bean soup and a few pieces of bread. The family sat on rocks as they took their meal. As Roys rose to put some things in the wagon, Lorenzo looked down the road that descended the face of the cliff and spotted a large group of Indians walking up toward them.

Roys Oatman had often bragged to his family and others that when he was traveling around Iowa, preaching the gospel and receiving converts into the Mormon church, he had learned how to "handle" the Indians. But as Lorenzo watched these southwestern Indians approach in the waning afternoon hours of February 18, 1851, he could not help but wonder if his father would be able to "handle" them as he had the Indians of Iowa.

The events that now transpired atop the mesa can be reconstructed only from recollections left years later by Olive and Lorenzo and such bits of corroborating evidence as later white visitors to the site were able to gather. No Indian account of the events was ever recorded.

Olive and Lorenzo remembered that their father invited the Indians to sit down, then said a few words to them in Spanish. They answered in the same language. The brother and sister estimated the band's size at seventeen Indians—a formidable number, if accurate— but they were badly unnerved by the intrusion, and they likely did not count heads.[33]

They said that the Indians asked for tobacco and a pipe, which their father promptly produced. When the Indians finished smoking, they volunteered the information that there were "two horses down in the brush." (This recollection has a ring of authenticity, for Dr. Le Conte and his guide had lost two horses to Indians the day before, and the Indians who stole them could well have joined the party that approached the Oatmans on the mesa, although neither Olive nor Lorenzo could have known about the connection. Perhaps the Indians hoped to trade the stolen animals for a part of the Oatmans' supplies.) They asked for pinole (corn meal). Roys Oatman said that they had almost no food in the wagon and what little there was he had to save for his family. But the Indians were persistent. (While the Oatmans had little food, the Indians had even less. They were struggling with a terrible drought that year and almost certainly suffering from famine. If the family's bean soup and bread seemed a paltry meal to the Oatmans, it may well have seemed a feast to the Indians.) Roys reluctantly offered the Indians some bread. When this was eaten, they asked for more. When Roys refused this last request, one of the Indians climbed into the wagon and began to push the contents around. He came out to speak to the others, then announced that they wanted meat. When the request was not met, the Indians began to take objects from the wagon and conceal them in their clothing. After the family protested, the Indians withdrew into a little circle and began talking among themselves.

Pretending to ignore the intruders, Roys began to reload the wagon with items that had been strewn about on the ground. Mary Ann Oatman went inside the vehicle to arrange things, while her older children stood outside. Lorenzo was so frightened that he turned his eyes from the scene.

Now something provoked the Indians into action—the available evidence provides no clue as to what it was. In their recollections Olive and Lorenzo protested that their father had done nothing to offend the Indians, that to the contrary, he had treated them courteously. What is more, neither Olive nor Lorenzo even hinted that their father had made any show of arms. If he (or Lorenzo) had waived guns in the Indians' direction or fired a warning shot, the Indians would almost certainly have retreated.

Without warning the Indians let out what Lorenzo later remembered as a "deafening yell" and rushed toward the family, swinging clubs. The boy was struck on the top and back of his head with a blow that sent him to the ground. He attempted to regain his feet, but received another blow that sent him sprawling. Within a few seconds, Roys, his wife, his daughters Lucy and Charity Ann, and his sons Roys, Jr., and Roland were all beaten to the ground. Olive saw Lorenzo fall, the top of his head covered with blood. She saw her bloodied father lying on the ground and her mother, one baby in her arms and another still in her womb, lying not far away. Olive guessed that she too had been struck, for she collapsed unconscious on the ground.

The Indians now began to strip the fallen bodies of anything of value. They searched the wagon for food, broke open boxes, and rifled through their contents. When they came on a feather bed, they tore it open and scattered its feathers to the wind. They took the wheels off the wagon, tore the canvas canopy off its frame, and unyoked the cows and oxen. Then they bundled their plunder and, taking thirteen-year-old Olive and her eight-year-old sister, Mary Ann, by their arms, quickly headed down the hill. Behind them they left seven bodies, broken and bloodied, lying among the rocks and cacti.[34]

CHAPTER 4

The Captives

The Indians who had attacked the Oatmans hurried down the trail with their loot and captives, retracing the path they had followed to the top of the cliff. They crossed the river and headed into the brush and the hills to the north. The attack had occurred in Mexico, and the Indians retreated into the United States; but if they were aware of the invisible lines the whites had drawn on the land, they gave no sign of it.

Olive later remembered that the Indians divided themselves into two parties, one that took charge of her and Mary Ann and another that herded her father's cows and oxen. The group that had responsibility for the girls followed a trail for half a mile, Olive reckoned. It led through a narrow opening in the hills to a campsite, where the Indians took off their packs and made a fire. They boiled some beans taken from the Oatman wagon and mixed flour with water to form little cakes. They offered the girls some food, but they refused it. After the Indians finished eating, they rested for a while, then shouldered their packs and set off again on the trail.[1]

Olive and Mary Ann walked along with their captors, but reluctantly. The Indians had removed the girls' shoes, probably to make it difficult for them to escape, and as they moved across the rocky desert, their bare feet became bruised and bloody. At one point, the

Indians realized that Mary Ann was too weak to continue, and one of
them hoisted her onto his back. The party stopped several times to
make camp. At one of the camps, they were rejoined by the Indians
who had taken the animals. Only two of the oxen were with them; the
other animals had already been killed and butchered. Now the two
remaining animals were slaughtered, cut up, and packed for carrying.

Taking again to the trail, the Indians seemed surprised when they
came round a large rock and encountered another party of Indians.
Olive got the impression that these Indians did not belong to the
same tribe as her captors. One of them, apparently outraged to see
white people so deep in Indian territory, attempted to shoot her with
an arrow, but her captors interceded to protect her, and an angry
confrontation followed. When the captors were satisfied that the
other Indians no longer presented a danger, they resumed their
journey. After three or four days of exhausting travel, the party arrived
at the Indians' village.[2]

In the recollections she recorded years later, Olive gave vague and
not always consistent descriptions of the village and its location. In
Stratton's *Captivity of the Oatman Girls,* she described it as "a cluster
of low, thatched huts, each having an opening near the ground";[3] in
the lectures she gave some years later, it was "a small village of half
underground huts surrounded by a rocky range of hills."[4] Neither
description was specific enough to distinguish the place from scores
of similar Indian villages scattered through the Gila country in 1851,
and Olive did not give the village's name. She can hardly be faulted
for the vagueness of her recollections, however, for the shock of the
Indian attack and the rigors of her forced flight through the desert
would have dulled the senses and muddled the memory of any
young girl in similar circumstances.

Olive's statements about the village's location were even less satisfactory than her description of it. When she arrived in San Francisco
in 1856, she told a newspaper reporter that the village was "about
one hundred miles . . . from the place where we were attacked" and

that she, Mary Ann, and the Indians traveled "on foot all that night and the next day" to reach it. At one point in Stratton's book, Olive is quoted as stating that the village was 200 miles away and that it took three days to get there;[5] at another point in the same book she sets the distance at more than 250 miles and the travel time at eighty hours. In her lectures, Olive did not specify the distance in miles, saying only that it took the party until the "fourth day" after the attack to reach the village. She never gave the direction in which the party traveled, although in Stratton's account she stated that at one point in the journey, they traveled over "a succession of small bluff points of high mountain chains, these letting down to a rough winding valley, running principally northeast."[6] It is unlikely, however, that any of these descriptions accurately represented the trip that she and Mary Ann made to the Indian village. If they had in fact traveled 200 miles (let alone 250) in a northeasterly direction from the attack site, they would have passed through all of the Yavapai country north of the Gila; crossed a range of high mountains; penetrated the territory of the Western Apaches in the mountains beyond the Verde River; climbed another, even higher mountain; and arrived somewhere on the broad plateau occupied by the Navajos and Hopis. If they had gone such a distance due north, they would have arrived at the Grand Canyon of the Colorado, well beyond the Yavapai country and deep into the territory of the Yavapais' bitter enemies, the Hualapais and Havasupais. If they had proceeded to the west or northwest, they would have crossed over the Colorado River, a formidable geographic feature never mentioned in any of Olive's accounts of the trip. While the southwestern desert is vast and the Indians of the region were capable of covering large distances in short periods of time, two hundred miles is simply too great a distance for barefooted white girls to have walked in only three or four days. The conclusion is inescapable that either Olive's reckoning of the distances covered on this trip were greatly exaggerated or Royal Stratton badly overstated the estimates she gave him.[7]

If Olive was vague about the village and its location, she was emphatic in identifying her captors as Apaches, more specifically as Tonto Apaches. (A word that the early Spanish misapplied to these Indians, *tonto* means "dull," "stupid," or "foolish.")[8] The territory of the Tontos stretched from the Verde River valley (about 120 miles northeast of the place where the Oatmans were attacked) to the lofty San Francisco Peaks (about 170 miles north of the attack site) and thence eastward into high and wooded mountains. Although the Tontos shared the raiding lifestyle of other Western Apaches, they differed from them in the degree to which they mingled with the Wipukepas and Kwevkepayas, the Eastern Yavapai peoples. In fact, relations between the Tontos and some of the Wipukepas were so close that they shared a common territory, hunted together, and spoke each other's languages. French and American fur trappers and the gold seekers of 1849 applied a confusing and inaccurate array of names to the people living where the Western Apache and Eastern Yavapai territories intersected, sometimes calling them "Tontos," "Apaches," or "Tonto Apaches," sometimes "Mohave-Apaches," "Apache-Mohaves," or "Apache-Yumas." (The last three labels were particularly inappropriate, for neither the Apaches nor the Wipukepas had anything at all to do with the Mohaves or the "Yumas" [Quechans], who lived far to the west.) Given this jumble it would hardly be surprising if Olive Oatman (and Royal Stratton, writing for her) were confused about the real identities of these peoples. But the confusion in nomenclature is enough at least to raise serious questions about Olive's identification of the Indians who captured her as "Apaches" or "Tontos." Were they in fact Indians living to the east of the Yavapai territory? Were they perhaps the mixed Kwevkepaya-Tonto peoples who lived along the Apache-Yavapai border? Or were they members of one of the four principal Yavapai groups?

The identity of the attacking Indians will probably never be established with certainty, for the evidence is too fragmentary. There are signs, however, that point toward an answer.

First, Olive Oatman's identification of the attackers as Tonto Apaches—accepted by Stratton and repeated by scores of later writers—deserves attention. Tontos may in fact have traveled upwards of 120 miles (perhaps even 200) from their own territory before encountering the Oatman family on the Gila. If they did so, however, they would have had to cross the territory of other Indian peoples—the Yavapés, Wipukepas, Kwevkepayas, Tolkepayas, Pimas, or Maricopas—to do so. Indians who were a long way from home would be less likely to take captives—who might not survive the trek back—than to kill all members of the family, pillage their wagon, and be done with the whole affair. The attackers decision to take the two girls captive suggests that they did not think it would be too difficult to get them back to their village.

Second, Olive made it very clear in her recollections that the attacking Indians had regular, friendly contacts with the Mohaves—in fact, that "almost the only tribe with whom they had any intercourse was the Mohaves"[9]—and she and Mary Ann were ultimately taken by the Mohaves to live in the Mohave Valley. The Mohaves' territory was about 175 miles west of the Tonto Apaches'. While the Tontos did maintain some contacts with the Mohaves, they had to traverse the territories of other Indian peoples to do so. Olive's recollections contain no suggestion that, when a party of Mohaves took her and Mary Ann from the captors' village to the Mohave Valley, they crossed through any other Indians' territory along the way.

The Indians who lived closest to the attack site were the Western Yavapais, or Tolkepayas. In fact, the part of the Gila River where the Oatmans were attacked then marked the time-honored southern boundary of the Tolkepaya territory. If nothing else, the proximity of their territory to the attack site justifies a close examination of the Tolkepayas as the probable attackers.

The territory occupied by the Tolkepayas constituted about half of the extensive Yavapai domain. A broad desert plain interrupted at intervals by craggy mountains, it was an unremittingly dry land (in some places the average annual rainfall was only two inches), sparsely watered by springs hidden in mountainsides or canyons. Most of the region's plants—cacti, leathery shrubs, and low trees—were protected from foraging animals by spines, nettles, and thorns. To casual observers the Tolkepaya land seemed a desolate stretch of sand and rock in which human beings would never willingly seek to make their homes. But the desert's lifeless appearance was deceptive, for people who accepted its challenges found it a hospitable home. To be sure, agriculture could never thrive there. Crops might be planted along the rivers or in the beds of desert washes where rainwater rushed in torrents during the desert's infrequent storms; but the bulk of the land was suitable only for hunting and gathering and for people willing to be perpetually on guard against famine and thirst.

The Tolkepayas farmed on a small scale. Like other Indians of the Southwest, their favorite crops were corn, beans, and squash. They planted seeds in the early summer and left them virtually untended until later in the year, when they returned to harvest whatever a benevolent—or in dry years, unyielding—nature had provided. The people spent most of their time ranging over the desert in search of the fruits, seeds, nuts, vegetables, and animals that formed the bulk of their diet. Mescal (the fleshy heart of the agave plant) was their most important food; it grew on rocky slopes throughout the Yavapai territory and could be harvested year-round.[10] In midsummer they picked the figlike fruit of the giant saguaro cacti; in November they gathered sunflower seeds in the mountains. Rabbits, deer, elk, antelopes, bighorn sheep, tortoises, wood rats, squirrels, and lizards were hunted all through the year.[11]

From late spring to early fall the Tolkepayas lived in small camps, often not much larger than extended families. In late fall, winter, and early spring, they gathered in larger villages. Their houses (called *uwas*) were domed huts supported by poles and covered with grass, bark, branches, or animal skins.[12] The winter villages were located where they could be easily defended and where game was abundant and water sources dependable. Tolkepaya hunting parties typically contained ten to fifteen men, though sometimes more, and were occasionally transformed into raiding or warring parties that set out, not to bag game, but to attack the Tolkepayas' bitter enemies, the Pimas, Maricopas, and Hualapais. Oral traditions of all the Yavapais record frequent and often brutal struggles between the rival peoples of the southwestern desert.[13] When an enemy village was attacked, club-swinging Tolkepayas killed or disabled as many of the inhabitants as they could. Sometimes, however, they spared the lives of women and children, who were taken back to their villages as captives. When Tolkepayas lost some of their own in battle, their tradition required vengeance, and they did their best to inflict equivalent losses on their enemies.[14]

Like other peoples of the southwestern desert, the Tolkepayas were concerned first and foremost with satisfying the basic needs of life: searching for food and water, building houses and fashioning clothes, and protecting themselves from weather, wild animals, and their human enemies. Warfare—both offensive and defensive—also played a prominent role in their lives. The warfare was often bloody and cruel, but probably not much more so than that of other peoples in Europe, Asia, or Africa.

The practice of taking captives and holding them in degrading and often brutal bondage was, as historians have demonstrated, widespread among all of the southwestern Indians and, in fact, common among almost all Native peoples of North America. Captives were often enslaved; sometimes they were ransomed back to the peoples from whom they were taken; not infrequently they were adopted into their captors' families or tribes. In the course of their capture or enslavement, captives were sometimes wounded or killed. In a region in which an overall rule of law could not be imposed, because there was no supratribal authority to impose it, taking captives and enslaving them was often the only means of exacting revenge or redressing past wrongs. Captivity and enslavement constituted a kind of self-help system in which justice was exacted when there was no other way of doing so.[15]

But there were other, more ambiguous motives for taking captives: the desire to replenish population stocks depleted by war, disease, and famine; the determination to seize something for which the enemy would pay a ransom, thus helping to equalize wealth between tribes; the impulse to acquire girls or young women who might marry into the captors' tribes, forming bonds of kinship that would make future conflicts less likely. It is no more honest to deny that captivity and slavery were pervasive among the Tolkepayas, and among other Indians of the region, than to suggest that the Indians were obsessed with such practices. It was a hard, cruel, often degrading part of life in the southwestern desert.[16] Acknowledging that fact may help to explain the fates that ultimately befell Olive and Mary Ann Oatman.

Tolkepaya culture is not hard to reconcile with Olive Oatman's description of the Indians who captured her and her sister Mary Ann. As described in Stratton's book, the Indians were residents of a small village that subsisted entirely on hunting and gathering. Their principal foods were deer, quail, rabbits, and roots. (Olive said that the villagers "knew nothing of cultivating the soil," but the limited agriculture practiced by the Tolkepayas led other observers to make this same mistake.)[17] Olive remembered that her captors made the most of the meager food resources available to them ("it was a marvel to see how little was required to keep them alive") and that, when put to the test, they were capable of great displays of endurance and strength. They always traveled on foot, apparently not yet having acquired the habit of riding horses (there were many horses in the region in 1851, but only the Apaches had become really expert horsemen). The village derived its water supply from one or more springs (Olive described at least one "gurgling spring" in the vicinity). Olive said that she and her sister were treated badly by their captors; they were forced to work, as burden bearers and food gatherers under the stern supervision of the women and children of the village. If the girls did not obey the commands given them, they were beaten. Olive later characterized the life she and Mary Ann led while among their captors as a "dark prison life."[18] They had very little to eat, she said, and most of that they had to gather themselves. She may not have known of the drought that beset the whole region in 1851, but she was clearly feeling its effects.

What is the evidence that the attackers were Tolkepayas? First, the attack took place at the edge of Tolkepaya territory but at a great distance from the Tonto Apache homeland. Second, Olive and Mary Ann were taken to live in a village that closely resembled a typical Tolkepaya village. Third, the assertion of Dr. Le Conte's guide that the Indians who stole their horses (probably members of the same party that later attacked the Oatmans) sounded like "Yumas"[19] can be explained by the fact that the Tolkepaya language (a dialect of Yavapai) is a Yuman language. Fourth, the Tolkepayas' territory touched that of the Mohaves on the northwest, and the Mohaves were frequent (and according to Olive "almost the only") visitors to her captors' village. And fifth, years after the girls were taken captive, one of the Mohaves who was present when the girls arrived in the Mohave Valley, when asked to identify the capturing Indians, recalled straightforwardly: "They were Yavapai who did it."[20] (Tolkepayas, again, were the Yavapais who lived closest to Mohave territory.) While this evidence does not answer the question conclusively, it at least supports a strong probability that the Oatmans were attacked by Tolkepayas, not by Tonto Apaches, as Olive later asserted.[21]

A plausible scenario by which a party of Tolkepayas would have come to the banks of the Gila River when the Oatmans were there is not difficult to imagine: A group of Indians was hunting in the desert for food, gathering whatever fruits, seeds, or roots they could find in the drought-parched desert, watching for any game they might kill and bring back to their village. Part of the group encountered Dr. Le Conte and his guide and stole their horses, and the following day, the whole group came on the Oatmans atop the mesa overlooking the river. When Roys Oatman refused to give them any substantial food, and when he allowed them to poke through his wagon and wander freely through his campsite, they realized he would make an easy target. They attacked him and his family, stole his cows and oxen, and captured two of his daughters. It was an ugly but familiar scene in the struggle for survival in the southwestern desert.

If Tolkepayas were in fact the attackers, where might they have held Olive and Mary Ann Oatman as captives? The Tolkepaya territory had many villages, some that were occupied on a permanent basis, others that were used only intermittently, and almost any of them could have been the site of the Oatman captivity. One, however, stands out as more likely than the others to have been the attackers' village: a place called Wiltaika, located in the long, troughlike depression between the Harquahala and Harcuvar mountains that Americans later named the McMullen Valley.[22] It was probably the closest of all the Tolkepaya villages to the attack site, about sixty miles north. The valley was guarded on the southeast and northwest by rugged mountains but open on its southwestern and northeastern ends to the desert plain. Springs in the nearby mountains provided a good supply of water. It would have been feasible (although by no means easy) for Olive and Mary Ann, accompanied by their Indian captors, to walk to Wiltaika from the attack site in three days and convenient for the Mohaves to visit the place, encounter the girls, and ultimately decide to take them to live in the Mohave Valley. Of course, Wiltaika can be identified as the attackers' village with no more certainty than the attackers can be identified as Tolkepayas. If the Oatman girls were captured by Tontos, they obviously did not take them to Wiltaika. If, however, they were captured by Tolkepayas, as seems probable, it is at least likely that Wiltaika was their destination.

The good relations that prevailed between the Mohaves and the Tolkepayas were attributable not only to the proximity of the two people's territories but also to the similarity in their Yuman languages. Mohaves made at least two visits to the attackers' village during the time that Olive and Mary Ann were held there. The first was apparently a trading trip made by a large group of Mohaves in the fall of 1851. The Mohaves brought vegetables, grain, and other products that they hoped to exchange for furs, animal skins, and other items. The second, in the spring of the following year, was for the specific purpose of taking Olive and Mary Ann to live among the Mohaves. Preliminary arrangements for the transfer were apparently made during the first trip but could not be finalized until the Mohave chief gave his approval. The second party was headed by a young woman who, Olive later learned, was the daughter of the Mohave chief. Olive remembered this woman as beautiful, intelligent, and well-spoken. She was fluent in the language of the capturing Indians (Yavapai?) as well as her own Mohave, and she was sympathetic to the plight of the white captives.[23]

The girls were asked whether they would prefer to stay with their captors or leave with the Mohaves, but they declined to express a preference lest it later be held against them. A council was convened to discuss the proposed transfer, and an agreement was reached: the Mohaves would give the captors two horses, some vegetables, a few pounds of beads, and three blankets in return for Olive and Mary Ann. Olive later characterized the agreement as a "sale," but it could just as easily be seen as an adoption. The Mohaves told the girls that they could provide better homes for them than the Indians who had captured them, that they wanted to take the girls with them because of their kindly feelings toward them. The captors were apparently willing to concede those points, but they were giving up something valuable and demanded compensation. Arrangements like this were not foreign to the southwestern desert; indeed, comparable transactions often occurred among European Americans, who were no strangers to child adoption.

Olive later remembered the day she and Mary Ann left the captors' village with the Mohave party. A full year had passed since they had first come to live there, and in that time they had grown used to

the routine of village life. Many of the villagers were angered by their
willingness to leave. Some hurled insults at them, even threatened to
harm them physically. Others, feigning indifference, merely laughed.
But a few of the children cried.[24]

Accompanied by the Mohaves, Olive and Mary Ann set out once
again on a long trip through the desert. In Stratton's book Olive
remembered that the journey took more than ten days and covered
350 miles;[25] like her reckoning of the distance between the attack
site and the captors' village, however, this was an exaggeration. If the
party had traveled that far, they would have gone well beyond the
Mohave Valley toward the Sierra Nevada of east-central California.
More likely, they traveled much less than ten days, following a leisurely
pace to cover the actual distance that separated the captors' village
from the Mohave Valley. (If the village was Wiltaika, the distance
would have been only about 90 miles.)

Straddling the Colorado River where the states of Arizona, Nevada,
and California intersect, the Mohave Valley is one of the most distinc-
tive geographic features of the southwestern landscape. It measures
about thirty miles from north to south and two to five from east to
west and is walled off from the surrounding desert by high mountains.
Though the mountains are as barren as the surrounding desert, the
valley floor is more inviting, a slightly sloping bed of sand and grass
slashed down the middle by a ribbon of trees and water. The water
is the Colorado River, the most important watercourse in the Southwest, a fifteen-hundred-mile-long channel that begins high in the
Rocky Mountains; flows through a succession of plateaus, canyons,
and valleys; and eventually finds its mouth at the head of the Gulf of
California in Mexico. Because of its length and volume, because much
of it flows through a desert, and because it overflows its banks every
year to fertilize the surrounding soil, the Colorado is often called
the American Nile. Olive and Mary Ann Oatman caught their first
sight of the river and of the surrounding Mohave Valley from the

crest of a long trail that approached the valley from the east, paused at a break in the mountains, and then led down into the valley. Not surprisingly, Olive's was impressed with "the loveliness that nature had strewn upon that valley."[26] With the Mohave chief's daughter and their other Mohave companions, the girls proceeded down the slope.

On the valley floor, the party went directly to the home of the Mohave chief, where, surrounded by family and friends, he welcomed the new arrivals. Olive later described the chief as a "tall, strongly built man, active and generally happy."[27] But this description could have applied to any number of Mohave men, for adult Mohave males were characteristically tall (averaging six feet), with lanky physiques and long faces. Their complexions were dark, but not so dark as those of many other southwestern peoples; their black hair was cut squarely across their foreheads but allowed to grow long in back, where it was woven into ropclike strands that often hung to the hip.[28]

Olive and Mary Ann entered the chief's house with some trepidation. They wondered why he had bothered to bring them all the way from the captors' village. Was it so they would be even farther away from their white friends and relatives than they had been and thus less likely to return to their own people? And could they expect their lives to be any easier among the Mohaves than it had been among their original captors? The chief received them politely but coolly, providing a place for them to sleep and food for them to eat. But it was clear from the start that he expected them to work for their keep. They had to carry water from the river to the chief's house; gather wood along the river banks, tie it in bundles, and lug the bundles into the village; pick wild roots, mesquite beans, and berries; help other Mohaves sow seeds near the river; and later in the year, join in the work of harvesting and storing the wheat, corn, beans, pumpkins, and melons that would sustain them through the fall and winter.

Agriculture, like most other aspects of Mohave life, was dominated by the great river that flowed through the valley. In the spring, when snow melted in the distant mountains, the river spilled over its banks, rushing through the northern canyons with incredible force and spreading rich deposits of silt over the valley bottoms (it was the waterborne silt, richly colored, that prompted Spanish explorers to name the river the Rio Colorado, or Red River). When the river was running high (as it was when Olive and Mary Ann first saw it), the Mohaves knew it would be a fertile year. As the waters receded, they planted seeds in wet fields on either side of the stream. Left to their own devices, the seeds sprouted and grew into plants. But the Mohaves never plowed or irrigated their fields; and because they frequently harvested their crops before they reached maturity, their yields were low. Even in good years, the harvest was enough to feed the people only through the summer and autumn; by winter the people began to look elsewhere for food. There was little game in the valley, so they rarely hunted, although fish were occasionally taken from the river and a small lake nearby. The wild berries, nuts, seeds, and roots that were gathered in remote corners of the valley and on the lower slopes of the surrounding mountains were always a more important part of the Mohave diet than fish, game, or farm crops.

Olive later remembered that when she and Mary Ann first arrived at the Mohave chief's house, neither he nor any of his family showed much interest in them. They made no efforts to converse with the girls, inquire about their former lives, or probe their feelings. (The language barrier that separated the Mohaves and their white charges was of course responsible for much of this seeming indifference.) After Olive and Mary Ann began to understand the Mohave language, the Mohaves spoke more freely with them. Some of the Indians heard the girls singing among themselves—hymns they had learned in church—and asked them to repeat them. The music was strange to their ears, but the Mohaves enjoyed it, and some even offered to pay the girls for their performances. Olive remembered that they gave her and her sister treasured pieces of red flannel (probably manufactured in Mexico or the United States and traded from one

Indian people to another) and strings of beads that the girls wore around their necks.[29]

In time, some Mohaves confided their religious beliefs to the girls, recounting Mohave creation stories and reciting long and detailed descriptions of the Mohave spirit world. They spoke of the spirits who lived at the top of a mountain called Avikwame ("Spirit Mountain") that towered over the northern end of the valley. In an account reminiscent of the biblical story of Noah, they told the girls that there was once a great flood that covered all the land; after the waters receded, a canoe containing one family came to rest on top of Avikwame, and from this family all the Mohaves were descended. Avikwame was a place sacred to the spirits, and ordinary mortals were forbidden to approach its summit; but shamans might go there on special occasions to receive messages that the spirits wished to relay to the people.[30]

Olive recalled, however, that some of the Mohaves were persistently unfriendly, even hostile, to her and her sister. Some challenged them with provocative questions about white life and taunted them with thinly veiled threats. These Mohaves, according to Olive, believed that Americans were dishonest, weak, and prideful, that they had "forsaken nature" and were consumed by a desire to "possess the earth."[31] They told her that when a Mohave killed an American, the American's spirit was sent in chains to Avikwame, where it was doomed to eternal torment.[32]

Americans, however, were not the only objects of Mohave ill feelings. Over the centuries the Mohaves had formed durable friendships with some of the neighboring tribes and equally durable hatreds for others. They were traditional allies of the Yavapais and Quechans and enemies of the Maricopas and Pimas. They were also bitter enemies of the Cocopas, a Yuman tribe who lived on the Colorado near the Gulf of California. In the spring of 1854, the Mohaves and Quechans organized a military expedition against the Cocopas. While the Mohave warriors were gone, Olive was told that if any of those warriors were killed in the struggle with the Cocopas, an equal number of the Mohaves' captives back home would be "sacrificed" to the Mohave "spirits."[33] This threat would naturally have struck fear in Olive and Mary Ann. Olive later remembered that during the whole time the war party was away, she lived in fear that the Mohaves would suffer losses on the battlefield and that her own life might also be forfeit. But the Mohaves and Quechans were able to surprise the Cocopas and, in the ensuing battle, kill three Cocopa men and capture two Cocopa women. When the warriors returned in triumph, Olive was at last able to breathe easily. But her relief was short-lived. One of the Cocopa captives, a beautiful woman of about twenty-five, attempted to escape to her homeland by plunging into the Colorado River and swimming south. The woman was pursued, recaptured, and subjected by her Mohave captors to an agonizing death: her arms and legs were fastened to an upright wooden cross (a practice much like crucifixion, which the Mohaves may have learned about by listening to the sermons of Catholic missionaries or seeing religious pictures in the missions at Yuma), and thus impaled, she was made the target of dozens of Mohave arrows. Olive said that she was horrified by the spectacle and took it as a warning of the fate that might befall her if she ever attempted to leave the Mohave Valley.[34]

The accuracy of Olive's story of the Cocopa captive's gruesome death is impossible to determine. There is no question that Mohave warriors frequently took captives and that, once taken, the captives were often treated brutally. Studies by the anthropologist A. L. Kroeber indicate that the capture of girls or young women was "a constant object of Mohave war parties."[35] Mohaves typically spoke of these captives as "slaves," although Kroeber thought the Mohave word used for this purpose (*'ahwe*) in fact meant only "strangers."[36] A more accurate translation is probably "enemy," a concept that was not as brutal as "slave" but still denoted contempt.[37] Kroeber believed that Mohave captives were not "abused" except when they were suspected of "trying to escape." The Mohaves' "curious attitude in the matter," Kroeber wrote, "is distinctly southwestern."[38]

However much the death of the Cocopa captive might have terrified Olive, there is no suggestion in any of her recollections that she or Mary Ann were ever mistreated by the Mohaves; on the contrary, her accounts reveal that some Mohaves treated them with special kindness and that, in time, warm friendships were formed between Mohaves and the white girls.

Almost from the start, the chief's wife, whom Olive identified as Aespaneo, took a motherly interest in Olive and Mary Ann. She prevailed on her husband to have a small plot of ground set aside as the girls' private garden and to see to it that they had seeds for planting and a secure place in which to store their crops. And when the girls' supply of seeds was exhausted, she gave them more from her own modest stores. The chief's daughter, whom Olive called Topeka, was a good friend to Olive and Mary Ann. She shared food and blankets with the girls and took every opportunity to demonstrate warm and protective feelings for them. Olive recalled that her experiences with Aespaneo and Topeka convinced her that kindness "is not always a stranger to the untutored and untamed bosom." "They seemed really to feel for us," Olive admitted. In time, too, Olive came to feel that she and her sister had become a part of the chief's family. The chief's wife had become their surrogate mother, his daughter their sister, and the chief himself their adopted father.

Who was this Mohave chief who took Olive and Mary Ann into his family in the spring of 1852—and where was the house he and his white charges lived in? Olive's recollections leave us with unsatisfactory answers to these intriguing questions. She remembered that the village in which the chief lived (there were several in the valley) occupied both sides of the river, but she did not specify whether his house was on the east or west bank. In describing her first approach to the house from the east, she did not mention crossing the river, thus implying that it was on the east side. Half a century later, however, a Mohave with vivid recollections of Olive's time in the Mohave Valley placed the house squarely on the west bank, within the boundaries of what had by that time become the city of Needles, California.[39]

Olive said that the house stood on a small elevation above the river and that it was surrounded by two enclosures, one a square of stakes embedded in the ground and measuring about fifty feet on each side, the other completely enclosing the first and consisting of cottonwood trees planted in a square measuring about a hundred feet on each side. The house itself was about twenty feet square, with walls of poles set in the ground and a roof with a ridgepole and rafters that sloped on either side to eaves. The top was covered with a thick mat of limbs and mud. Although the house was rudely built and furnished, the compound about it, surrounded by trees and grass, made a pretty sight.[40]

In the book that Royal Stratton later wrote for Olive and Lorenzo Oatman, the chief was identified by a curious (and somewhat puzzling) assortment of names: "Espaniola," "Aespaniola," "Espaniole," "Espanesay," and "Aspenosay."[41] What meaning (or meanings) should be assigned to these names, or whether Stratton's transcription of them bears anything more than a vague resemblance to their Mohave originals, may never be known. Olive, after all, came to know the chief's name only by sound and never saw it written down, and Stratton's attempt to render it in English was almost certainly awkward. Disregarding the differences in spelling, the names given by Stratton could all be variants of a single word, all deriving from the Spanish word español and all translating into English as "Spanish" or "Spaniard." If this is the case, it would not be surprising, for Mohave men and women commonly had more than one name, sometimes simultaneously, and they adopted and discarded names almost at will. The Mohaves were particularly protective of their own, Mohave names and seemed willing (even eager) to assume fanciful, often Spanish names for the benefit of "outsiders," regardless of whether the outsiders were Spanish, Mexican, or American.[42]

It is equally possible, however, that the name (or names) given by Stratton were not of Spanish origin at all. One student of the Oatman story has suggested, though without persuasive explanation, that the name was based on a Mohave word describing a woman's genitals.[43] This suggestion, is not incredible. In his study of Mohave naming practices, Kroeber learned that Mohaves often used "names of the most undignified sort." "A phrase that strikes as apt or novel," Kroeber wrote, "or alludes to a trivial incident is the basis of many names. There is not the least shrinking from obscenity." Kroeber further asserted that Mohave men sometimes assumed names with sexual connotations "in the hope of attracting or impressing women."[44]

Whatever the meaning of the name "Espaniola," there is no doubt that it was not the chief's sole or formal name. Olive described the chief as "the Mohave magnate," by which she meant that he was the principal leader (or "head chief") of the Mohaves.[45] There were other "chiefs," of course, but none (not even the "magnate") had much political or military authority. The Mohave nation (properly "Aha macave," or "the people who live by the water")[46] was a relatively small group, numbering three thousand or four thousand in the 1850s,[47] whose cohesiveness derived more from feelings of national unity than any fear of authority. The head chief (called the *pipatahon* or *Aha macave pipatahon*)[48] was a man to be admired rather than obeyed; he maintained his leadership through personal integrity and professional competency but had no authority to give orders or command obedience. Other chiefs, called *kohots*, were religious or ceremonial leaders. When Mohaves gathered for celebrations, the kohots were expected to provide food and to entertain the guests with orations. Although they had no more political or military authority than the pipatahon, the kohots commonly acted as spokesmen for the nation when strangers entered the valley. Although Olive's recollections suggest that Espaniola was the pipatahon, other evidence reveals that he was one of the Mohave kohots. In fact, a well-known chief named Homoseh quahote was the Aha macave pipatahon during the time that Olive was in the Mohave Valley. While Homoseh quahote undoubtedly had other names (including Spanish ones), it is possible to determine with some certainty that he was not the chief who gave a home to Olive and Mary Ann Oatman and whom Olive later remembered as "Espaniola."

For as long as any of the Mohave people could remember, they had been divided into hereditary clans. The clan names were patrilineal (that is, passed from one generation to the next through fathers) and were based on the names of familiar animals, plants, or natural objects (such as "Hipa," the coyote; "Vermacka," the bean; "Shulia," the beaver; "Whalia," the moon; and "Chacha," the corn).[49] All of a father's daughters bore his clan name; in fact, all of the girls born into the same clan bore the same clan name. (The sons also bore the clan name, although silently; only the daughters actually answered to the clan name.) Although the daughters also used familiar or affectionate names, their clan designations were their formal names; the clan name enabled a Mohave to quickly and certainly determine a girl or woman's paternal descent. When Kroeber visited the Mohave Valley in 1903, Mohaves who still remembered Olive Oatman told him that she was known by the clan name "Owich" (signifying the clouds, rain, and wind).[50] Kroeber thus concluded that the chief who took Olive into his home was of the Owich clan. She can have derived this name only from a Mohave man who had assumed the role of father to her. It is well established, however, that Homoseh quahote belonged to the Malika (wood rat or ground squirrel) clan.[51] If Olive was an Owich, as Kroeber's informants assured him, she could not have lived in the house of the Malika Homoseh quahote. The conclusion is thus clear that the man Olive knew as "Espaniola" was a kohot and not the Aha macave pipatahon.

Kohots were responsible for taking charge of captives who from time to time were brought into the valley.[52] As Olive later made quite clear, Espaniola took her and Mary Ann into his house from the first day of their arrival among the Mohaves, assuming responsibility for their welfare and, in time, accepting them into his family. By custom they would have born his clan name, though they might also be known by familiar or affectionate names. One of Olive's familiar names was probably "Spantsa," although it is likely that she also had others.[53]

CHAPTER 5

The Tattoos

Around the time they became members of the *Owich* clan, Olive and Mary Ann received more tangible recognition of their new status as Mohaves. In Stratton's book Olive claims that she and her sister protested when Mohave shamans first approached them with the suggestion that they be tattooed. They may in fact have objected, if only because the process of being tattooed entailed some pain. Since the girls had undoubtedly seen other Mohaves receive tattoos, however, they must have known that the pain was not very great (after the process began, a kind of numbness set in). In fact, Mohave tattooing was relatively simple. The shaman pricked the skin (usually the chin, but sometimes other parts of the face or body as well) with what Olive called "sharp sticks" (perhaps long cactus spines) to form lines that bled freely; the "sticks" were then dipped in the juice of a weed that grew along the river and in blue powder ground from river rocks and used to rub the powder into the bleeding lines. At the same time that Olive and Mary Ann received tattoos on their chins, Olive (and perhaps Mary Ann as well) also received tattoos on their arms—a single straight line on each.[1]

The tattoos Olive and Mary Ann received while in the Mohave Valley raise some of the most intriguing questions presented by the Oatman story. Olive later claimed that the tattoos were "slave marks" that permanently branded her and her sister as Mohave captives and made it easy for other Indians to identify them if they ever attempted to leave the valley. But this claim is problematic. First, Mohave tattoos were not limited to captives but given to almost all Mohaves, men as well as women. Following no regular pattern, the marks were selected by the person tattooed or sometimes the tattooer. Further, the tattoos had a clear religious or spiritual purpose: they were designed to permit deceased persons to obtain entrance to "Sil'aid," the Mohave "Land of the Dead." A Mohave who died without a tattoo would be denied entrance to Sil'aid and condemned "to go down a rat-hole." Some Mohaves, aware that tattooing was painful, refused to have the procedure done when they were young; but old and still-untattooed Mohaves, contemplating the approach of death, almost always had themselves so marked to protect their immortal spirits. A Mohave tattoo could thus be likened to Christian baptism, a purification rite that prepares the soul for entrance into heaven.

Mohave women seem to have been tattooed around the time of puberty, not before. The ritual may have prepared them for marriage, or at least signified that they were ready for marriage. Olive reached what Mohaves considered marriageable age during the time she was living with Espaniola's family (she turned fifteen during the first year she spent in the Mohave Valley and eighteen during the last full year she lived there). Though younger, Mary Ann may well have entered puberty during that same span of years. The notion that these white girls could have taken, or even thought of taking, Indian husbands—Indians who had never embraced Christianity and still practiced a "heathen" religion—was an abomination to devout white Christians in mid-nineteenth-century America. Stratton took pains to refute any suggestion that the girls "lost their innocence," as he put it, during the years they lived with the Mohaves. He acknowledged that Olive's age, sex, and "exposure" made her vulnerable to advances by Mohave men, but he denied that these men had done anything improper. "To the honor of these savages,"

Stratton wrote (speaking for Olive), "let it be said, they never offered the least unchaste abuse to me."[2] Stratton and Olive undoubtedly believed that this assertion would silence the wagging tongues that suggested she had entered into some kind of marriage or other sexual relationship with a Mohave man. They must have known that rumors to that effect had been circulating and had already achieved a degree of acceptance. Olive's protestations of sexual innocence, repeated often and emphatically,[3] undoubtedly satisfied many Americans. But there were others who were not convinced by her denials and who continued for years after she left the Mohave Valley to repeat stories that she (and perhaps Mary Ann as well) had married and borne children.[4]

Did the Oatman girls marry while they were among the Mohaves? And did either of them have any Mohave children? Any attempt to answer these questions requires a consideration of various factors, some peculiar to Mohave culture, others more general to both whites and Indians.

First, Olive's assertion that she was not subject to the "least unchaste abuse" by Mohave men finds some support in Mohave sexual mores. It was a rule among the Mohaves that female captives were not to be "violated." This rule was not based on simple etiquette but on the deeply held belief that sexual relations with a captive would bring "sickness into the land."[5] To avoid this "sickness," a purification ceremony had to be performed over the captives. Even after the ceremony was performed, captives generally were not married to Mohave men but lived out their lives as single women. Olive and Mary Ann may not, however, have been regarded as captives when they arrived in the Mohave Valley (they had been captured, but not by the Mohaves). And even if they were initially so regarded and were thus "off limits" to Mohave men, their status could have been changed through purification ceremonies, very likely through the tattoos they received from the shamans. By the time they received their tattoos, if not earlier, the girls may well have been accepted as Mohaves rather than as captives, so the taboo against sexual relations with them would not have applied.

Second, after Olive and Mary Ann became Mohaves, they may have been less constrained by the sexual inhibitions of their Christian upbringing than other Americans. The Mohaves were an uninhibited people who engaged in sexual relations without embarrassment. Their traditional dress was scanty and would certainly have been regarded by most Christians as immodest. Children habitually went naked, while adult males wore nothing but a breech cloth and perhaps a blanket thrown round their shoulders in cold weather. Adult females wore skirts woven of strands from the soft inner bark of willow trees but were naked above the waist. The Mohaves had no formal wedding ceremonies: if a man and woman wished to form an intimate relationship, they simply lived together; they were divorced when one or the other left the marriage house. Older Mohaves did not exhort the younger generation to chastity; on the contrary, they encouraged them to "enjoy themselves" while they could.[6]

Two or three years after Olive and Mary Ann were captured on the Gila, they surely had despaired of ever again living among whites. They were of the age when sexual feelings are stirring, and their daily familiarity with the Mohaves may well have persuaded them that these men (or at least some of them) were worthy of their affection. They had every reason to believe that they would live the rest of their lives as Mohaves, and if they wanted to have families and raise children, there would have seemed no other realistic way of doing so than by acceding to Mohave ways.[7]

The notion that Olive (and perhaps Mary Ann) married Mohave men is supported by certain admissions that Olive made about her feelings for the Indians. Stratton went to great lengths to describe the Indians' "savagery" and demonstrate why any white person who had fallen into their hands would do everything possible to escape. Yet Olive admitted that she had developed strong attachments to the Mohaves, that she looked on some of them with special affection.

This affection may well have extended to sexual attraction, perhaps even to romantic love.

Another fact suggests that Olive was not as anxious to leave the Mohaves as Stratton suggested. In February 1854 a large party of Americans (more than a hundred men and twice as many mules and horses) came into the Mohave Valley under the command of U.S. Army lieutenant A. W. Whipple. Whipple had been ordered by the War Department in Washington, D.C., to survey the country along the thirty-fifth parallel west of Fort Smith, Arkansas, to find a route for a railroad from the Mississippi River to the Pacific Ocean. His party entered the Mohave Valley from the south on February 24, traveled up the east bank of the Colorado to a point near Espaniola's house, then crossed the river on pontoons. Whipple found the Mohaves friendly and even obtained their consent to building the railroad through the valley. He and his men met with several of the Mohave chiefs, offered gifts to their followers, and enlisted the services of one chief to guide them westward toward California. Before leaving the valley on March 2, Whipple made detailed entries in a journal, later published by order of Congress. The artist who traveled with his expedition, a German named Balduin Möllhausen, also kept a journal that was later published.

Where were Olive and Mary Ann during the seven days the Whipple party was in their midst? If they longed for an opportunity to escape the Mohaves and return to their own people, there is no indication in Whipple's or Möllhausen's journals that they did any-thing to establish contact with the Americans. It is possible, of course, that the Mohaves concealed the girls from the army surveyors, or removed them from the valley while they were there. There is no hint, however, in any of Olive's statements after she returned to the white world, in Stratton's book, or in the script she prepared for her lectures that the Mohaves hid her or her sister from Whipple. Her silence on this tantalizing point makes it doubtful that the Mohaves tried to prevent either of the girls from contacting Whipple. It also suggests that at least by February 1854, neither Olive nor Mary Ann were so unhappy with their lives among the Mohaves that they wanted the surveyors to take them out of the valley.[8]

But if the girls were happy, this would soon change. Since the day in February 1851 when the Oatman family was attacked on the Gila River and Olive and Mary Ann were carried away as captives, Mary Ann had never been robust. She had suffered more than her older sister during the drought of 1851, when food was scarce in the captors' village, and she seemed less able than Olive to endure the hard labor that life as an Indian captive required. By the time she arrived in the Mohave Valley, she was probably already suffering from chronic malnutrition, and the valley's unreliable food supplies made it difficult for her to regain her strength. When the Colorado overflowed, she and Olive ate well; but when drought returned to the valley and Mohave supplies of wheat, corn, and vegetables ran low, it was Mary Ann who suffered more from hunger.

In her recollections Olive detailed the months of hunger that eroded her sister's strength. When the valley's food supplies were nearly exhausted, the girls were asked to join a gathering party and travel into the mountains to search for berries. Olive recalled that Mary Ann started out with the party but, owing to her weakness, had to drop out and return to the village. Olive continued on, but worried about her sister the whole time she was away. While Olive and the others were gathering berries in the mountains, Mohaves were dying in the valley and in the mountains. When Olive returned to the chief's house, she found her sister even weaker than before. Olive wandered through the valley searching for birds' eggs in the hope they might help Mary Ann, but the few she found did little to restore her sister's fast-ebbing vitality. For a few days Olive sat close to her sister's bed, which was laid outside the chief's house, and begged food of passersby. Though she was given scraps (Aespaneo and Topeka were generous, but only within their limits), they were too little and too late.

Mary Ann's death was a blow to Olive. When the end finally came, Olive showed her grief by alternately wailing (in Mohave fashion) and praying (in Christian fashion). Aespaneo and Topeka shared her loss, coming to Mary Ann's lifeless body, bending over it, and weeping bitterly. After the wailing and praying, the Mohaves began to prepare Mary Ann's body, in Mohave fashion, for cremation. Olive protested, pleading for the privilege of burying her sister's body in the ground, according to Christian custom. Burial was wholly foreign to Mohave ways, and the Indians protested. Olive recalled that she had almost given up hope of changing their minds when Aespaneo came to her and told her that she had interceded with Espaniola and he had agreed to Olive's request. The chief himself gave Olive two blankets in which to wrap Mary Ann's body and prevailed on two Mohaves to dig a grave. Olive selected a spot in the garden that Aespaneo had given her and Mary Ann, and when the grave was ready, the body was lowered into it and covered with earth.[9]

After she left the Mohave Valley, Olive gave conflicting accounts of Mary Ann's death. She left no doubt that the death was from starvation and that it was caused by the failure of the Colorado to overflow its banks, but she was ambiguous, even equivocal, about when the death occurred. Her recollections in Stratton's *Captivity of the Oatman Girls* suggest that Mary Ann died in the third or fourth year of their captivity—1853 or 1854. But in the lectures she delivered some years later, she stated that the death happened in 1852, which was the first year she and her sister spent in the Mohave Valley. If Mary Ann died in 1852, she would have been only nine years old; if in 1853, ten; if in 1854, eleven. But none of these dates was correct. Soon after Olive arrived at Fort Yuma in February 1856, the post commander asked her when Mary Ann had died and Olive stated quite clearly "one year ago" (which would have been in the spring of 1855). Shortly thereafter, a newspaper reporter who had spoken to Olive wrote that Mary Ann had died only six months before Olive was brought to Yuma (in the late summer of 1855). Mary Ann was twelve that year.

Why did Olive have so much trouble remembering when her sister died? Her confusion about dates is understandable, given the difficulty she must have had in keeping track of time during the years she lived among the Indians (the Indians did not reckon time in months and years but by the lapse of "moons," a method that was effective only to account for short periods of time). When Olive got to Yuma, she was not even certain how old she or Mary Ann had been when they were captured. But beyond the normal uncertainty that might be expected under these circumstances, there is a suspicion that when Olive told the public about her Indian captivity, she decided to "rearrange" events to better suit her purposes. If Mary Ann did not die until 1855, she was still living when Whipple led his surveying expedition through the Mohave Valley in 1854, and if she had asked the explorers to help her return to the Americans that year, she probably would not have starved to death the following year.

Like many other aspects of the Oatman story, the precise time of Mary Ann Oatman's death would be almost impossible to establish on the basis of the available historical record. In this instance, however, it is possible to supplement historical records with scientific evidence: studies of tree rings in the watershed of the Colorado basin. Dendrochronological tests clearly show that 1855 was the only year of the four Olive and Mary Ann Oatman spent in the Mohave Valley during which water flows in the Colorado River were below average. The 1852 and 1853 flows were above average, while those of 1854 were about average; in 1855, however, the flows were only three-quarters of the average. This evidence supports the conclusion that Mary Ann Oatman died sometime between the spring and early summer of 1855, not before.

Olive was still suffering from hunger after her sister died. But she was older and stronger than Mary Ann and had Aespaneo's help in satisfying her hunger. Olive later recalled that this unceasingly kind woman again showed her affection for Olive by drawing from the store of corn she had set aside for planting the following spring, grinding it, and boiling the coarse meal to make a gruel that she offered to Olive. Olive took it gratefully, and Aespaneo brought her more. The older woman was discreet in her ministrations, conscious that she would be criticized if she was seen favoring Olive over equally hungry Mohaves. But she persisted. Olive gradually regained her strength and, with it, the ability to forage for some of her own food. "Had it not been for her," Olive later said of the chief's wife, "I must have perished."[10]

During all the time that Olive and Mary Ann were living with the Indians, an air of mystery hung over their disappearance. Whites who heard about the attack on the Oatman family were sure that the girls had been captured by the Indians (their bodies had not been found among those of their parents and brothers and sisters). But where had they been taken? With what tribe or band of Indians were they living? If they had survived the initial attack on the Gila River, had they survived the hardships they would almost certainly have faced living with Indians in the desert? As months, then years, passed, interest in the fate of the Oatman girls abated somewhat but never died, for the girls' surviving brother, Lorenzo, clung to the belief that they must still be living and that, if he could only find where, he would bring them back to the world of the whites.

In the first hours after the attack, Lorenzo cannot have given much thought to rescuing his sisters. When Olive and Mary Ann last saw their brother, he was lying motionless on the rocky cliff top, his head covered with blood, and it was only through a series of fortuitous circumstances that the fourteen-year-old managed to save himself. Stratton's *Captivity of the Oatman Girls* laid out those circumstances as Lorenzo himself remembered them: He had awakened several times after the Indians left the cliff top, but finding himself covered with blood and unable to move he lapsed again into unconsciousness. Night fell and dawn broke again on the following day before he awoke a final time and summoned up the strength to move. By this time he was lying, not on top of the cliff, but at the foot of the rocky slope that led up to the top. Glancing upward, he saw traces of blood marking the way by which he had come down the slope and reasoned that he had either fallen or been thrown over the edge—he was not sure which.[11]

Crawling painfully, he started up the slope; but nearing the top, he realized that the Indians might still be watching and that if he went any farther, he might be attacked again. So he reversed his direction and returned to the bottom, reasoning that if he had any chance of surviving, he had to find help, and the closest help seemed to be in the direction of Maricopa Wells.[12] Heading east, he retraced the route his family's wagon had followed the preceding week. He was weak and sore, wary both of the Indians and of the desert sun, so he proceeded slowly, seeking the protection of bushes and trees as he went. He later remembered that for a few hours, he was trailed by a pack of animals (wolves, perhaps, or coyotes) but eventually drove them off by throwing rocks at them. Several hours later, still covered with blood, he collapsed and fell asleep.[13]

About noon of the following day, he encountered two Pimas riding along the trail. One was an Indian he knew from the Pima villages, and Lorenzo was overjoyed to see him. When the Pimas learned about the attack, they were shocked. They gave him a little food and water and told him to wait by the side of the trail while they rode on to the attack site. A little while later the boy saw some objects approaching in the distance. He was afraid at first that they were more unfriendly Indians but greatly relieved when they came closer and revealed themselves to be two wagons. One was occupied by the Kelly brothers, John and Robert, the other by Willard Wilder and his family. Robert Kelly looked disbelievingly at the battered figure in the road before finally recognizing him as Roys Oatman's oldest son.[14]

The men in the wagon listened quietly as Lorenzo told his story, but Mrs. Wilder wept. The Kellys and Wilders had intended to drive their wagons all the way to Yuma, but Lorenzo's shocking tale persuaded them to reconsider. With murderous Indians on the trail, they agreed that the prudent course was to return to the Pima and Maricopa villages and wait for other travelers who might accompany them across the desert.[15]

Back at the Indian villages, the Pimas and Maricopas were quick to blame the Quechans for the attack. Lorenzo seemed to agree with the accusation, but the Kellys and Wilders discounted it, knowing that the Quechans were the traditional enemies of the Pimas and Maricopas. It was agreed that Willard Wilder and Robert Kelly would go to the attack site while Lorenzo remained behind with the others. When Kelly, Wilder, and two Maricopa companions reached the site, they found the ruined wagon and six dead bodies. Though wild animals had already scavenged the corpses, they were still recognizable. The men tried to dig graves, but the ground was hard and they had no shovels, so they gathered the remains in a pile and covered them with rocks.[16]

Back at the villages, Wilder and Kelly told their companions that Olive and Mary Ann had almost certainly been taken by the Indians. The knowledge did little to encourage Lorenzo's recovery (he was dangerously ill for about a week); but it steeled his resolve to obtain his sisters' rescue. At length, the boy's wounds healed and he recovered at least some of his former strength. Meanwhile he and his companions continued to wait for other travelers to come through the villages.

Their wait was rewarded on March 14, when a curious party of seven men riding six mules came into the villages. The men confided the strange news that they were American soldiers who had deserted their U.S. Army post in the New Mexico mountains and, in their haste to get away, lost one of their mules. So each of the seven had to take turns walking while the others rode. The dissident Mormons may have been shocked by the soldiers' confession, but they were in no position to be choosy about traveling companions and readily took up positions beside them. It proved to be a wise decision, for the combined party made it across the desert and past the first crossing of the Gila River without even the hint of an Indian threat. When the Mormons reached the site where the Oatmans had lost their lives, they paused to offer their respects, then resumed their westward march. With the danger of Indian attack safely behind them, the deserters decided to pick up their pace and bade their slower companions good-bye. The wagons finally reached the confluence of the Gila and Colorado rivers on March 27, 1851. Crossing the river in a small ferry boat, they were met by the commanding officer of Camp Yuma (the post was not designated a fort until the summer of 1852), Brevet Major Samuel P. Heintzelman of the 2nd U.S. Infantry.

Lorenzo, the Kellys, and the Wilders were not impressed by their first sight of Yuma. Just four months old, the post consisted of a few dozen tents pitched on the summit of a hill overlooking the river juncture and some rudely constructed Indian huts nearby. It was manned by three companies of infantrymen assisted by a ragtag crew of civilians recruited in California. Heintzelman was a West Pointer who had fought with General Winfield Scott in Mexico, and his subordinate officers, seasoned veterans of western warfare, were dedicated men. But they did not form a harmonious corps, for the major was a thoroughly disagreeable man who made life miserable for his subordinates. The camp was surrounded by a sea of Quechans, three thousand or four thousand in all, who were kept in uneasy subjection by Heintzelman's threat to "destroy" them if they did not obey the wishes of the "Great White Father" in Washington. The commander's threat was bold, but he was far from confident that he could carry it out, not because his troops were unequal to the task but because the army was unable to keep them reliably supplied. Yuma was a little more than two hundred miles east of San Diego, and supply wagons took as long as two weeks to cross the high mountains and sandy desert that separated the two places.

If the uneasy military equilibrium of Yuma did not disquiet the Brewsterites, the surrounding desert did. This, after all, was Colin

Brewster's "Land of Bashan," the "earthly Eden" with rich bottom-
lands, good stands of timber, and "friendly" Indians. It was, to be
sure, green and inviting along the two rivers, where cottonwoods and
willows lined the banks. But the surrounding country for miles in
every direction was one of the hottest and driest places in all of
North America, a region where rocks far outnumbered trees, where
cactus competed with creosote bushes to wring moisture from the
sandy soil, and where hungry coyotes hunted for lizards and leathery
jackrabbits. Not long after her family arrived at Yuma, Mrs. Wilder
wrote her father:

> It seems that it never rains here, to do any good or hurt. The
> ferrymen say that they have been here ten months, and it has
> not rained enough to wet their shirts through.
>   In consequence of there being no turf here, it is very dusty,
> as the wind blows two days out of seven; and when the wind
> does not blow, about three o'clock, mi[d]gets (gnats) bite
> unmercifully.[17]

The harsh landscape and constant Indian danger were not the
only unpleasant facts the newcomers encountered in Yuma. They
also found disagreement among the officers as to what, if anything,
should be done about the attack on the Oatmans. When Dr. Le
Conte arrived at Yuma at the end of February with Roys Oatman's
urgent letter asking for horses, he had demanded that Heintzelman
send immediate help. The commander refused on the ground that
he had no animals fit for the journey, all the while fuming at the
entomologist's "arrogant and presumptuous" manner. But the
following day, he managed to find four mules he could spare and
sent them upriver with two of his soldiers. When Heintzelman's men
returned with news that the Oatmans had all been killed, the commanding officer angrily turned on Le Conte (whom he contemp-
tuously called "Dr. Bugs"), saying he should have stayed with the
Oatmans (especially since Mrs. Oatman was expecting a child) and
grumbling that "some people like charity at other people's expense."[18]

After Le Conte left for San Diego, some of Heintzelman's officers urged the commander to organize a search party to locate Olive and little Mary Ann and, if possible, take them back from the Indians. Captain Delozier Davidson was vocal in urging such an undertaking, as was the post surgeon, Henry Stuart Hewit. But Heintzelman refused both Davidson and Hewit, pointing out that the attack on the Oatmans had occurred on Mexican territory and that as a U.S. army officer, he had no authority to send soldiers into Mexico. (He did not know, or apparently care to find out, that Olive and Mary Ann were being held on the American side of the border, where he had a legal right—some would argue a responsibility—to look for them.) Dr. Hewit responded by filing a complaint charging Heintzelman with "neglect of duty." Heintzelman was hardly fazed by the charge, which he attributed to Hewitt's "ill will."[19]

While Heintzelman and his subordinates feuded, the Kellys and Wilders asked the commander if he could give them work and shelter. He obliged them with jobs and permission to occupy some of the Indian huts at the camp. Heintzelman soon learned that the new arrivals were Mormons,[20] but he did not care what their religion was as long as they did their work. They told him they had come to the confluence of the Gila and Colorado with the intention of settling but quickly realized that the surrounding country was not as it had been described in their prophecies.[21] When Heintzelman learned that their "prophet" was a young man named Brewster, that he had described the country around Yuma "in glowing terms," and that he had proclaimed the nearby desert as "good for grazing," the major noted in his journal: "I wish he could see our starved mules."[22]

While the Kellys and Willard Wilder worked, Lorenzo continued to regain his strength under the care of Dr. Hewit. The boy lived with Hewit in his tent and watched him as he tended his patients. He also listened as the surgeon and the post's other officers grumbled about Heintzelman. Not surprisingly, Lorenzo agreed with Hewit's assessment of the commander and quickly developed a special dislike for him.[23]

Alternately frustrated and infuriated with Major Heintzelman, Hewit now submitted his resignation to the Department of the Pacific in California. About the same time, the army decided that Yuma could no longer be provisioned from San Diego and ordered Heintzelman to bring his troops back to California until more reliable supply lines could be established. When the commanding officer and his men abandoned Yuma early in June, Hewit and Lorenzo traveled west with them. On their way, the surgeon received the welcome news that his resignation had been accepted,[24] and he and Lorenzo pushed on to the coast. From San Diego they traveled by ship to San Francisco, where they arrived on June 26, 1851.[25]

Hewit had decided to return to his family in Connecticut, but before he left, he got Lorenzo settled in San Francisco with a job and a place to live. The doctor's final departure for the East left Lorenzo very much alone in the world. He was not yet fifteen and had no relatives or close friends within a thousand miles. He suspected that Olive and Mary Ann were still living, probably with the Apaches, but he had no idea where, or how he might find them. Lorenzo's San Francisco job required hard labor. He had little choice, however, for he was poorly educated and could not qualify for a less menial position. When he injured himself while lifting a heavy load and was compelled to leave, he tried unsuccessfully to get another job. After two years, he left San Francisco for the California gold country, hoping to strike it rich in the mines. But he had no luck, and after a year or so, he returned to San Francisco to look again for work.

He wrote to friends and relatives, hoping to reestablish contact with families he had known in Illinois and become friendly with on the road to Bashan. But the mail was slow and unreliable, and he waited in vain for answers. Finally replies came from two of the families who had joined his own on the first leg of their journey west. John Richardson and his family, who had remained loyal to Colin Brewster after the original train split in two in New Mexico, had made it through to the Colorado River sometime in 1852, then continued

on to southern California, where they settled just east of Los Angeles.
Ira Thompson and his family, who had remained in Tucson when
the Kellys, Wilders, and Oatmans pushed on to the Pima and Maricopa villages, had also made it through and had set down roots a few
miles from the Richardsons in a little town called "the Monte"
(rechristened El Monte a few years later). After exchanging letters
with the Richardsons and the Thompsons, Lorenzo decided in the
spring of 1854 to go down to the Monte, where Ira Thompson was
running a stage station called the Willow Grove Inn. Lorenzo was at
the inn in May 1854 when he received a letter from Asa Abbott
inviting him to come back to Whiteside County, Illinois. Lorenzo
replied that he would like to see his Uncle Asa and Aunt Sarah again
but didn't think the time was right for such a trip. He had just been
paid $200 for his interest in a crop he had helped to set out. He
described the facts of the attack on the Oatman family (the Abbotts
had not yet received a satisfactory explanation of the tragedy) and
said that he was thinking of going back to school ("I thing that it will
not doo me eny harm for I cannot read my one writing it is spelt so
bad and impraper," he wrote his uncle, amply proving his point).[26]

Despite his bad spelling, Lorenzo wrote letters to people he
thought might help him find Olive and Mary Ann. He also sent
letters to Yuma (which Heintzelman had now regarrisoned as "Fort
Yuma"), inquiring if anyone there knew anything about his sisters.
After the summer of 1854, when Heintzelman was succeeded by
Brevet Major George Henry Thomas, officers at Yuma felt freer to
look into the girls' fate. Soon Lorenzo learned that some information about Olive and Mary Ann had filtered into the fort.

In April 1855 a Mexican citizen by the name of Federico Augusto
Ronstadt informed Major Thomas that he had heard from a Mexican
soldier that the two Oatman girls were then living with the Mohaves.
The soldier had told Ronstadt that a Quechan named Francisco had
said that, if asked, he could "acquire true information . . . about
the unhappy captives." The German-born Ronstadt had put this

information in a letter addressed to Thomas and left it at the major's headquarters. Although the letter contained obvious misinformation (it said that the Oatmans had been killed in 1852, that the Mohaves were the perpetrators of the outrage, and that Francisco was a Mohave), it was still a promising lead. Thomas placed Ronstadt's letter in his official file but seems not to have followed up on the suggestion that he contact Francisco—or if he did, no record of his action has survived.[27]

Other reports were received in Yuma to the effect that the Cocopas were holding Olive and Mary Ann some distance south of the fort. This latest intelligence was passed on to Lorenzo, prompting him to write to two members of the California legislature asking if the state government could organize a hunt for his sisters. But the legislators gave him no definite reply, so he went to Los Angeles and hired a lawyer to go to San Francisco and see what could be done there to get assistance. While awaiting news from the north, Lorenzo joined eight other men on a prospecting trek into the mountains east of Los Angeles. He thought that by accompanying the gold seekers he might learn something about his sisters. The party found an abundance of bear but no precious metal, and Lorenzo learned nothing about Olive and Mary Ann.

Early in January 1856 Lorenzo received a letter from a California rancher named Duff Weaver informing him that a man named Black had recently crossed the Colorado River into southern California with news that an offer had been made to the commander at Fort Yuma to ransom an "American woman" held captive by an unidentified tribe of Indians. Black said that the woman could have been "bought" for a "small sum in blankets" but the commander refused the offer. The commander in question was the new officer in charge of Yuma, Brevet Lieutenant Colonel Martin G. Burke. It was generally understood, of course, that the "American woman" was one of the Oatman girls, probably Olive. Weaver's letter created a stir when it appeared in the *Los Angeles Star* of January 5, 1856. When confronted with the newspaper article at Yuma, Burke denied that he had refused an offer to ransom Olive Oatman or any other white woman. Brevet Lieutenant Colonel George Nauman, on the staff of the Department of the Pacific, promptly launched an investigation into the charges.[28]

Duff Weaver's letter included an offer to help Lorenzo organize a search party to hunt for his sisters. About the time Weaver's letter arrived, Lorenzo received news from Yuma that one of his sisters had died while living among the Mohaves but that the surviving sister was still living with the tribe. Lorenzo and some of his neighbors at the Monte responded by drawing up a petition asking California governor J. Neely Johnson for "men and means" to rescue the survivor from the Mohaves. The petition was delivered to Johnson at his office in Sacramento and promptly denied. The governor stated that he had no authority to disburse public funds for private purposes but suggested that Lorenzo might appeal to the federal Indian Department in Washington, D.C.[29]

When Nauman arrived at Yuma, he quickly satisfied himself that Lieutenant Colonel Burke had not turned down an offer to ransom an "American woman" from the Mohaves. In fact, he had actively pursued leads to any white woman who might be held by Indians in the neighborhood of the fort. Nauman then joined Burke in sending runners out to the neighboring tribes, offering ransoms for all white prisoners being held by the Indians. The offers apparently had the desired effect, for on February 22, 1856, the Quechan named Francisco came forward with positive information that a white woman was living with the Mohaves about ten days north of Fort Yuma and that "under certain conditions, and for certain considerations," he would go to the Mohave Valley and bring her back.[30]

Francisco did not go directly to Burke with this information, but to a New Yorker named Henry Grinnell who was employed as post carpenter at Yuma. Though he had grown up far from the southwestern deserts, Grinnell had established an easy rapport with the local Indians after he came to Yuma in 1853 and soon acquired the reputation (rare for the time) of a white man the Indians could trust. For some months he had heard rumors whispered among the Quechans that two white girls were being held by the Mohaves. When Francisco not only gave him definite information that one of the girls was still living with the Mohaves but also offered to personally go north and bring her back to Yuma, Grinnell had reason to hope that a breakthrough was imminent. Although the Quechans lived more than two hundred miles south of the Mohave Valley, they maintained friendly relations with the northern tribe and had more than a passing acquaintance with events in the Mohave Valley.

The carpenter took Francisco to Burke, who made out a special "pass" authorizing Francisco to visit the Mohaves as his representative. The pass was inscribed by Burke's secretary in large, elegant script. On one side of a sheet of paper, he wrote the words "Francisco a Yuma Indian, going to the 'Mohave' nation," and on the other:

> Francisco[,] Yuma Indian, bearer of this[,] goes to the 'Mohave' Nation to obtain a white woman there, named SPANTSA. [I]t is desirable she should come to this post, or send her reasons why she does not wish to come.
> Head Quarters Fort Yuma, Cala.
> 27th January 1856.
> Martin Burke
> Lieut. Col., Commanding[31]

Francisco took the paper, left the commander's office, and melted into the desert.

Olive Oatman in Santa Clara, California, in 1857 or 1858. Taken while she was a student at the University of the Pacific, this photograph clearly shows the Mohave tattoo on Olive's chin. Courtesy History San José.

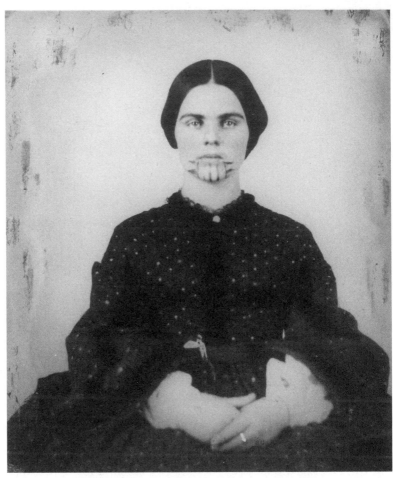

Olive Oatman shortly after leaving the Mohave Valley in 1856. She looks strong and well-fed in this tintype image, and the Mohave tattoo on her chin is readily apparent. Courtesy Beinecke Library, Yale University.

Lorenzo Oatman shortly after he was reunited with his sister Olive in 1856. This tintype image was made at the same time as the tintype of Olive. Courtesy Beinecke Library, Yale University.

Olive Oatman by Powelson Photographic Studio. One of a series of *carte-de-visite* photographs taken in Rochester, New York, after publication of *Captivity of the Oatman Girls.* Courtesy Arizona Historical Society, Tucson (AHS no. 1927).

Olive Oatman in Rochester. This *carte-de-visite* photograph reveals that Olive had learned how to conceal her tattoos under a mask of cosmetics. Courtesy Edward J. Pettid Papers, Special Collections, University of Arizona Library, Tucson.

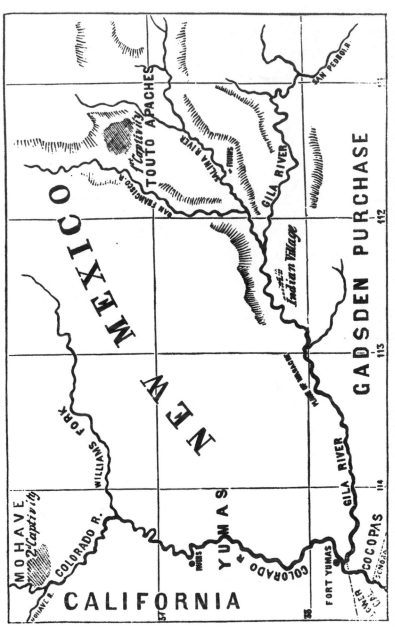

Map of New Mexico Territory in 1851. Prepared for the second edition of Royal Stratton's *Captivity of the Oatman Girls*, this was a rude approximation of some of the places featured in the book. Courtesy The Bancroft Library, University of California, Berkeley.

"The Massacre." This artist's conception of the Indian attack of February 18, 1851, appeared in the New York edition of Royal B. Stratton's *Captivity of the Oatman Girls.* Courtesy The Bancroft Library, University of California, Berkeley.

Engraving of Olive Oatman. This portrait, clearly showing the tattoos on her chin, was used as a frontispiece for *Captivity of the Oatman Girls* and helped to make the book a best seller. Courtesy The Bancroft Library, University of California, Berkeley.

Engraving of Lorenzo Oatman. This portrait appeared in *Captivity of the Oatman Girls*. Courtesy The Bancroft Library, University of California, Berkeley.

A typical Mohave man and woman. This lithograph is based on a drawing made by Balduin Möllhausen, a German artist who visited the Mohave Valley with a U.S. Army expedition in 1854, while Olive Oatman was living with the Mohave Indians. Courtesy The Bancroft Library, University of California, Berkeley.

A typical Mohave house. This lithograph is based on a drawing made by Balduin Möllhausen during the time that Olive Oatman lived in the Mohave Valley. Courtesy The Bancroft Library, University of California, Berkeley.

Artist's depiction of Mohaves executing one of their captives by crucifixion. This engraving was made for the New York edition of Royal Stratton's *Captivity of the Oatman Girls*. The event depicted may be apocryphal. Courtesy The Bancroft Library, University of California, Berkeley.

Handwritten pass issued January 27, 1856, to Francisco, a Quechan Indian (misidentified as a Yuma). Signed by Brevet Lieutenant Colonel Martin Burke of Fort Yuma, the pass authorized Francisco to go to the Mohave Valley and bring Olive Oatman (identified as "Spantsa") to Yuma or "send her reasons why she does not wish to come." Copy in Olive Ann Oatman Papers, Center for Archival Collections, Bowling Green State University, Bowling Green, Ohio. Location of original not known.

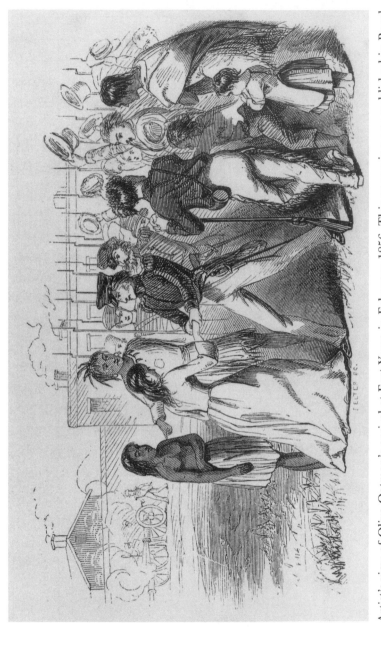

Artist's view of Olive Oatman's arrival at Fort Yuma in February 1856. This engraving was published in Royal Stratton's *Captivity of the Oatman Girls.* Courtesy The Bancroft Library, University of California, Berkeley.

SACRAMENTO THEATER!

The public are respectfully informed that this popular place of amusement is now open for the purpose of presenting to the citizens of Sacramento an ENTIRE NEW DRAMA, written by Mr. C. E. Bingham, portraying in life-like colors the incidents in the narrative of the CAPTIVITY and MASSACRE of the OATMAN FAMILY, which will be produced with a full and efficient company.

SECOND NIGHT

Of the new original play, dramatized by Mr.

C. E. BINGHAM

Which was well received by a full and fashionable house on its first presentation, on Saturday evening last.

MISS SOPHIE EDWIN . . AS . . OLIVE CATMAN
MISS LOUISA PAULLIN . . AS . . MARY ANNE
FANNY DEMING HANKS . . AS . . DUNDENAH
PROFESSOR RISLEY IN NEW ENTERTAINMENTS

This (Monday) Evening, July 27th,

Will be presented, for the second time an entire new Drama, in three acts, written by Mr. C. E. Bingham, entitled The

CAPTIVITY AND MASSACRE

OF THE

OATMAN FAMILY!

BY THE

APACHE & MOHAVE INDIANS!

OLIVE OATMAN	MISS SOPHIE EDWIN
DUNDENAH (Indian)	FANNY DEMING HANKS
Mrs. MARY OATMAN	MRS. PAULLIN
MARY ANN OATMAN	MISS LOUISA PAULLIN
MASTER LORENZO D. OATMAN	MISS ANNIE SMITH
Mr. George Oatman	Mr. POTTER (Grief)
Loquor (an outcast and fugitive)	PAULLIN — PEMBERTON
Kamelo (Indian Chief)	GRAY
Walter Wilder	B. S. MORTIMER
Kowmalen (Indian)	CHARLES
Peter Kelly, (whisk-sodd-if Indians)	Potton (Indian) — JAMES
Dr. Leond.	ARTHUR — Toman, ch dress't
Sagot II ...ne.u.	PROFESSOR RISLEY

Between the pieces.

SONG - - BY - - MISS LOUISA PAULLIN
BALLAD . . . BY . . . MISS ANNIE SMITH
BUNKER HILL POLKA . . BY . . PROFESSOR RISLEY
FAVORITE DANCE - - BY - - LA PETITE CERITO

The whole to conclude with the laughable farce of The

YANKEE HEIRESS

Winterblossom	Mr. POTTER
Perry Seymour	MORTIMER
Charles Hanes	ARTHUR
Ira	GRAY
Caroline Morton	FANNY DEMING HANKS
Miss Winterblossom	MRS. PAULLIN
Sally	MISS LOUISA PAULLIN

PRICES OF ADMISSION:

Dress Circle and Parquet	$1 00
Pit	50

Box office open from 10 A. M. to 4 P. M., when seats can be taken.
Doors open at half-past 7, performance to commence at 8 o'clock.

DAILY BEE PRINT.

Handbill for the play titled *The Oatman Family*. Based on the story of the Oatman family, this drama was produced in San Francisco and Sacramento in the summer of 1857. Courtesy Everett D. Graff Collection, The Newberry Library, Chicago.

Handbill for Olive Oatman's lectures. Olive spent seven years on the lecture circuit, speaking about her Indian experiences and promoting the sales of Royal Stratton's *Captivity of the Oatman Girls.* Courtesy Everett D. Graff Collection, The Newberry Library, Chicago.

Royal B. Stratton. The charismatic Methodist preacher was the author of the best-selling *Captivity of the Oatman Girls.* Confined to an insane asylum about 1873, he died in Worcester, Massachusetts, on January 24, 1875, at the age of forty-eight. Pencil drawing by the author after a photograph on glass negative in the archives of the First Congregational Church in Worcester, Worcester, Massachusetts.

Olive Oatman at age forty-two. In her later years, Olive was painfully
sensitive about her Mohave tattoos and wore a veil whenever she left her
house. This picture shows, however, that she had learned to almost
completely hide the tattoos with powders and creams. Courtesy Abbott
Collection, Morrison, Illinois.

John Brant Fairchild. He married Olive Oatman in Rochester, New York, on November 9, 1865. Courtesy Edward J. Pettid Papers, Special Collections, University of Arizona Library, Tucson.

The Fairchild home in Sherman, Texas. John and Olive Oatman Fairchild lived in this handsome Victorian-style home for almost thirty years. Courtesy Sharlot Hall Museum, Prescott, Arizona.

Lorenzo Oatman in later years. No portrait of Roys Oatman is known to exist, but this photograph of his son Lorenzo may approximate what Roys looked like. The elder Oatman's sister-in-law once wrote that, as an adult, Lorenzo was "very much like his Father in looks and manners." Courtesy Abbott Collection, Morrison, Illinois.

The Oatman plot in the Red Cloud Cemetery in Red Cloud, Nebraska. Lorenzo Oatman was buried here in 1901. His wife, Edna Amelia Canfield Oatman, was interred here following her death in 1919. Photograph by the author.

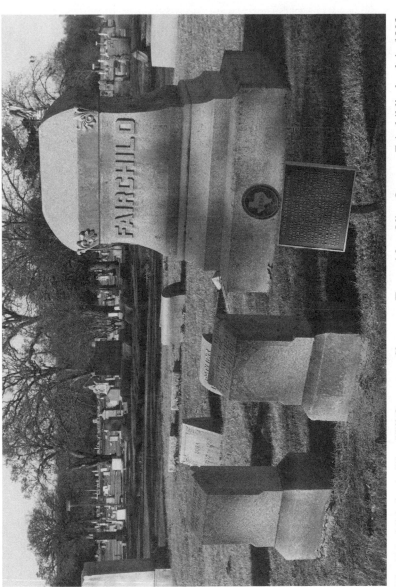

The Fairchild plot in West Hill Cemetery, Sherman, Texas. After Olive Oatman Fairchild's death in 1903, her wealthy husband erected these monuments to mark her grave, his own, and the family plot. Photograph by the author.

The Oatman Massacre site near Gila Bend, Arizona. Here, on February 18, 1851, Roys Oatman, his wife Mary Ann, and four of their children were clubbed to death by a band of Indians, probably Western Yavapais, or Toklepayas. Olive and Mary Ann Oatman were taken into the distant hills as captives. Photograph by the author.

SITE OF OATMAN MASSACRE

FEB. 18, 1851

YUMA COUNTY HISTORICAL SOCIETY

Metal sign marking the Oatman Massacre site. This marker stands atop a cliff overlooking Oatman Flat, near Gila Bend, Arizona. Photograph by the author.

CHAPTER 6

The Return

By the beginning of 1856, Olive had fully recovered from her close encounter with starvation. Now eighteen years old, she spoke the Mohave language habitually, dressed in Mohave skirts, and answered to a Mohave name. Long exposure to the sun and other elements had turned her skin a weathered brown. As she looked around the Mohave Valley, she saw mountains, canyons, and fields that were as familiar to her as the prairies of Illinois had once been. It was almost as if Olive Oatman had never lived, or having once lived in a remote time and place, had transformed herself into a contented Mohave woman.

In February of that year, however, events again conspired to set Olive's life on a different course. She later recalled that she was in front of Espaniola's house one day when a young Mohave came running up to her. He said that a Quechan was on his way to the Mohave Valley, coming from far down the river "to try and get me away to the whites," as Olive put it. A few hours later the village erupted in excitement as the Quechan arrived with three companions and announced that he had authority from the commander of Fort Yuma to take "Spantsa" back with him. His name was Francisco.[1]

News of Francisco's arrival spread quickly through the valley. As a crowd began to gather around Espaniola's house, the chief summoned a council. Meanwhile two Indians took Olive to another part of the village where, as she later recalled, she was "shut up alone, unattended, unprotected."[2]

What happened during the three or four days that Francisco remained in the Mohave Valley? It is clear that his mission was to obtain custody of Olive and take her back to Yuma and that the Mohaves resisted his request, at least at first; but the historical evidence tells us precious little about how the Quechan set about his goal. Olive's own account of this time differs sharply from the only known Mohave recollection of the same events and is suspect on several grounds. Olive said that the council that Chief Espaniola presided over was long, noisy, and contentious. Although she was excluded from the meeting, participants later told her what transpired there. After three days and three nights of debate, she was informed that the council had denied Francisco's request and ordered him and his companions to leave the valley. Instead of leaving, however, the Quechan crossed the river and continued to press his case with Mohaves who lived there. He argued, pleaded, and threatened, and eventually persuaded these Indians of the rightness of his cause. They then agreed to return with him to Chief Espaniola's house, where another council was convened. This time Olive was allowed to be present.

In the second council, Olive learned that the Mohaves had used all sorts of deceptions to dissuade Francisco from taking her away from them. They claimed that she was not an American at all, but a member of a little-known race "living away to the setting sun." They ordered her to speak to Francisco in some language other than English and to deny that she was an American. But she defied these orders and, in broken English, told Francisco the true story of how she had come to the Mohaves. When Francisco learned of the Mohaves' deception, he launched into a "vehement" address. Olive noticed the pass that Burke had given him and asked if she could look at it. She struggled at first to make sense of the document (it

had been five years since she had read any English), but after a while
the letters and words came back to her, and she was able not only to
read the document but to translate it into Mohave for the council's
benefit. Francisco then issued an ominous warning: the whites were
determined to recover Olive, and if he returned to Yuma without
her, the soldiers there would kill him and all the Quechans. What
was more, he said, there were now five million whites "all through the
mountains," and they would destroy all the Mohaves if the council
refused to give Olive up.[3]

The council was sharply divided. Some members favored releasing
Olive at once; others bitterly opposed such action; yet others wanted
her killed so the Mohaves could deny that she had ever lived among
them. After a while the chief asked Olive and Francisco to leave his
house while the deliberations continued. Sometime after sunrise he
called them back and announced the final decision: she could go.[4]

Years later a Mohave named Tokwatha ("Musk Melon") left quite
a different account of the circumstances under which Olive left the
Mohave Valley. He had known both Olive and Mary Ann during the
whole time they lived in the valley, and after Francisco arrived in
February 1856, he paid close attention to the goings-on at Espaniola's
house. He said that Francisco and his companions went straight to
the chief with the message that the officers at Fort Yuma had
demanded that Olive be turned over to them. Tokwatha's recollection
of what was said, like Olive's account, was based largely on what
firsthand participants later told him.

The chief and his advisers debated Francisco's request through the
night. "Well, I would like to raise this girl," Espaniola is supposed to
have told Francisco. "We traveled far to buy her. We like her. And we
want to make friends through her. When those who come by us know
how we treat her, they will treat us well too. If the officers want to see
her, they had better come here and talk with me, and I will let them
have her." But the women in the chief's house were distraught at the
prospect of losing Olive. "[We] like you much," they said to her.[5]

The Indians continued to deliberate for another night. Then Francisco said to his companions, "We might as well return; we cannot get her." But Tokwatha went with the Quechans to the other side of the river, where another chief and another company of Indians had gathered.

Francisco told this assemblage that Espaniola had refused to surrender Olive, even though the Quechan had told him that was what the army officers wanted. The other chief advised him to go back to Espaniola and offer the Mohaves a gift, "because they did pay for her and they do like her. And if you pay, you will surely get her." According to Tokwatha, the other Quechans proposed giving Espaniola a horse.[6]

The next morning the Quechans, accompanied by Tokwatha, went back across the river to Espaniola's house, where Francisco again pressed his case. "A man called Carpenter sent us," Francisco said (referring to the post carpenter Grinnell). "You did not agree to what he wants, but we have returned, because he will not let up. He will go on bothering you about it. The reason you did not agree is that we were not offering you anything; we know that. Well, we have a white horse downriver at Yuma; we will give you that."

Another Mohave chief was present at this meeting. Tokwatha remembered that he was "a head man"—an "old man, above everybody"—and that he was asked whether he thought Olive should be permitted to leave. "I am satisfied," the old chief said. "That is why we kept her; we raised her so that if anyone wants her back, they can have her. If Carpenter wants me to give her to him, I will do so. Let's take her down and go to get the horse."[7]

The basic facts of Olive's and Tokwatha's accounts of this episode are consistent: Francisco's request was met with a long consultation among the Mohaves; they were reluctant at first to give her up but finally agreed to do so. The tenor of the two accounts, however, could hardly be more different. In Olive's version the Mohaves were devious, even malicious, in their attempts to keep her; in Tokwatha's they preferred to keep her but were easily persuaded to give her up.

Both of these recollections may contain grains of truth, and the way that truth is shaped in each may reveal the unstated purposes of the witness. Years after Olive left the Mohaves, Tokwatha clearly wanted to avoid the impression that his people had mistreated the white girl or stood in the way of the whites' desire to be reunited with her. His account was likely designed to demonstrate that the Mohaves felt real affection for her and that their initial reluctance to comply with Francisco's request was rooted in a traditional Indian desire to uphold their dignity—for if they were not offered anything for her, they would feel slighted. Olive's account of the same episode was almost certainly motivated by a desire to show that she had lived with the Mohaves against her will, never abandoning the hope of returning to her own people; that she had remained so long with them only because they had threatened her. Royal Stratton doubtless played a large part in shaping this account, as he did in many other parts of his *Captivity of the Oatman Girls*. But other, disinterested descriptions of Olive's demeanor soon after she left the Mohave Valley belied this explanation and showed that Olive in fact was reluctant to leave the Mohaves and, at the least, ambivalent about her return to the world of the whites.

Chief Espaniola insisted that his daughter Topeka accompany Olive on her trip south to Yuma[8]—perhaps so that she could take possession of the horse waiting for him in Yuma, perhaps because she had shown genuine love and respect for Olive for so long and wanted to stand by her on what was certain to be a long and exhausting journey. Tokwatha also joined the party. Olive was deeply affected by her departure from the Mohave Valley. She could not resist the desire to look around her one last time: "Every stream and mountain peak and shaded glen I was as familiar with as with the dooryard of my childhood home," she recalled years later. She paid her last respects to the grave of her sister Mary Ann, the unmarked mound of sand that had become a "temple and a tomb" not only of her sister's body but also of her own memories. Some of the Mohaves were sorry to see her go. Some seemed genuinely happy that she was able to rejoin her own people after so many years away from them. But some were outwardly contemptuous. And others, Olive thought, were simply petty and mean-spirited.

Chief Espaniola's own son insisted on stripping Olive of the meager possessions she had intended to take with her as souvenirs of her sojourn in the Mohave Valley: small, tattered pieces of blankets that she was wearing and a few strings of beads. She said she was deeply hurt by this evidence of the son's "littleness and meanness."[9] But was the chief's son Olive's Mohave husband? And was he only insisting on the return of the marriage gifts he had bestowed on her, much as a white husband might expect the return of an engagement or wedding ring in the event the engagement or marriage was terminated? Why else would this Mohave (among all the others in the tribe) claim the right to retrieve the gifts made to Olive? And why would the other Mohaves—including the chief himself—permit him to do so? If there was in fact an intimate relationship between Olive and the chief's son—what white Americans would recognize as a marriage—then the son's actions seem not so much little and mean as reasonable and, under all the circumstances, understandable.[10]

Whatever Olive thought of the chief's son, she must have been moved by the genuine affection displayed by the chief's wife. When Aespaneo first realized that Olive was to leave the valley and that in all likelihood she would never see her again, she began to cry, and she continued to cry for a full day and a night, as if she were losing her own child.[11]

The journey southward that Olive, Francisco, Topeka, Tokwatha, and the others made was long and demanding. The travelers hewed to the banks of the Colorado where there was a passable trail, and where there was none, they plunged into the river's swift waters (Olive had become an excellent swimmer during the years she lived on the Colorado). They crossed from one side of the river to the other, sleeping at night under trees that hugged the riverbank, or overhanging rocks, or sometimes the open sky. They had little food to take with them and were glad to find berries, seeds, or nuts along the way. As they approached Yuma, one of the Quechans in the party instructed another, younger Quechan to run ahead to the fort and let Henry Grinnell know that they were near. He was to ask the carpenter to obtain a calico dress and send it upriver for Olive to put on so that she would arrive at the fort "properly" clothed. The travelers knew that the whites would be shocked if they saw Olive in only her willow-bark skirt.[12]

But the calico dress had not yet arrived when, on the morning of the ninth day, the party approached Fort Yuma from the opposite side of the river.[13] A group of Quechans had gathered to greet them. When Grinnell crossed the river and Olive saw a white man approaching for the first time in perhaps years, she threw herself on the ground and would not rise until a dress had been brought for her. Grinnell provided one, which Olive quickly donned. Then the party crossed the river: Olive, Francisco, Topeka, Tokwatha, and Grinnell on the ferry, with the Quechans swimming the stream.[14]

It was February 22, 1856,[15] exactly five years and four days since Olive had been snatched away from her family on the banks of the Gila River. But for Olive it might as well have been ten years, even fifty, so much had happened in the interim. Olive and her party were quickly brought before Colonel Burke. The post commander welcomed her back to the world of the whites, but was puzzled by her reluctance to speak. Her English—rarely used during the five years she lived with the Indians and virtually abandoned since Mary Ann's death—was halting. Browned by the sun, she was nearly as dark as the Indians who brought her into the fort (though on close examination, light patches could still be seen on her neck where her hair covered her skin). And her chin was clearly marked by the dark blue lines of the Mohave tattoos.

Burke put Olive in the care of a white family then living at Yuma. Who this white family was, and how long Olive was in their charge,

is not clear. Two men who were familiar with affairs at Yuma during
the 1850s later recalled that Olive was cared for by Sarah Ann Bowman, a remarkable woman who supervised the mess and laundry at
Fort Yuma but wielded greater influence than either of those respon-
sibilities might suggest.[16] Bowman was an imposing figure both
because of her stature (she stood over six feet tall) and her considerable reputation. While traveling with General Zachary Taylor's army
during the Mexican War, she had demonstrated extraordinary
composure in the face of enemy fire, inspiring the general's soldiers
to dub her the "Great Western" in allusion to a famous steamship of
the same name. The sobriquet followed her the rest of her life. While
she cooked and washed for soldiers in Texas and New Mexico, the
"Great Western" also provided local girls to satisfy their sexual needs.
At Yuma she lived with her husband, Albert Bowman, in a house
across the river from the fort. She kept her mess hall there, her
laundry, and rooms for the Mexican girls who washed the soldiers'
clothes by day and visited their rooms at night. Although she violated
some Victorian mores, Sarah Bowman was, as Colonel Burke knew,
a dependable woman with a strong motherly instinct who could be
trusted to take good care of Olive Oatman.

Stratton's book did not identify the family that cared for Olive at
Yuma, stating only that she "was taken in by a very excellent family
residing at the fort."[17] This statement might support the two men's
recollections that the "Great Western" was Olive's Yuma guardian,
but only if a good-hearted camp follower and her husband could
meet Stratton's definition of an "excellent family." Olive's own statement to a San Francisco reporter, made four months after her arrival
at Yuma, suggests that some other person or persons may have cared
for her. Olive then said that, after her departure from the Mohave
Valley, "I was taken to Fort Yuma and remained there a month in the
family of Sergeant Reuben Twist."[18] It is possible, of course, that Olive
spent time with both Mrs. Bowman and Sergeant Twist or that there
was some sort of business or personal arrangement between the

"Great Western" and the sergeant (she might, for example, have provided him with living quarters, prepared his food, done his laundry, or
acted as his housekeeper). Beyond the fact that Twist was stationed
at Yuma while Olive was there, however, virtually nothing is known
about him or any connection he might have had with Bowman.
Barring the discovery of further evidence on the point, it must be
assumed that Twist was Olive's primary custodian and that her actual
care was provided by another person or persons—perhaps Twist's
wife or housekeeper, perhaps even the "Great Western."

On the same day that Olive arrived at Yuma, Burke addressed a
letter to the editor of the *Los Angeles Star* informing him of Olive's
safe arrival at the fort. He briefly sketched the sequence of events by
which Francisco had come to Henry Grinnell with news that the girl
was living among the Mohaves and a promise that he would bring
her back to the fort. And, he announced, Francisco "has now complied with his promise." Burke asked the editor to report the relevant
facts in his newspaper, "with a view that Miss Oatman's friends may
be aware of what has occurred."[19]

Lorenzo Oatman was working in the woods some distance from
the Monte when a friend showed him a copy of the *Star* containing
the news of Olive's arrival at Yuma. He immediately went to Los
Angeles to try to get more information from the newspaper's editor.
He owned no horse, and could not afford to buy one, but some friends
helped him assemble an outfit for the long journey to Yuma. His
friend Jesse Lowe, a carpenter from Tennessee, agreed to accompany
him. Together, nineteen-year-old Oatman and twenty-four-year-old
Lowe left the Monte on March 10. After an exhausting trip of eleven
days, they arrived at Yuma on March 21.[20]

If Lorenzo was overjoyed to actually see his sister alive, Olive must
have been amazed to discover that her brother—whom the Indians
had left for dead on the cliff above the Gila River—had survived the
attack, made it back to the white settlements, and spent years trying
to find her. In the five years that had passed since Olive and Lorenzo

last set eyes on each other, both had changed. Olive's brown skin, mysterious tattoos, and well-developed arms, wrists, and hands marked her as a mature Indian woman, not the slender white girl Lorenzo had known in Illinois and on the western trail.[21] For his part, Lorenzo was no longer a callow boy, but a husky, worldly-wise young man. So it is hardly surprising that Olive and Lorenzo had some difficulty recognizing each other when they met at Yuma. They regarded each other for an hour in silence. Then they began to talk, to share memories of their childhoods, their mother and father and brothers and sisters, and the bloody afternoon above the Gila River when an Indian attack had changed the course of their lives.[22]

It was March 26 when Olive and Lorenzo left Yuma. They went together in the government wagon train that regularly crossed the desert between Yuma and San Diego. The Mohave Tokwatha was there when the wagons left the fort. Years later he remembered seeing the long train of wagons, with Lorenzo and Olive seated in one of them. Olive saw Tokwatha and got out of the wagon to speak to him.

"You are going?" the Mohave asked her. But almost before Olive could answer, Lorenzo jumped out of the wagon and came up to the Indian, brandishing a club.

"Don't!" Olive cried out. "He is a nice man; he took good care of me."

Realizing his mistake, Lorenzo put his weapon aside and, to make amends, presented Tokwatha with a box of crackers.

"This is the last I shall see of you," Olive said. "I will tell all about the Mohave and how I lived with them. Good-bye."

Tokwatha and Olive shook hands. Then she climbed back into the wagon and, with Lorenzo at her side, rode away to the west.[23]

Olive and Lorenzo arrived in San Diego at the end of March, then immediately left for Los Angeles County. At the Monte, they were welcomed by Ira Thompson, who put them up in his Willow Grove Inn. Thompson's daughter, Susan, now married to a man named

David Lewis, was delighted to welcome Olive back to the world of the whites. On the trail west from Illinois, Susan and Lucy Oatman had been almost inseparable. But Susan also knew Olive well enough to share confidences with her. Years later, she remembered Olive's sojourn at the Willow Grove with dismay, describing her as a "grieving, unsatisfied woman" who "somehow shook one's belief in civilization." Susan firmly believed that Olive had been the mother of two children while she lived among the Mohaves and that having to leave these children behind when she left the Mohave Valley was the source of her sadness.[24]

Susan was not the only Californian who sensed a pervading sadness in Olive. When William A. Wallace, editor of the *Los Angeles Star*, visited the Monte in mid-April, he found Olive "timid" and "lacking in confidence." On April 19 Wallace published an interview with her that occupied two columns on the *Star*'s front page. In the interview, he asked her a host of probing questions, but because she was unable to give "the full details unassisted," her brother and friends had to help her with some of the answers. "Her faculties have been some-what impaired by her way of life," Wallace wrote, "but her friends assured us that in the short time she has been among them she has made very perceptive improvement."

Aided by Lorenzo and the Thompsons, Olive told the editor a great deal about her experiences among the Indians. She said that the "Apaches" (Tolkepayas?) had treated her and Mary Ann "cruelly," that while they lived with those Indians, they had been overworked, and that "when they could not understand what was said to them they were beaten." When they arrived in the Mohave Valley, however, the chief "took them into his own family, and they were treated in every respect as his own children. . . . Lands were allotted to them, and they were furnished with seeds, and raised their own corn, melons and beans as the Indians did." The Mohaves always told Olive that she "could go to the white settlements when she pleased," but they dared not go with her for fear that "they might be punished for having kept a white woman so long among them." She could not go alone, for she did not know the way back to the whites.

Wallace thought Olive "rather a pretty girl." Her skin "was as fair as most persons who have crossed the plains," but her face was "disfigured by tattooed lines on the chin, running obliquely and perpendicularly from her mouth," and her arms were marked "in a similar manner by one straight line on each." She "conversed with propriety, but as one acting under strong constraint." She was "very ambitious to learn," the editor noted, and spent "most of her time in study."[25]

Wallace's interview with Olive was reprinted in newspapers in San Francisco, Sacramento, and even Oregon. She became an object of sympathy and concern all along the Pacific Coast. Though she and Lorenzo were comfortable enough at the Monte, their situation there was neither permanent nor settled. They were orphans, without any close relatives to protect them from the dangers of the world. In San Diego, county judge D. B. Kurtz suggested that Olive be placed under the care of a San Diego resident named Thomas Collins. Joseph A. Fort, the Pacific Express Company's agent in southern California, hoped that "some of our philanthropic San Francisco ladies will offer their services to either provide a home for her, or use their influence in procuring her admission to the Orphan Asylum."[26] Fort's suggestion was taken up by the northern city's Sisters of Mercy who offered to accept Olive into their San Francisco orphanage.

Closer to the Monte, a colony of Mormons also extended the hand of friendship to the orphans. Loyal to Brigham Young, these Mormons had been living at San Bernardino, about twenty-five miles east of the Monte, since the fall of 1851, when they established a supply station for Young's Salt Lake City "Zion." Swelled in the succeeding years by Mormons happy to exchange the hot summers and icy winters of Utah for southern California's temperate climate, San Bernardino was now the largest single town in southern California, with a population of about three thousand. Jefferson Hunt, one of the leaders of San Bernardino, was a member of the California State Assembly and pleased to help Olive and Lorenzo cope with their uncertain futures. He introduced a bill in the assembly calling for the state to pay $1,500 for Olive's relief. The *Star* welcomed the measure as "cheering intelligence," while San Francisco's *Golden Era* hailed it as "gallant and opportune."[27] Although Hunt's relief bill passed both houses of the legislature, it apparently failed to get Governor Johnson's signature and did not become law.[28]

While Olive and Lorenzo were awaiting action on Hunt's legislation, federal officials were considering a petition that Lorenzo had sent to far-off Washington in January. Requesting help in locating the still-captive Olive, it was similar to Lorenzo's petition to Governor Johnson, which he had denied. Congress moved much more slowly than the California legislature, however, and it was not until January 1857, a year after Lorenzo's federal petition was submitted, that the House Committee on Military Affairs denied it. Since Olive had already been rescued from the Indians, the committee reasoned, Lorenzo no longer needed the federal government's help.[29]

As Olive and Lorenzo pondered their futures at the Monte, a man whom neither could be expected to know was on his way to southern California to assume their care. Harvey B. Oatman was a nephew of Roys Oatman and a first cousin of Olive and Lorenzo. He and his brother Harrison had begun their lives in New York, where their father (Roys Oatman's older brother Harvey) died while they were still very young. They had gradually moved westward through Ohio, Indiana, and Illinois, finally arriving in 1853 in the Rogue River Valley of southern Oregon, not far from the California border. There is no evidence that Roys and the elder Harvey Oatman were ever very close or that either Olive or Lorenzo had more than a passing acquaintance with his sons before the younger Harvey appeared in Los Angeles on June 3, 1856, and announced that he had come to take them back with him to the Rogue River Valley. The Oregon Oatmans had first learned of the attack on Roys Oatman's family three years earlier, and after Olive was brought out of the Mohave Valley, they read about her in newspaper articles published in Oregon. Reckoning that they were now Olive's and Lorenzo's nearest relatives, in geographical if not familial terms, they decided that they had a responsibility to care for them. From Los Angeles the twenty-seven-year-old Harvey Oatman made his way to the Monte, where he was put up in the Willow Grove Inn.

Ira Thompson was not pleased to meet Harvey Oatman. The Thompsons were providing good homes for Olive and Lorenzo, he thought, and Harvey's public announcement that he was going to take them away seemed presumptuous. Thompson wondered why Harvey had not shown any interest in the orphans before the newspapers began to bathe them in publicity. In a letter to the *Star*, he vented his displeasure, complaining that Harvey had known since the summer of 1853 that Lorenzo was living alone in California but had never spent "an hour's time or one dime to advertise for information in regard to his young cousin." In fact, Harvey's connection with Olive and Lorenzo was regarded as so tenuous that somebody (perhaps Thompson) challenged him to produce proof that he was related to them. Harvey was able to do so with old family documents he had brought from Oregon, but Thompson still was not satisfied. His attitude may have been motivated at least in part by religious rivalries. It is not known whether he was still sympathetic to Mormonism. (The shattering of Colin Brewster's dream of an earthly paradise along the Colorado and Gila rivers had persuaded many Brewsterites not only that Brewster was an unworthy prophet but that the whole Mormon business of prophecy and revelation was a sham.) Whether or not his affections still lay with the church founded by Joseph Smith, Ira Thompson was no friend of Methodism, the evangelical religion Roys Oatman had followed before his conversion to Mormonism. Thompson may have suspected that if he surrendered Olive and Lorenzo to Harvey Oatman, who was still a practicing Methodist, they would soon return to the faith of their father and grandfather. If in fact that was his suspicion, events would soon prove him right.

After a prickly two weeks at the Monte, Ira Thompson finally agreed to let Harvey take Olive and Lorenzo to Oregon. It was mid-June when the brother and sister joined their cousin on a north-bound coastal steamer. They arrived in San Francisco on June 22 and took rooms at the Clinton Hotel. Public interest in Olive's reappearance after five years with the Indians was, if anything, even stronger in San Francisco than it had been in Los Angeles, and a reporter for the bay city's *Daily Evening Bulletin* promptly sought an interview. In a story published on June 24, the *Bulletin* reported that Olive was "a young lady apparently about nineteen years of age, large, stout and healthy. Her chin is tattooed with five or six lines, made with Indian [sic] ink, and running from the lip downwards."[30]

Probably while she was in San Francisco, perhaps resting at the Clinton, Olive took pen to paper to write a letter to Robert Kelly, one of her closest friends from the Brewster wagon train. After leaving Yuma and arriving in California, Kelly had come to live on a ranch near San Diego, and he had prospered wonderfully. He was still unmarried, a fact that might have reached Olive before she wrote him. "I feel once more like my self," Olive wrote to Robert,

> since I have risen from the dead and landed once more in A sivalized world . . . the events of the past five years of my life has been misery and dispare I have ben A slave to those friends [fiends?] that comited the bloody masicree to toile and worke for them that had the blood of then that ware near and dear to me stained up under thare hands that driven the happy smiles from my brow and be diewed my life with tears. . . . It seems like a dream to me to look back and see what I had ben thrue and just now waking up.[31]

Nothing is known about this letter except that it was written, sent, and received by Robert Kelly, who kept it for the rest of his life (when Kelly died in 1890, he was still unmarried and Olive's letter was still among his possessions). Is it evidence that a romance had blossomed between Olive and Robert while they were following the tragic trail to Bashan? If so, were Olive's feelings for Robert still alive? The available evidence provides no good answers to these questions, though the letter itself is ample proof that three months after she left the Mohave Valley, Olive's remastery of English was far from complete.

Olive, Lorenzo, and Harvey Oatman did not stay long in San Francisco. A day after their arrival, they boarded a boat for a voyage northward through San Francisco Bay and up the Sacramento River to the town of Red Bluff, where they boarded a stagecoach that took them over the Siskiyou Mountains into the Rogue River Valley of southern Oregon.

The Rogue River country was a rugged land of deep valleys, high mountains, and dense forests, only recently occupied by whites. The bulk of the white population had been lured there by gold and silver discoveries in the mountains that bordered the Rogue and its principal tributary, Bear Creek. In the two or three years since the first miners had arrived, whites had dramatically changed the landscape, laying out several towns, fencing off the valley floors into farms, and erecting a chain of gristmills and sawmills to process wheat and timber. They had also killed or driven out virtually all the Indians who had once occupied the region. In 1851, the year the Oatman family was attacked on the Gila River, there were an estimated ninety-five hundred Indians in the Rogue River country. But increasingly bitter clashes between the Natives—called Rogue River Indians or sometimes just "Rogues"—and the flood of white settlers prompted some white leaders to declare a "war of extermination" in the fall of 1855. Many Indian "outrages" were cited as justification for the "war," including a well-publicized incident in which Harvey Oatman's brother Harrison and some companions were attacked while driving wagons over the Siskiyous toward California. Two men were killed in the attack. Harrison Oatman escaped with his life by bolting from his wagon and seeking protection in a white-owned cabin nearby. Before the

"Rogue River War" ended, in June 1856, an astounding number of Indians—perhaps as many as seven thousand—had been killed (many in a barbarous fashion); all of the Indians' ancestral homeland of some eight thousand square miles had been seized by the whites; and the surviving Natives had been forced to move two hundred miles to the north to a "reservation" on the Oregon coast.[32]

Thus memories of the bloody struggle against the Indians were still fresh in Oregonians' minds when Olive and Lorenzo arrived in Oregon with Harvey Oatman. Harvey and Harrison had started their lives in the Rogue country as farmers, but they had soon moved into the town of Phoenix, where they now operated a store and hotel. In Oregon Lorenzo found work, probably in the Oatman hotel or store, while Olive sought to improve her skills as a seamstress. She had learned the basics of sewing from her mother, and ladies in Phoenix were willing to teach her their techniques. Under their tutelage she became a good seamstress who was very particular about the making and fitting of her clothing.[33]

Olive made several friends in the Rogue River country. One was Abby Taylor, daughter of the Reverend S. P. Taylor, who lived on a farm not far from Phoenix. Olive spent a good part of her time in the Taylor home, not only sewing but also trying to improve her English. Under Abby's tutelage she studied grammar and spelling, punctuation and penmanship. Though she would always have a difficult time with spelling and punctuation, she quickly acquired a flowing hand that made her letters pleasing to look at if not to read.

All the young women of Phoenix were impressed by Olive's skill as a swimmer. She had developed her ability, she told them, on the Colorado River, where the Mohave women threw her into the water and compelled her to swim to shore. One of Olive's Phoenix friends was Florinda Davenport. Olive took Florinda and several other women down to Bear Creek, where she demonstrated her swimming prowess and gave them lessons.[34]

The young ladies of the Rogue River country found Olive a good companion. But it was apparent to some of them that she was a troubled young woman. Years later Rev. Taylor's granddaughter remembered that Olive was "painfully sensitive about the tattooing on her chin, and on meeting a stranger her hand invariably went to her face to hide the cruel disfigurement." The granddaughter also recalled that Olive was "subject to the deepest fits of melancholy and despondency, often walking the floor at night weeping and wringing her hands."[35] Olive had left the Mohave Valley. But it was apparent, at least to her friends in Oregon, that the valley had not yet left her.

CHAPTER 7

The Book

It was not long after Olive and Lorenzo arrived in Oregon that they became acquainted with the Reverend Royal Byron Stratton, pastor of a Methodist church in Yreka, California, a mining town about fifty miles south of the Rogue River country.

Stratton is an interesting figure apart from his connection with the Oatmans. Born in Potsdam, New York, in 1826, he embarked on a course of religious studies while still a boy and, by the age of twenty-one, began his life as a minister. He served as a Methodist pastor in and around New York until 1851, when, with his wife, Lucia, and four-year-old son, Albert, he set out for California by way of Panama. Arriving in San Francisco, he took up pastoral duties with the California and Oregon Conference of the Methodist Episcopal Church, first in Sacramento, then in San Francisco, and beginning in 1854, in Yreka.[1]

Stratton quickly made an impression on the Methodists of Yreka, leading a fund drive that resulted in construction of a new Methodist church for the town and building a reputation as a spellbinding preacher. He made frequent trips into the Rogue River country to speak to gatherings of Methodists, perform baptisms, and counsel the faithful; and late in 1854 he joined a party of white men who climbed to the summit of Mount Shasta, which towers 14,162 feet above Yreka, to deposit a specimen of the town newspaper and a copy of the New Testament as evidence of their feat.[2]

Although Stratton had no experience as a professional writer, he was interested in the Oatman family's travails in the southwestern desert and offered to help Olive and Lorenzo write a book about them. His eloquence as a preacher must have persuaded the young Oatmans that he was equal to the task, for they quickly reached an agreement to work with him on the project. The volume was planned to consist of Olive's and Lorenzo's recollections, put down in their own words, with background and description by Stratton. The finished book followed that plan, up to a point, but the minister could not resist the temptation to reword and rephrase Olive's and Lorenzo's raw testimony. In the course of this rewording, he stripped their recollections of much of their authenticity, making it difficult to determine which words were originally theirs and which were his. And he stamped the whole work with the strong opinions he brought to the subject of the American Indians.

It is not likely that Stratton had had any notable personal experiences with Indians before he met Olive and Lorenzo Oatman in 1856. He had heard many stories about the Indians in his native New York State, where Indian traditions were many and varied, and he had read widely about the continent's first inhabitants in works of both fiction and nonfiction. His reading almost certainly included some examples of the Indian captivity narrative, an already classic literary genre that had, from colonial times on, fascinated American readers.[3]

The Indian captivity narrative was a quintessentially American form, a literary reflection of the long struggle between the European invaders and the Native peoples of North America for control of the continent. The narratives were first-person accounts written by whites who had been snatched away from their homes and families by marauding "savages," made to endure unimaginable cruelties, and later (as a result of either escape or rescue) "redeemed"—that is, returned to their white families. Although typically attributed to the captives themselves, the narratives were almost always shaped, if not entirely composed, by other writers. Many of the writers were clergymen, in part because the Indian-white struggle for control of North America was seen largely in religious terms, in part because clergymen were, at least in colonial and revolutionary times, the most literate members of white communities and, as such, the best prepared to help less educated men and women complete a difficult literary undertaking. As the captivity narratives became more popular, fictional elements were added to them, enhancing their "thrilling" tone and increasing demand for them even more. Eventually, some of the most widely read examples were wholly fictional (James Fenimore Cooper's *Last of the Mohicans* won the most readers). Although the captivity narratives were a popular source of literary entertainment, most Americans believed that they provided accurate pictures of the Indians and their customs. As the Indian frontier receded to the west, white contact with American Indians became increasingly sporadic, and captivity narratives became one of the principal sources of white information about Indian life. Few whites had any idea that the captivity narratives badly distorted the essential characteristics of that life or that they were works of propaganda designed to justify whites' relentless encroachment on Indian lands. And if they had known, they may not have cared, for captivity narratives told whites what they wanted to hear about Indians.

In addition to his probable reading of captivity narratives, Stratton had closely followed events in the bloody "Rogue River War" of 1855–1856, which had been depicted in the white press as a heroic crusade against Indian "savagery." Stratton read newspaper reports of the "war," talked with whites who had participated in it, and formed very definite opinions about the Indians who were its victims. Not surprisingly, his opinions were quite unfavorable.

In Stratton's mind the Indians were first and foremost "heathens"[4] and, as such, were to be scorned by pious men and women. His vocabulary of epithets was rich and evocative. He described the Indians by turns as "savages," "brutes," "wretches," "land pirates," "ferocious man-animals," "human devils," and "objects of disgust and loathing." He dismissed their speech as "gibberings," their religious beliefs as "superstitions," their mode of living as "barbarity" and "squalidness." He argued quite blandly that the European conquest of America was directed by the Almighty and applauded the heavenly directed process by which "barbarians, the remnant of a decaying race," were being "rooted out."[5] Whatever opinions Olive and Lorenzo held about the Indians when they first met Stratton in 1856, he was to influence the written account of those opinions in a definite direction.

The book was written almost entirely in Yreka, although it is possible that some work was done along the Rogue River in Oregon. It was in Yreka, on February 1, 1857, that Stratton signed the preface, signifying his completion of the manuscript. The book was then taken to San Francisco, where it was published by Whitton, Towne & Co.

The text was illustrated with engravings of scenes from the story: the first night's encampment of the Brewster wagon train, the Indian attack on the Oatman family, Olive and Mary Ann during their time with the Mohaves, and a portrait of Olive showing her tattooed chin. Numbering twelve in all, the illustrations were drawn by San Francisco artists (probably the celebrated German-born painters and lithographers Charles and Arthur Nahl) and engraved on wooden blocks by a San Francisco artisan named William F. Herrick. The drawings were based on descriptions supplied by Olive and Lorenzo, as supplemented by the artists' own experience of western life. Readers would appreciate the realistic tone of the engravings, and the hint of salaciousness in the images of Olive and Mary Ann, bare breasted and nubile, during the time they were held captive by the Indians (neither Stratton nor the publishers could have doubted that these pictures would do much to increase interest in the book).[6]

The text followed a more or less chronological outline beginning with the scene at Independence, Missouri, in August 1850, when the

Oatmans joined the Brewster wagon train, and ending at the Monte in southern California in February 1856, when Olive and Lorenzo began their short stay with Ira Thompson and his family. Extensive portions of the text were written in the first person and presented as if they were Olive's and Lorenzo's own words. Other sections were written in the omniscient voice of the author. In his preface Stratton admitted that he was not a professional writer, but he defended his work on the ground that its interesting subject matter would command the attention of readers despite its literary shortcomings. There was apparently some disagreement about the book's title, for when it was finally issued, its cover and title page bore different inscriptions. The latter read (in the inflated style of popular Victorian literature) *Life Among the Indians: Being an Interesting Narrative of the Captivity of the Oatman Girls, Among the Apache and Mohave Indians, containing also An interesting account of the Massacre of the Oatman Family, by the Apache Indians, in 1851; the narrow escape of Lorenzo D. Oatman; the Capture of Olive A. and Mary A. Oatman; the Death by Starvation of the latter; the Five Years Suffering and Captivity of Olive A. Oatman; also, her singular recapture in 1856; as given by Lorenzo D. and Olive A. Oatman, the only surviving members of the family, to the author, R. B. Stratton.* The cover was simply inscribed *Captivity of the Oatman Girls.*

Stratton's work reprised the classic Indian captivity narrative. It described a "brutal" Indian attack on an innocent white family and the forcible capture of two members of the family. It detailed a long list of cruelties that the captives suffered at the hands of the Indians. It related heroic efforts to "rescue" the captives, and it concluded with the "redemption" of one of them. It followed the pattern of many of the narratives in that it was written by a clergyman and adopted a vehemently anti-Indian tone. Interestingly, it also conformed to the classic narrative pattern of insisting that the captives were never subject to "sexual abuse" by the Indians.[7]

Beyond this classic denial of sexual abuse, however, the book did not explicitly address the question of whether Olive married a Mohave man or gave birth to a Mohave child or children. It did not discuss Mohave marriage practices. Of course, many readers would assume that if Olive was not a victim of sexual abuse, there could have been no husband and no children. But what if there had been a fully consensual relationship, involving sex but no abuse? What if Olive had entered into a Mohave marriage but chose not to reveal the fact because she knew that it would inflame white opinion against her? If so, Stratton would almost certainly have been privy to Olive's secret and willing to help her conceal it from a disapproving public. In a section of the book devoted to Olive's "five years of captivity," the minister made a curious statement. "Much of that dreadful period is unwritten," he wrote, "and will remain forever unwritten."[8] The statement is as provocative as it is enigmatic. What was "unwritten" in the published text and destined to "remain forever unwritten?" Was it something trivial, inconsequential, unworthy of notice? If so, why does the statement so closely follow his description of the Mohave period of Olive's life as "dreadful"? What else could have been so "dreadful" that Olive would devoutly wish to conceal it from readers?

The finished book was ready for sale in early April 1857. The first copies were made available in San Francisco, but stocks of the book were quickly sent to more remote locations, such as Yreka and the Rogue River Valley. On April 3 the San Francisco *Bulletin* reminded its readers that the paper had reported the Oatman story in its own pages and repeated Stratton's claim that the book's value lay in its subject matter, not in "any literary merit."[9] Eight days later the *San Francisco Herald* wrote of the book: "The story is a thrilling one, though poorly written."[10]

When Royal Stratton read the words "poorly written," and other, equally unfavorable comments about the book, they must have troubled him, for he later became very defensive about his contribution to the volume, arguing that he never aspired to a fine literary style but defending his work on the ground that he had spoken in public for some eleven years and, during all that time, he had almost always had a "carefully prepared" script before him. He claimed that he had sought "plainness, brevity, and an unadorned style." But his claims rang hollow. His sentences were long, his vocabulary pretentious, his narrative relentlessly repetitious. He missed no opportunity to wring the last drop of pathos from a scene and, in the process, frequently smothered the natural emotion that it evoked. Although the Oatman story was intrinsically dramatic, Stratton sought at every turn to heighten the drama. Some years after the book was published, the western historian Hubert H. Bancroft described Stratton's style as "literary fustian" and observed that the story's essential interest "was, or should have been, well nigh destroyed" by it.[11]

But ponderous writing was not the book's only defect. The text contained factual lapses, misspelled names, and incorrect dates, and it omitted whole elements of the story that the author was either unaware of or chose to ignore. Nowhere does the book suggest, for example, that the Oatmans were Mormons or that they had any relationship to Joseph Smith, Jr., or James Colin Brewster. Stratton revealed only that the Oatmans were members of an emigrant company who were going to establish "a colony of the Anglo-Saxon people" near the head of the Gulf of California. Of course, he knew perfectly well that Olive and Lorenzo's parents were Latter-day Saints; that after Smith's murder, they rejected the leadership of Brigham Young and set out on a quest for a new Mormon leadership, eventually finding it in James Colin Brewster. He chose not to reveal this rather messy religious history because it would not comport with the picture he wanted to portray of a virtuous family of Anglo-Saxons set upon by a "fiendish" band of "heathens" on the banks of the Gila. The Oatmans were representatives of the "superior race."[12] If his portrait of them showed their "feet of clay," their superiority would be neither as clear nor as convincing as he pictured it.

Despite its defects, *Captivity of the Oatman Girls* sold very well. Readers found it a compelling chronicle of real human beings subjected to enormous perils; a story showing how some of these people succumbed to the perils while others endured and even overcame them. And its depictions of the Indian threat to white culture and institutions, exaggerated as they were, elicited sympathetic responses from white settlers in remote parts of the West, settlers who lived in constant (if not always rational) fear that they themselves might one day be attacked by "savages." Like other Indian captivity narratives, it told white readers what they wanted to hear about the Indians. It provided literary justification for the long war the whites had waged against them, and it made it clear that the war was now being fought in the southwestern desert.

The book sold so briskly that the first edition of five thousand copies was exhausted in just over three weeks. The San Francisco *Bulletin*, calling this an "astonishing run," announced on July 29 that a second edition was ready for sale.[13] Stratton made a few changes in this edition, adding a new preface and a crudely drawn map showing some of the places referred to in the text. Three of the twelve original engravings were redrawn, and the one of Olive that appeared near the end of the first edition was moved to the front of the book (readers were fascinated by Olive's tattoos, and the publishers wanted to ensure that potential buyers saw them before they put the book down). And a poem titled "Stanzas to Olive Oatman" was added. Signed with the pen name "Montbar" and dated at Marysville, California, April 27, 1857, it was a soppy paean to the white girl who had endured five years of Indian captivity. It read in part:

> In captive chains whole races have been led,
> But never yet upon one head did fall
> Misfortune's hand so heavy. Thy young head
> Has born [*sic*] a nation's griefs, its woes, and all
> The serried sorrows which earth's histories call
> The hand of God.[14]

Six thousand copies of the second edition were printed, bringing the total in print to eleven thousand.[15] As the second San Francisco edition was put on sale, another printing of the same edition was issued in Chicago (identical to the San Francisco printing except for the name of the publisher, Charles Scott & Co., inscribed on the title page). Arrangements for the Chicago printing were made by mail, probably by Stratton himself.

As sales of the book continued to mount, Stratton realized that the little volume he had dashed off in Yreka had tapped a rich vein. He announced in his preface to the second edition that proceeds from sales of the book would permit Olive and Lorenzo to secure the educations that thus far had been denied them. And he had already made arrangements for those educations.

Early in 1857 the minister left Yreka for Santa Clara, about fifty miles south of San Francisco, where he took a seat on the Visiting Committee of the Methodist-run University of the Pacific and the pastorate of the local Methodist church. Olive and Lorenzo joined Stratton in Santa Clara, where in July 1857 Lorenzo enrolled in the university's Male Preparatory Department and Olive entered its Female Collegiate Institute. They could be grateful that *Captivity of the Oatman Girls* was selling well, for tuition at the university ($20 per term per student) would otherwise have been well beyond their means.[16]

In late July or early August the students learned that the story of their family's tragic experiences had been transformed into a stage play. With a script by San Francisco playwright C. E. Bingham, the drama was ponderously titled *The Captivity and Massacre of the Oatman Family by the Apache and Mohave Indians,* though audiences soon began calling it *The Oatman Family.* The premier performance was given on July 25 in Sacramento. In early September the play came to the American Theater in San Francisco in a production that featured Junius Brutus Booth, Jr., as "Langee" (a fictional Indian) and Booth's wife, Harriet Mace (billed as "Mrs. J. B. Booth"), as Olive Oatman. Booth was the scion of one of the country's most celebrated acting families (his father was Junius Brutus Booth, Sr., his younger brothers Edwin and John Wilkes Booth), and his name added cachet to the

Oatman drama. Since no script of the play has been found, it cannot
be determined how closely it followed the story line of Stratton's
book. There is little doubt, however, that it increased interest in Olive
and Lorenzo's plight and added to the mounting sales of the book.

Olive and Lorenzo began but did not complete their studies for
the spring 1858 term of the University of the Pacific. Stratton had
grown increasingly enthusiastic about the commercial potential of
Captivity of the Oatman Girls and now sought to transfer his base of
operations (and that of Olive and Lorenzo as well) from California
to New York. And so on March 5, 1858, the minister, his wife, and
their two children, joined by Olive and Lorenzo, boarded the steamer
Golden Age in San Francisco for the first leg of a long voyage to New
York. They arrived on the Pacific Coast of Panama on March 17 and
promptly debarked for a land journey across the isthmus. On March
18, at the Caribbean port of Aspinwall, they boarded the steamer *St.
Louis* for the last leg of their voyage to New York, where they arrived
on March 26.[17]

<<< • >>>

Stratton had probably corresponded with eastern publishers
before leaving San Francisco, for very soon after he, Olive, and
Lorenzo arrived in New York City, they made arrangements with the
firm of Carlton and Porter to produce a new edition of *Captivity of
the Oatman Girls*. Carlton and Porter were closely associated with the
Methodist Publishing House in New York (the senior partner, Thomas
Carlton, was a Methodist minister and director of the Methodist
Publishing House) and an important agency for the dissemination
of Methodist ideas and doctrines.[18]

The contents of the projected volume were ready for the publishers by April, when Stratton wrote a "preface to the third edition."
In it he stated that he, Olive, and Lorenzo had received many letters
urging them to have the book published in an edition that could be
distributed all over the country. Three new illustrations had been
prepared for the new volume: a portrait of Lorenzo, an artist's

depiction of Olive and Mary Ann's arrival at their captors' village, and another depiction showing a "skulking" Indian eavesdropping on a private conversation between the two girls. All of the previous illustrations had been redrawn and reengraved "in a much improved and more perfect style." (Not surprisingly, no effort had been made in the new illustrations to hide Olive's and Mary Ann's very revealing Indian costumes.) Stratton was as sanguine as ever about the book's broad appeal, reminding his readers of its "thrilling" contents.[19]

With improved illustrations, larger type, and better-quality paper, the book issued by Carlton and Porter was more attractive than either of the first two editions. The red cloth covers were embossed with a filigree design and stamped on the spine with gilt—"fripperies" that the utilitarian Methodists had once frowned on but that Thomas Carlton had long since accepted as necessary concessions to popular taste. The manuscript had been carefully edited, with some (but not all) of the misspellings corrected and much of the punctuation regularized. No effort was made to rewrite the text, however, so the book that went to the New York press was as burdened as the earlier editions with Stratton's overwrought prose.

After their business arrangements in New York were completed, Olive and Lorenzo headed north along the Hudson River, then westward through upstate New York toward the town of Chili, a few miles southwest of Rochester. They traveled on one of New York's new steam-powered trains. As they glided smoothly over the iron rails, they were reminded how rapidly the country was changing. Only seven years before, they had spent six months in a covered wagon between Independence and the Gila River; now they could cover the distance between New York City and Rochester in a few hours.

They went to Chili to visit their great-uncle Moses Sperry, brother of their grandfather Joy Sperry. While Moses and his wife, Sarah, welcomed them into their home, Stratton took his family to Albany. The minister's arrangements with Carlton and Porter required that he and the two Oatmans remain in close contact with the publishers

and with each other. At Chili on April 4 Lorenzo wrote to his Uncle
Asa and Aunt Sarah Abbott in Whiteside County, Illinois. He informed
them of his and Olive's arrival in New York and their journey upstate
by "the cars." The book would be out in only three weeks, he said, and
then they would start promoting it. "We intend to make a business of
it," he said.[20]

Moses Sperry was well-known in Rochester, where he had served
in important public offices since the 1830s, and he took Olive and
Lorenzo into the city to introduce them to some friends. He also took
Olive to the Powelson Photographic Studio on State Street, where,
dressed in a demure, floor-length dress, she posed for a series of
carte-de-visite photographs. The Powelson photographs revealed the
former Indian captive as a sober but attractive young woman, con-
siderably slimmer now than when she came out of the Mohave Valley
in the spring of 1856. Apparently satisfied with the photographs, Olive
returned to the Powelson studio at least one more time. Olive's Rochester portraits were made for distribution to friends and relatives, but
extra copies may also have been prepared for sale to members of the
public who longed to see a photographic likeness (not just an artist's
engraving) of the already celebrated heroine of *Captivity of the
Oatman Girls*.[21]

In Powelson's photographs the tattoos on Olive's arms were hidden
by the long sleeves of her dress. In at least one of the pictures, the dark
blue lines on her chin were also hidden, probably by cosmetics. In
other Powelson shots, her chin tattoos appear in almost shocking
clarity. That some pictures reveal the chin tattoos while others conceal
them suggests that, with the aid of powders and creams, Olive was now
able to turn the marks on and off, almost at will.

Carlton and Porter's edition of *Captivity of the Oatman Girls* went
on sale in New York and other cities near the end of April. Attrac-
tively priced at one dollar a copy,[22] it enjoyed a small boom in the first
few days. Not content to let sales take their own course, Stratton and
the two Oatmans immediately began their promotional campaign.

On May 3 the trio met a *New York Times* reporter who interviewed Olive and Lorenzo and inspected a copy of the book. The next day, the *Times* published a long article summarizing the volume's contents and reminding readers of Olive's and Lorenzo's experiences among the Indians.[23]

On Monday evening, May 10, Olive, Lorenzo, and Rev. Stratton appeared together at New York's Trinity Methodist Episcopal Church. The event was advertised on the front page of the *New York Tribune* under the provocative heading "Lo! The Poor Captive!" Stratton was the featured speaker, delivering a lecture on "The Indians of California and the South-West," while Olive and Lorenzo related "some incidents of their horrid captivity of five years among the Apaches and Mohavies; also of the massacre and starvation of Mary Ann, of which the Oatman Book treats." The advertisement was clearly designed to promote sales of *Captivity of the Oatman Girls,* for it referred several times to the "new and thrilling work, more startling than any romance, yet every word true."[24]

Who originated the idea for promoting sales of *Captivity of the Oatman Girls* with lectures—Stratton or Carlton—is unclear. In any case, it was a brilliant strategy and, as events were soon to demonstrate, ideally suited to Olive's natural talent for public speaking. Although no reviews of the May 10 event have been found, it must have gone off well, for it set the pattern for a host of similar appearances over the ensuing months, and even years. Stratton appeared at some of the events, but it soon became obvious that Olive was the real star, and before long, she assumed sole responsibility for the lectures.

Both Stratton and Carlton were aware, of course, that by sending Olive Oatman out on the lecture platform, they were defying strong conventions against permitting women to speak in public, especially in churches—and most especially before "promiscuous audiences" (including men as well as women). From an early date, most devout Christians had honored St. Paul's injunction: "Let your women keep silence in the churches: for it is not permitted unto them to speak;

but they are commanded to be under obedience, as also saith the law."[25] When American women first attempted to give public lectures early in the nineteenth century, they were met with an almost deafening chorus of disapproval. Women who defied the taboo against public speaking were deemed "not respectable," and some were even suspected of sexual impropriety. During the 1850s, however, some brave women began to make inroads against the taboo, appearing on the lecture platform as "trance speakers" (women who were speaking not in their own stead but as representatives of "departed souls") or before audiences of abolitionists as advocates of social reform. Olive was one of the first women to defy the social stigma attached to women speaking in public. Her personal history was well calculated to attract audiences, and she had the voice, poise, and presence to hold their attention. But she almost certainly shared the trepidations, the sometimes acute stage fright, that struck other women who attempted to defy the prohibition.[26]

Although a complete list of Olive's many lecture appearances cannot be assembled, scattered reports in newspapers, letters, and promotional handbills reveal that she toured over a large geographic area (stretching from New York to Ohio, Michigan, Indiana, and Illinois) from the spring of 1858 until well into the Civil War years. During this time Olive made a few appearances with Stratton. On February 10, 1859, for example, she and the minister made a joint appearance in Rome, New York. But by November of that year she was traveling alone through Indiana. In March 1860 she made a solo appearance in Syracuse,[27] and in April 1863 two more in Victor and East Bloomfield, New York. While she made these lecture tours, her residence shifted between her great-uncle Moses Sperry's home in Chili, the Stratton house in Albany, and the Abbott farm in Whiteside County, Illinois.

Olive's first visit to Whiteside County since her return from California was made with Lorenzo in the summer of 1858. Since Uncle Asa and Aunt Sarah Abbott's acreage adjoined the former Oatman farm, Olive and Lorenzo felt a special attraction to the place. With the Abbotts, the brother and sister walked along familiar country roads, visited the homes of neighboring families, and shared memories of the days before Roys and Mary Ann joined the Brewsterites on their journey to "Bashan." Lorenzo worked on the Abbott farm and attended school. When he was not helping with the farm work or attending classes, he traveled the nearby prairie, selling copies of *Captivity of the Oatman Girls.* Olive left Illinois in January 1859 to return to New York, where more lecture dates had been set, while Lorenzo remained with the Abbotts. Sarah Abbott was impressed with both of the young Oatmans. In a letter to her sister Betsey Hoyt in Utah, she noted that Olive was an "intelligent girl for one that has not had better advantages" and that Lorenzo was "very much like his Father in looks and manners." But Lorenzo was subject to "spasms," Sarah said, and "cramping fits that come on him when he is asleep." Lorenzo thought his attacks were caused by a blow he received to his head during the Indian attack in 1851.[28]

Olive was a gifted lecturer. The day after her appearance before a full house in Rochester in April 1865, the *Rochester Daily Union and Advertiser* commented on her "dramatic power" and the ability "she possesses of awaking in the minds of her audience a lively sense of the blessings of civilization."[29] She delivered her lectures from a script, written in her own graceful hand but still rife with the poor spelling and erratic punctuation of her California letters. Though the script may have been revised during the years she delivered the lectures, at least by the spring of 1864 she had settled on a standard text, which she titled "A Narative."[30] This text clearly owed much to Stratton's book: some of the book's factual errors were carried over into the lecture script, and some awkward expository passages were copied almost verbatim. In preparing these parts of her script, Olive did not draw on her own memory but repeated much of what Stratton had written. More important, the entire script was suffused with an anti-Indian bias that closely reflected Stratton's own prejudices.

Olive detailed the almost daily cruelties inflicted on her and little
Mary Ann, not only by the Indians who captured them in 1851 but
also by the Mohaves. She insisted that the tattoos she received while
living with the Mohaves were "slave marks," ignoring the fact that
tattoos were worn by native Mohaves as well as captives. "You per-
ceive," she told her audiences, "I have the marks indelibly placed
upon my chin."[31]

Olive's willingness to call attention to her tattoos is striking. In
Oregon she had been painfully self-conscious about the tattoos and
had constantly attempted to hide them from new acquaintances.
Later in life she would resume the attempt to conceal the marks with
cosmetics and veils. In her lecture appearances, however, she was not
at all reluctant to invite her audiences' attention to the tattoos. She
must have recognized that the blue lines were, at least potentially, a
double-edged sword. While they might excite sympathy for her as a
victim of Indian "cruelty," they might also be taken as evidence that,
while living among the Mohaves, she had been sexually "violated"
or, even worse, had willingly entered into a sexual relationship with
a Mohave man. Why did Olive choose to wield this very sharp sword?
Perhaps she had simply surrendered to commercial pressures,
deciding to exploit the tattoos to promote her appearances and book
sales. But she may also have come to realize that she could manipulate
the marks, highlighting them when it was to her advantage to do so
and concealing them when it was not.[32]

Perhaps by the time Olive took to the lecture platform she had
accepted Stratton's view of the Indians who captured her in 1851,
and of the Mohaves as well, as "wretches" and had become convinced
that their way of life was "unmitigated barbarism."[33] If she truly held
these views, however, they must have been developed after she met
Stratton, for she did not express any such notions in the first weeks
after she left the Mohave Valley. In any case, Olive's lectures never
rose to the level of an anti-Indian diatribe. She was generous in
acknowledging the kindness of some of the Indians she met in the

Mohave Valley, notably the wife and daughter of Chief Espaniola. She expressed genuine sympathy for the young Cocopa woman who suffered a painful death at the hands of the Mohaves after she was captured by a Mohave war party in the spring of 1854. Most important, Olive related a fascinating incident that occurred in New York in February 1864.

A Mohave chief named Irataba had come to the eastern city in the company of a prospector and guide from Arizona named John Moss. Moss wanted Irataba to see American cities and converse with leaders of the American government (perhaps President Abraham Lincoln himself) so that he would understand the overwhelming power of the whites and encourage his people to adopt their ways. Olive was understandably surprised when she read in the newspaper that a party of Mohaves was to be staying at the elegant Metropolitan Hotel in Manhattan. In her lecture script, she explained what happened next:

> Having learned that among the number, was the Chief, I sought an interview with him & found it was not the same *chief* that *reigned* when I was there among them, but his Brother.
>
> The old one had died & his Bro. had been elected in his place.
>
> It was a singular coincidence, that after the laps of 8 years the wild savage & the *released captive* should again *meet*; not among the mountain solitudes of the Paciffic slope; amid the filth & degradation of an unmitigated barbarism; but in the metropolis of the highest civilization; not in the wigwam; but in the beautiful adorned reception room at the Matrepolitan.
>
> We met as friends giving the left *hand* in friendship, which is held as a sacred pledge, among some tribes.
>
> I conversed with him in his own language, making many enquiries about the tribe. I learned from him, that his tribe had been enspired with a desire to become sivalized. I learned too that the chiefs daughter was yet living & that she still hoped that I would tire of my pail faced friends & return to *her.* The Picture of sadness is upon her countinance & she goes too &

from her daily labors, *alone* & *lonely.*
May God *bless* this poor forest *Girl.*[34]

Olive's emotional description of this meeting in New York is one
of the most telling of all her remembrances of the Mohaves. It reveals
that, eight years after she left the Colorado, she still felt affection
and concern for the Mohaves. She wanted to speak (in his own
language, no less) with the chief in whose household she had lived
for four years; she inquired about members of the Mohave tribe; and
she extended her left hand in a "sacred pledge" of friendship. If she
truly believed that the Mohaves had treated her cruelly, that their
way of life was "unmitigated barbarism," why did she choose to renew
old links that had once bound her to these people? Had the emotional ties connecting her to the Mohaves been completely severed?
Or did she wish to learn how some of them (perhaps her former
husband, perhaps a child or children she had been forced to leave
behind when she left for Fort Yuma) had fared in the intervening
years? Did she want to give the chief a message to transmit to those
loved ones when he returned to the valley?

The anti-Indian bias of Olive's lectures might be explained on
grounds wholly separate from her own inner feelings. The lectures,
after all, were never really about the Indians but about *Captivity of the
Oatman Girls* and Olive's desire to promote its sales. Her effectiveness
as a speaker certainly helped increase the book's sales, and in time
she came to rely on the income from her lectures. Well past her mid-
twenties, she was still unmarried and, despite the occasional generosity
of family members, obliged to make her own financial way in the
world. Admission fees (which apparently varied from venue to
venue) were charged at most, if not all, of the lectures. And though
the fees had to be shared with those who hosted the events (mainly
Methodist churches or associated groups),[35] a small profit was left
over for Olive to live on. Books were also sold at her appearances,
and, as her lecture script makes clear, Olive was not at all shy about

reminding her listeners of the book ("my book," she sometimes called it) or referring them to its pages for a more detailed treatment of the Oatman story. By 1863, at least, Olive was lecturing often enough, and selling enough books, to make her occupation "quite profitable."[36]

While Olive was making her living as a lecturer, sales figures for *Captivity of the Oatman Girls* continued to climb. The first print run in New York in 1858 was only three thousand, but it brought the total number of copies then in print to fourteen thousand. That was followed within the first year by six thousand additional copies; this printing announced that the book was being sold not only by Carlton and Porter in New York but also by the firm of Ingham and Bragg in Cleveland, apparently now a copublisher. In 1859 there were another three printings totaling five thousand copies. When the number of copies in print totaled twenty-four thousand, the name of J. H. Seeley of Potsdam, New York, was added to the title page. Apparently this firm, located in Stratton's home town, had agreed to become the third copublisher. The final printing brought the total number of copies in print to twenty-seven thousand—quite an impressive number for a mid-nineteenth-century book.

The book's healthy sales must have pleased Olive, Lorenzo, and Rev. Stratton, all of whom had a financial stake in the venture. Beyond its commercial success, however, the book had some wholly unexpected consequences. It made Olive and Lorenzo—but especially Olive—into celebrities. Her prominence in the book (in both the text and the engravings) and the many lecture appearances she made to promote its sales assured her at least a modest measure of fame. Her name became something of a household word among many American families; some even named their baby girls after her. Thus a fair number of Olive Oatman namesakes were born in the late 1850s and 1860s—Olive Oatman Cribbs, Olive Oatman Fretts, Olive Oatman Hooker, Olive Oatman Pearce, Mary Olive Oatman Raley, Olive Oatman Smith, Olive Oatman Stockett, and Olive Oatman Willett, among many others.[37]

Olive's celebrity also aroused popular interest in tattoos among white Americans. The practice of adorning the human body with permanent markings had been known to Anglo-Americans at least since the 1770s, when Captain James Cook brought a tattooed South Sea Islander back to England,[38] but widespread public fascination with the practice dated only from the 1860s, when P. T. Barnum introduced tattoos into his popular freak shows. The Connecticut-born John Hayes appeared in Barnum's "Greatest Sideshow on Earth" in the 1880s, claiming that the 780 tattoos on his body had been forced on him while he was a captive of American Indians. Although Hayes's claims were spurious (his tattoos were the work of a professional artist), they were obviously inspired by Olive's real-life experiences. The leap from Olive Oatman to John Hayes was not implausible. Like Hayes, Olive exhibited her tattoos to curious audiences for a fee. He did it in a circus, she in well-publicized lectures. If he was Barnum's most famous tattooed man, she was America's first bona fide "tattooed lady."

CHAPTER 8

The Legacy

Olive's lectures not only provided her with income and celebrity. They also brought her in contact with men and women who were interested in her life experiences and shared her religious values, in the process helping her ease what must essentially have been a lonely life. During an appearance in Farmington, Michigan, in late 1864, she met a thirty-four-year-old man named John Brant Fairchild who was to dramatically shape the rest of her life.

Born in New York in 1830, Fairchild had come to Michigan with his large family (originally five boys and three girls) while still a boy. In 1849, when he was nineteen, he made the first of several trips across the continent to California. Eventually, two of his brothers joined him on these overland adventures, helping him drive herds of cattle from Mexico and Texas to California, where gold seekers were willing to pay good prices for them. On one of these journeys the Fairchilds met disaster when a band of Apaches attacked them and their herd, shooting and killing John's brother Rodney. John managed to make it on to California and, from there, returned to Michigan, where with the proceeds from his cattle drives, he bought a farm near the town of Farmington, nineteen miles west of Detroit. After Olive gave her usual lecture in a Farmington church, she was introduced to John Fairchild and his three sisters. Intrigued by the former Indian captive, the Fairchilds invited her to visit John's farm. Olive and the Fairchilds got along so well together that she came back to Farmington for a longer visit in July 1865. It was then that she accepted John's proposal of marriage. Their wedding took place on November 9, 1865, in the First Baptist Church of Rochester, New York. Olive was twenty-eight years old and her husband thirty-five. Olive later remembered the months that led up to and immediately followed her marriage as the "happiest period of my life."[1]

On marrying, Olive gave up all her lecture activities. She and her husband lived on the Fairchild farm while he sought business opportunities. Beginning in the spring of 1866, he led another cattle drive, this time buying a herd of Mexican longhorns in Texas and bringing them north through Arkansas to Missouri, where the railroad took them to Chicago. By 1870 the Fairchilds were living in Niles City, Michigan, where John was occupied as a money broker. Then, late in 1872, they sold their Michigan property and headed south to Texas, where they settled in the budding farm center and railhead of Sherman, about sixty miles north of Dallas.

Fairchild plunged into the commercial life of Sherman, founding the City Bank and buying a large house at the corner of South Travis and Moore streets. Without children of their own, John and Olive adopted a baby girl in 1873. She was named Mary Elizabeth, but affectionately called Mamie. John became one of the wealthiest citizens of Sherman (the city directory listed his occupation simply as "capitalist"),[2] while Olive lived a comfortable life in her big home surrounded by lawns and trees.

As Olive was making a new life in Texas, Lorenzo was seeking his own destiny in the upper Midwest. He had chosen to remain on the Abbott farm rather than join his sister on the lecture circuit, admitting that he was more comfortable pitching hay and milking cows than telling church audiences about his experiences with the Indians. His attraction to Whiteside County was reinforced after he met the teenage Edna Canfield, who worked on the adjoining farm (the same farm that Roys Oatman had owned in the late 1840s). On August 3, 1860, Lorenzo Dow Oatman, twenty-four years old, and Edna Amelia Canfield, eighteen, were married in Morrison, Illinois.[3]

Lorenzo and Edna continued to live and work on the Abbott farm after their marriage. In the early 1860's, their two infant sons died and were buried in the country cemetery near the old Oatman farm. By 1864, however, they had moved from Illinois to Spring Valley in Fillmore County, Minnesota. There Lorenzo cleared a plot of prairie land and planted it in wheat, oats, and beans. He worked hard on his farm, but low prices made it difficult to turn a profit, and by the summer of 1870, he wrote his Uncle Asa back in Illinois that his purse was still empty. "I guess all the dollars that I get is what few I scratch out with my fingers," he complained. A few months later Asa's wife, Sarah, wrote her sister Betsey Hoyt in Utah that personal tragedy had again struck Lorenzo and Edna, when another of their children, a four-year-old son named Denver, was thrown from a wagon and instantly killed.[4]

By 1882 Edna Oatman informed the Abbotts that she and Lorenzo had moved again, this time to a plot of land in eastern Montana, near the town of Glendive on the Yellowstone River. Lorenzo had originally intended to start a small stock ranch there, but after Edna was offered the opportunity to run a nearby boardinghouse, they plunged into that work. "So here I am with warm meals at all hours," Edna wrote Sarah Abbott in September 1882. "Loren helps me all he can."[5]

Whatever she thought of Lorenzo's marriage to Edna Canfield, Sarah was pleased with Olive's marriage to John Fairchild. Soon after receiving news of her niece's Rochester wedding, she wrote her sister Betsey that Olive had "done well in getting a Husband."[6] Sarah's satisfaction was probably due as much to her belief that Olive's tattooed face and murky "Indian past" had hurt her marriage prospects as by the realization that John Fairchild was a solid man who wanted to give Olive a happy home.

In Sherman Fairchild demonstrated his devotion to Olive in many ways. He not only provided a comfortable house for her and their adopted daughter but also staffed it with servants and took pains to ensure that Olive's privacy was protected. He bought up and destroyed every copy of *Captivity of the Oatman Girls* that he could lay his hands on and he made it a rule that no guest in his home was ever to ask Olive any questions about the Indians. He knew that the subject was a sore one with her, and he may well have resented the part that Royal Stratton had played in making his wife the book's leading spokesperson. Beyond that, of course, he was sensitive about the whole issue of Olive's past. He knew that many Americans believed she had been sexually "violated" by the Indians and regarded the tattoos on her chin as evidence of a "shameful" past. There is no reason to believe that he found the tattoos physically repugnant. He may even have found them attractive, for, whatever else could be said about them, they were positive evidence that Olive was no ingenue, but a woman of "experience" in the world. She had a "past," and if that "past" was not in all respects socially acceptable, it marked her apart from other women.[7] Beyond that, John and Olive must have found a common bond in their experiences with the Indians. She had lost her mother and father and four of her brothers and sisters in an Indian attack; he had lost a brother in the same way. She had been captured by one tribe of Indians and tattooed by another. The fact that both had suffered at the hands of Indians inevitably drew them together in a way that other American men and women could only imagine.

If John Fairchild did not regard Olive's Indian "past" as repugnant, however, he did find discussion of it distasteful. By destroying copies of Stratton's book and banning any mention of Olive's Indian past in his home, he was not only protecting Olive from emotional distress but also shielding himself from the embarrassment of having taken an "Indian captive" as his wife. It is a measure of the low esteem in which Olive and John Fairchild held Rev. Stratton when they were married that the preacher was not told about their wedding, much less invited to attend it, and that he learned about it only secondhand.[8]

Although Olive had been very happy when she first married John Fairchild, and although no record indicates that he ever did or said anything to lessen her love for him, it soon became obvious that she was not an entirely happy woman. She suffered from a host of physical ailments, compounded by what doctors would later come to call depression and anxiety. In letter after letter to her beloved Aunt Sarah in Whiteside County, she complained of her poor health—debilitating headaches, sore eyes, and extreme nervousness. She left Texas often, to visit doctors farther north, to seek the solace of relatives (sometimes her own family in Illinois, sometimes her husband's relatives in Michigan), and even occasionally to seek care in a hospital or sanatorium. As early as 1866 she complained about pain in her eyes so intense that she was confined to her bedroom for nearly eight weeks. Four years later she was still suffering from this painful condition and had to seclude herself in a dark room. In March 1879 she wrote her Aunt Sarah that, again "on account of her eyes," she had been confined to her house, this time for more than four weeks.[9] Two years later, John Fairchild wrote the Abbotts that Olive had gone north to St. Catherine's, Ontario, Canada, where she was confined to her bed in a medical institution.[10]

While much of Olive's later life was marked by physical and emotional suffering, Royal Stratton's last years were punctuated by a series of strange controversies. Almost as soon as he arrived in New York in 1858, the California Conference of the Methodist Church reproved him for leaving its territory without permission. He began his pastoral life in Albany as minister of the Arbor Hill Methodist Church, where he demonstrated the same pulpit eloquence he had shown in Yreka, California. His Albany parishioners welcomed him to their midst—even holding open his position so that, in the early

months of the Civil War, he could briefly serve as chaplain of a
regiment of New York infantry.[11] But as he cemented relations with
his congregation, those with his church superiors deteriorated.
Within a few months after he delivered a highly publicized sermon
challenging the authority of the Methodist bishops,[12] he resigned
his Arbor Hill pulpit and took a similar position in a rival church.
At first denominated the "Congregational Methodist Episcopal
Church,"[13] the rival soon changed its name to the "Second Congregational Church of Albany." Stratton's determination to put distance between himself and the Methodist bishops was underscored
when, in 1864, he accepted the pastor's position at the First Congregational Church in Great Barrington, Massachusetts, the home state
of Congregationalism.[14]

Stratton was as eloquent in Great Barrington as elsewhere. On
Thanksgiving Day, November 24, 1864, he delivered an impassioned
sermon from his new pulpit, arguing that, as the Civil War entered
its denouement, Americans should be grateful not only for battlefield victories but also for the sure and steady progress of Christian
civilization across North America. Despite his forceful preaching,
however, the pastor was encountering personal opposition in his
congregation. A woman member of the church announced the
shocking news that while traveling in another state, she had learned
that Stratton had neglected his duties as army chaplain, gambled
while serving in the army, bribed an official "to protect his son from
prosecution" (for what offense, the records do not say), and even
committed "adultery of the worst kind." When the accuser was unable
to prove these charges, she was disciplined by the church. But doubts
about the minister were renewed a few months later when the long-
time deacon of the Great Barrington church resigned his post, saying
that he had repeatedly asked Stratton for copies of his ordination
papers but the minister had refused to produce them. The deacon
had finally concluded that Stratton was not legally ordained as a
minister. Soon, a petition was circulating in Great Barrington urging

Stratton to resign. He tried to hold out for a while, but ultimately bowed to his critics and left the church.[15]

By the end of 1867, he obtained a new position in the prestigious Old South Church of Worcester, Massachusetts. In the spring, the Worcester congregation received news that the pastor's twenty-one-year-old son, Albert, had committed suicide in Santa Clara, California. Albert had gone back to the Pacific Coast, where he had worked as a store clerk and schoolteacher before personal difficulties overwhelmed him. Albert's death would have aroused a wave of sympathy for his father if the pastor had not already begun to alienate Worcesterians with his own, erratic behavior. Soon his parishioners were openly questioning his sanity. By 1872 Stratton acknowledged that he had serious personal problems and submitted his resignation. He and his wife continued for a time to live in Worcester, but by 1873 his condition had deteriorated so badly that the mayor and aldermen had a guardian appointed for him. Apparently about this time, Stratton was confined to an insane asylum, where he remained for almost two years. On January 24, 1875, Royal Stratton died in Worcester. The newspaper reported the cause of death as "disease of the brain, which perhaps had been present for a long time." He was forty-eight years old.[16]

How Olive reacted to the news of Stratton's death—if, in fact, she ever learned about it—is not known. John Fairchild was so protective of his wife that he may well have shielded her from such unhappy tidings. He may also have taken pains to prevent her ever hearing of the ugly rumors being spread about her own mental stability. In 1877 a book titled *Picturesque Arizona* by newspaper reporter Enoch Conklin was published in New York. One of the first national publications to focus attention on the scenic wonders of the American Southwest, Conklin's book included the unhappy (and apocryphal) claim that after Olive left California, she went "to New York State, and afterwards died in an insane asylum."[17] If Olive had read this report, it would doubtless have pained her sharply. While there is no proof that she

was ever confined in an "insane asylum" (John Fairchild himself
denied the allegation),[18] it is easy to understand how such a rumor
might have gotten started. After she married in 1865, she withdrew
from public life and, in Texas, adopted a reclusive lifestyle. These
facts, coupled with reports about her chronic illnesses and occasional
hospital confinements, may have aroused suspicions that her problems were more serious than they actually were. Added to the reports
of Stratton's commitment to a mental asylum, these suspicions obviously resulted in journalistic confusion as to her own fate.

But Olive did not need to know that her sanity was questioned—
or that people in far corners of the United States thought she was
already dead—to suffer. Her chin and arms still bore the tattoos put
on them by the Mohaves in the early 1850s; she still had bad dreams
about her experiences in the desert; and she still complained of painful eyes, splitting headaches, and frightening nervousness. She wrote
her Aunt Sarah often, passing on family news, reporting her poor
health. In Olive's mind, at least, Sarah Abbott was a surrogate parent,
a substitute for the loving mother the Indians had robbed her of in
1851. In one moment of anguish, she scribbled a revealing note on
the back of an envelope addressed to Sarah:

> I long to have my dear Mother back; her memory is so Dear to
> me[,] all jentleness & goodness[.] I never felt the kneed of A
> mother [more?] I do so long for [a] long & confidential talk
> with you.[19]

Olive was saddened when she learned of her Uncle Asa's death in
1889 and devastated when news of Sarah's death came in 1900.

She was encouraged, however, by her daughter Mamie's progress
at Saint Joseph's Academy, a school near the Fairchild house run by
Roman Catholic nuns. Olive and John Fairchild worshiped at Saint
Stephen's Episcopal Church.[20]

Friends of the Fairchilds in Sherman developed affection and
respect for the couple. John was the essence of a small-town banker,

a handsome man with a long beard that grew progressively whiter as he aged. He was habitually called "Major" Fairchild in Sherman, in vague allusion to some kind of military background. Olive was shy and retiring, but to the small circle of friends who gained admittance to her house, she could be both warm and charming. One of the little girls of Sherman, a neighbor of the Fairchilds, often visited in the big Fairchild home on Travis Street. Years later, she remembered sitting by the fire, "watching Mrs. Fairchild and admiring her kind and gentle ways. Her sweet face was surrounded by beautiful white hair like a halo."[21]

With the passing years, Olive's tattoos seemed to fade a bit. By her sixtieth birthday, the blue marks of the Mohaves had become faint, though when they were not covered with powders or creams, they could still be seen. On her rare trips into the center of Sherman, she always wore a hat and a dark veil, pulled across her chin to obscure the Indian marks.[22]

Because they lived so far apart, Olive and Lorenzo had to keep in touch by mail. It seemed to Olive that Lorenzo and Edna were always on the move. After leaving Minnesota for Montana, they had pulled up stakes again, this time moving to Red Cloud, Nebraska, where they arrived in 1885 with their newest baby, a little boy born in 1883 and named Royal, or Roy (apparently in honor of Rev. Stratton). The Oatmans' experience running the Montana boardinghouse had given them the confidence to run a hotel, and in Red Cloud they invested their life savings in a series of three hostelries. They ran their first hotel, the Valley House, for about eight years, then moved on to another called the Gardner House. After two years they left the Gardner for the Holland House. Lorenzo was building yet another hotel when, in October 1901, he fell ill and died. Every business establishment in Red Cloud was closed on the day of his funeral, which was conducted in the Methodist church. He was sixty-five years old.

Olive survived her brother by only a year and a half, spending much of that time confined to her home, apparently suffering from heart

problems. Her end came on March 21, 1903, in her sleep. Funeral
services were held in the Fairchild house two days later, jointly
presided over by the Episcopal rector of Saint Stephen's and the
pastor of the Sherman Presbyterian Church. John Fairchild had an
elaborate grave prepared for his wife in Sherman's West Hill
Cemetery. In keeping with his status as one of the town's wealthiest
citizens, it was marked by a large granite monument and individual
headstones for Olive and himself. But before Olive's coffin was
lowered into the grave, according to the testimony of the undertaker
in charge of the burial, John had it enclosed in an iron container to
prevent the Mohave Indians from "reclaiming" her body.[23]

John Fairchild's own death came on April 25, 1907, four years after
Olive's. He was seventy-seven years old, the last survivor of those who
had been personally connected to the Indian attack of 1851 and the
desert captivity that followed it. But even his passing did not mark an
end to the Oatman story, for it had a durability of its own.

For all its faults, Royal Stratton's *Captivity of the Oatman Girls* continued to attract readers years after Olive and Lorenzo were gone.
Two years after John Fairchild's death a new edition of the book was
made available by the Oregon Teachers Monthly in Salem, Oregon.
Revised and abridged by Charles H. Jones, it retained the durable
title of *Captivity of the Oatman Girls* but added the subtitle *A True Story
of Early Emigration to the West.* Jones pared Stratton's text down to a
concise 119 pages but maintained the story's essentials and (alas for
the reader) much of the preacher's ponderous prose. The book was
issued again in 1935, this time in a fine-press edition illustrated with
modern woodcuts. The 1935 printing used the text of the second,
San Francisco edition and resurrected the title *Life Among the Indians,*
used on the title page of the first edition. A wider audience was
attracted to two facsimile reprints issued in the 1970s. In 1982 Time-
Life added a deluxe reprint of the third, or New York, edition to its
Classics of the Old West series, and in 1983 the University of Nebraska

appealed to scholars with a facsimile reprint of the New York edition, with an introduction by Wilcomb E. Washburn of the Smithsonian Institution. In 1994 the cycle of facsimiles was brought full circle with a facsimile reprint of the 1935 fine-press edition.

The Oatman story was also kept alive by Olive's and Lorenzo's descendants. Olive's adopted daughter, Mamie, left Texas after the death of John Fairchild, going to Michigan, where Fairchild relatives still lived and where, in 1908, she married Alistair Laing. Mamie and her husband had one daughter, named Olive for her grandmother, but the baby lived only a few days, and they spent the remainder of their days childless. Mamie Fairchild Laing lived in and around Detroit until her death there in 1938. During all that time, she treasured some of her mother's most valuable possessions, including the handwritten "Narrative" from which she delivered her Indian lectures for seven years and the original pass issued by Colonel Martin Burke at Fort Yuma in 1856, authorizing Francisco to bring her back to the fort or determine "why she does not wish to come." After Mamie's death these artifacts were given to a cousin, Louise Estelle Brown, and later to the cousin's daughter, Marjorie Brown, who died in Ann Arbor, Michigan, in 1989. Lorenzo's son, Roy Oatman, left Nebraska at an early age, eventually moving to Los Angeles, where he died in 1945, survived by a son, William.

Were there other children—half-Indian children, perhaps, or even grandchildren—who also shared memories of Olive? Several reports over the years had kept suspicions alive that Olive had taken a Mohave husband and borne children by him before she left the Mohave Valley in 1856. In 1863 an Austin, Nevada, newspaper reported that a local resident named George Washington Jacobs had taken several Indian children into his home and that one of them was "a beautiful light-haired, blue-eyed girl, supposed to have been a child of the unfortunate Oliv[e] Oatman." Jacobs had, according to the newspaper, acquired custody of these children (dubbed the "lost children of the desert") while he was in Arizona as a stage agent for the Butterfield Overland Mail Company. Ironically, Butterfield had run its coaches over the very trail that the Oatman family had followed in February 1851, and George Washington Jacobs himself had traveled the trail many times in the ensuing months and years. But Jacobs' blue-eyed Indian daughter met a tragic fate before her relationship to Olive Oatman could be proved or disproved, for while the stage agent was absent from his Nevada home, all four of his adopted children died of a mysterious malady. "It was a sad event," the Nevada newspaper commented, "bitterly wept over and not to be erased from memory."[24]

The story of Jacobs's "lost children" was not the only report suggesting that Olive had half-Mohave children. In 1893 a newspaper in Phoenix, Arizona, published a report (supposedly received from some Mohaves) that Olive gave birth to three children while she lived in the Mohave Valley and that one of them was a "half-breed" Indian, identified only as "Joe," who was then working in Phoenix. When questioned, "Joe" declined to either confirm or deny the report. The same newspaper reported that an Arizona pioneer named King Woolsey had known "Joe" some years earlier and believed that he might have been one of Olive's children; but Woolsey thought he might just as well have been the son of a French sea captain who had sailed up the Colorado River and taken up residence with a Mohave woman.[25]

In 1906 another Arizona pioneer, Joseph Fish, completed a manuscript history of Arizona that contained an interesting reference to one of Olive's supposed children. Fish was a Mormon loyal to the "Brighamites" in Utah and had spent many years studying the history of Arizona. In a tantalizing footnote, he related that Sharlot Hall, herself a noted historian of Arizona, had informed him that "Olive had two children while among her captors, [and] that one a Mohave sometimes visits Fort Yuma."[26] But in her own rather extensive study of the Oatman story, Hall made no reference to Olive's children.[27]

In 1922 a sensational story broke in Arizona newspapers about a Mohave Indian named John Oatman, who lived near (but not on) the Fort Mojave Indian Reservation and who was involved in a messy divorce suit. John Oatman claimed to be a wealthy man (the source of his money was apparently a gold mine in the Black Mountains above the Mohave Valley), though he lived in relative squalor. His claim that he was a grandson of Olive Oatman[28] was never proved or disproved, though observers thought it curious that, if he was in fact of mixed Mohave and white blood, he should bear his grandmother's (rather than his father's) name.

Memories of the Oatman story survived also among the Mohaves themselves. After Olive left the Mohave Valley, the people there struggled to adapt their lives to the ever growing influence of the whites. They resisted when immigrant wagons attempted to cross the valley on their way from the Great Plains to the Pacific Coast, going so far in 1858 as to waylay and kill some of the white travelers. But they soon realized that resistance to the tide of white settlement was hopeless. The U.S. Army established a fort in the Mohave Valley in 1859 and maintained a garrison there until 1890. Mohaves learned to live with the soldiers in their midst and also with the federal government's decision to relegate them to a reservation on the Colorado River south of the valley. After the Colorado River Reservation was established in 1865, Chief Irataba, who had clasped Olive's left hand in a gesture of sacred friendship in New York's Metropolitan Hotel in 1864, led his people south to the new preserve, determined to live in harmony with the whites. A sizable portion of the tribe, however, refused to follow him south, preferring to remain in the Mohave Valley.

Among the Mohaves, memories of Olive and Mary Ann Oatman never died. They were still vivid among some members of the tribe when A. L. Kroeber visited the Mohave Valley in 1903 to study Mohave customs and culture. Kroeber found many Mohaves who remembered Olive, but most were disinclined to talk about her on the ground "that it might be held against them as incriminating." Finally, however, the old Mohave named Tokwatha, who had known Olive during the time she lived in Espaniola's house and who had accompanied her and Francisco on their journey to Fort Yuma, sat down with Kroeber under the shade of a Mohave ramada to answer his questions and reminisce about Olive's departure from the valley. Years after Tokwatha himself died, other Mohaves continued to hold strong memories of the Oatman girls, though they were reluctant to share them with outsiders. Whenever they spoke to whites, it seemed, their words were misunderstood, twisted, turned against them. They believed that they had acted as humanitarians in rescuing Olive and Mary Ann from their original captors, providing a nurturing home for them in the valley. If Mary Ann starved to death while among them, her fate was no worse than that of many of their own people during that time of undependable food supplies. And Olive's final decision to return to the world of the whites was neither a repudiation of her Mohave background nor an indictment of the treatment she received while living with the tribe. It was, perhaps, a concession to the threats against the Mohaves first communicated by Francisco; an admission of the self-evident proposition that the whites had the raw physical power to destroy every last Mohave man, woman, and child; and an awful suspicion that, if they were defied, they might actually do so.

Memories of Olive Oatman—and of her mother and father and brothers and sisters—were also perpetuated on the Gila River, where the Oatman family was attacked in 1851. Sometime after Robert Kelly and Willard Wilder covered the remains of the victims with stones, a party of travelers passing by the site paused to remove the stones, gather up the bones, and carry them from the top of the rocky cliff (where no pick or shovel could penetrate the hard ground) down to soft, sandy earth in the flat that bordered the river. There they dug a grave, deposited the bones in it, erected a wooden marker (crudely carved with the words "The Oatman Family"), and enclosed the site with a fence. In 1862, when a column of Union Army troops marched along the same sandy flat (now known as "Oatman Flat"), they stopped to view the lonely fence and crudely carved board. Harvey B. Oatman, who had taken Olive and Lorenzo to Oregon in 1856, came to Arizona in 1878, announcing that he intended to erect "a substantial paling" around the Oatman grave and place a tablet on it. He told a newspaper reporter that he also intended to find little Mary Ann's grave in the Mohave Valley and transport her remains from there to Oatman Flat. (Harvey was unaware that the Mohaves had vowed that, after Olive left for Fort Yuma, they would disinter Mary Ann's remains and, following their own ritual tradition, cremate them). Eleven years later, in 1889, a family named Jordan acquired title to the bottomland adjoining the Oatman grave site (it had previously been part of the public domain) and started to farm it. They found the burial place enclosed with a "nice fence" and a neat wooden headboard that spelled out the names and the birth and death dates of the family (probably the work of Harvey Oatman). But cousin Harvey's work was destroyed in 1891, when the Gila went on one of its periodic rampages, flooding all of Oatman Flat and sweeping away the fence and wooden marker.[29]

The Arizona chapter of the Daughters of the American Revolution became interested in the grave site in the early 1920s. It persuaded Congress to pass a bill authorizing the secretary of the interior to grant the DAR title to the site and the surrounding acre,[30] and the chapter helped a government surveyor mark the corners with iron stakes. About the same time, Arizona governor George W. P. Hunt had a marker put up at the nearby attack site (now officially the "Oatman Massacre Site"). But Hunt's wooden marker rapidly deteriorated in the desert sun, and by 1940 its inscription was barely discernible. Frank Jordan, whose family farmed Oatman Flat, put a temporary monument over the grave site about 1948, but by 1950 Hunt's sign at the massacre site had deteriorated so badly that Jordan felt compelled to take it down. In the early 1950s the Daughters of the American Revolution was embarrassed to discover that it had not yet obtained title to the grave site (apparently the member in charge of the project had neglected to ask the secretary of the interior for a conveyance), so the organization renewed its efforts to complete the project begun thirty years before. Title to the acre plot was officially transferred to the DAR in 1954, and that year it dedicated a granite and concrete monument with a bronze plaque inscribed with the words

IN MEMORY OF
THE OATMAN FAMILY
SIX MEMBERS OF THIS PIONEER FAMILY
MASSACRED BY INDIANS IN MARCH 1851
ERECTED BY THE ARIZONA SOCIETY
DAUGHTERS OF THE AMERICAN REVOLUTION—1954

The Daughters deserved credit for finally seeing their project to completion, even if they did not get all the facts on their plaque correct (the massacre, of course, occurred in February, not March, of 1851), and even if the inscription failed to mention the fact that two of the Oatman girls were taken captive by the attacking Indians. Eventually, two piles of black rocks were erected atop the nearby cliff, at the spot where the attack took place. A white metal cross, tall enough to be visible from a considerable distance, was installed atop one of the piles, while a metal sign identifying the site of the "Oatman Massacre" was erected over the other.

The monument marking the Oatman grave and the cross and sign marking the massacre site did little to change the appearance of either place. Even into the twenty-first century, the place called Oatman Flat maintained a raw, unspoiled appearance. Black rocks still littered the cliff top where the Oatmans met their deaths, and traces of the old road, ground into the face of the cliff by the wheels of countless wagons and stagecoaches, still showed where the family labored to haul their wagon to the top.

More than a hundred miles northwest of Oatman Flat, reminders of the Oatmans lingered in some spots along the Colorado River. In

the early 1860s, gold was discovered in the mountains on either side
of the river, and white miners flocking to the area built a ramshackle
town of logs and mud bricks that they called Olivia (later Olive City)
in honor of the white girl who was captured by the Indians in 1851.
But the mines there soon gave out, and when they did, the town
crumbled into the desert. After 1900, however, another mining town
sprouted nearby. Built near the summit of the Black Mountains, not
far from the place where Olive and little Mary Ann caught their first
sight of the Mohave Valley in 1852, this town was called Oatman. No
reliable records have survived showing how or why this name was
selected, though pioneers there thought it was to honor Olive Oatman, the white girl who lived for four years in the nearby Mohave
Valley. Oatman was a rip-roaring frontier town between about 1910
and 1920, and after its one (and only) business street was made a
part of U.S. Route 66 in 1926, it became a way station on the most
widely traveled automobile road in the Southwest. By the end of the
twentieth century, the major flow of automobile traffic had been
diverted from Oatman, but the town found a new life as a popular
tourist stop, with restaurants, saloons, and an old hotel.

The Mohave Valley itself had changed much more than the mountains around Oatman. A large portion of the Mohave people still
lived in the valley, mostly in and around the railroad town of Needles,
on the California side of the Colorado, where Chief Espaniola had
his house when Olive and Mary Ann were in the valley. But the character of the Mohave homeland had changed, in part because of the
growth of Needles, in part because of the Colorado River's periodic
rampages. Sometime before 1903 the river changed its course through
Espaniola's village site, eroding the California side of the stream,
washing away the site of the chief's house and, with it, the site of Mary
Ann Oatman's grave. But after massive concrete dams were built on
the river in the early and mid-twentieth century (Glen Canyon, Hoover,
Davis, and Parker) the river became more tractable. The dams controlled the flow of the Colorado, ending the ancient cycles of flood

and drought and making abundant sources of water available for modern agriculture and the production of electricity. But they also changed the tenor of life in the valley. No longer were the Mohaves a hunting and gathering people who depended on the generosity of the river for their sustenance; now they were a half agricultural, half urban people dependent on government water and hydroelectric power.

After all the facts of the Oatman story have been told (or all of the facts that diligent research has been able to unearth), some important questions still remain unanswered.

First, what became of James Colin Brewster and the Mormon dissidents who followed him in his hapless quest for the "Land of Bashan"? After his party of emigrants split into two factions in New Mexico, he and the followers who remained loyal to him found a temporary resting place on the Rio Grande near Socorro, New Mexico. There they established a community that Brewster called "Colonia";[31] but in their letters back to Kirtland, Ohio, the "Boy Prophet" and his followers insisted that they still intended to push on to the confluence of the Gila and Colorado rivers. Brewster may eventually have made it there,[32] but if he spent any substantial time on either of those rivers, no record of his visit has survived. The bleak landscape, the lack of rain, the profusion of rocks and cacti must have quickly convinced him, as it did his followers, that there was something terribly wrong with his revelations. Here, certainly, no earthly Eden awaited the Saints of the Latter Days. Some of Brewster's followers did make it through to California in 1852, but they quickly passed over the "Land of Bashan" on their way to the coast. The San Francisco *Herald* reported on July 30 of that year the arrival from the Gila of "some five or six emigrant families. They belong to the Brewster division of Mormons, who left Missouri some two years since, for the 'land of promise,' said by one of their heads to be located on the Gila, according to a special revelation from Heaven. . . . The few families that have succeeded in reaching this place . . . state that they have been deceived and betrayed, by their own folly—renounce Mormonism, and are to return to the old folds."[33]

The official history of Brigham Young's Salt Lake church reported that Brewster did eventually make it to California and that, once there, he became an "itinerant lecturer" on spiritualism. But if this "Brighamite" report was true, Brewster's California lectures made no great impression, for his name is absent from the histories of that state. His father and mother, Zephaniah and Jane, eventually made it back to southern Illinois, where they were living in 1860. Zephaniah had by that time resumed his former trade as a carpenter. Ten years later, the elder Brewster, now seventy-four, had retired from carpentry and, when the federal census taker came to his house, he said only that he was "working in a garden."[34] There is no evidence of where Colin was during this time, except for a diary entry indicating that by 1867 he had made it to Peoria County, Illinois, where he and his wife, a woman identified only as Elizabeth, were baptized into a revived version of Sidney Rigdon's dissident Mormon church. After that, James Colin Brewster's trail disappears.

Brewster's followers left faint marks in the pages of history. A few of them may have joined the main body of Mormons under Brigham Young—although, if they did, they did not advertise their experiences with the "Boy Prophet," and traces of them in the history of Utah are all but indiscernible. The attack on the Oatman family sounded the death knell for Brewsterism: to a man and a woman, all of Brewster's followers abandoned his movement after they received news of the deaths of Roys and Mary Ann Oatman and their children and of the capture of Olive and little Mary Ann by the Indians. After they moved on from the Colorado River region, most of them went on to live ordinary lives, in Illinois, California, and elsewhere, like Olive and Lorenzo themselves, worshiping with the Methodists, Baptists, Episcopalians, or Presbyterians, relegating their experience with Mormon revelation to distant memory.

Second, what became of Francisco, the Quechan ("Yuma") who in 1856 played a key role in Olive's return to the world of the whites? Francisco may have seemed a heroic figure to the soldiers stationed at Fort Yuma in 1856, but to his own people he presented a different face. After Olive left Fort Yuma for San Diego, Francisco received some kind of promotion among the Quechans, and as soon as he did, he adopted a haughty and disdainful manner, looking down on his fellow Quechans and treating them disrespectfully, at least in the presence of whites. Then, in the late summer of 1857, the Quechans and the Mohaves united for one of their periodic wars against a neighboring tribe. Their enemies this time were the Maricopas, who lived with the Pimas near Maricopa Wells. In what proved a massive campaign, several hundred Quechans and Mohaves (some estimates went even as high as fifteen hundred) massed against an equal number of Maricopas and their Pima allies. Francisco joined his fellow tribesmen in this epic battle. But the fighting did not go well for the Quechans and the Mohaves, or for Francisco. Some of the Quechans and Mohaves began to grumble that their bad luck was owing to Francisco because he had become a friend of the whites and a traitor to his own people. When the Quechans returned home, they told a tale of death and humiliation on the battlefield: all of their boldest warriors had been slain by the enemy, among them Francisco. What they did not tell, however, was the manner of Francisco's death. Stratton learned about it secondhand. One of Francisco's own people, the preacher was told, killed him on the battlefield. Was this another white calumny against the Indians or a story based on fact? History has not recorded the answer to this question.

What conclusions can be drawn from the Oatman family's travails in the southwestern desert? Should the misfortune that befell the Oatmans on the Gila River in February 1851 be dismissed as just another tragic episode in the long and bitter history of whites and Indians in North America? Or can some larger lesson be drawn from the millennial vision, the quest for a "Zion" in the desert, the Indian attack, the captivity, the book, the lectures?

Alone among their family members, Olive and Mary Ann Oatman were made Indian captives—a condition that, in the eyes of many whites, was a "fate worse than death."[35] There is no question that the Oatman girls were captives when they were taken to the first Indian village (perhaps the Tolkepaya village of Wiltaika), though it is not clear that they maintained that status after they were taken to the Mohave Valley, accepted into the household of a Mohave chief, and admitted into full membership in the Mohave nation. The remoteness of the Mohave Valley effectively prevented them from leaving the Mohaves. But even if the valley had been less remote, there is no assurance that the girls would willingly have returned to the world of the whites. All the other members of their immediate white family were, so far as they then knew, dead. They had formed bonds with Mohave men and women. They were bound to the land and the people by ties of familiarity and habit. The Mohave Valley had become their home.

If Olive and Mary Ann remained captives after their arrival in the Mohave Valley, their captivity was more emotional than physical; they were restrained not so much by chains or threats as by their own hearts and minds; they were fearful perhaps of how they might be received in a world that held "savages" in contempt; they were conscious that their Mohave tattoos and their backgrounds as Indian captives would make it difficult for them to gain acceptance in a world in which, after all, they no longer had any places.

But if Olive and Mary Ann remained captives of the Indians, their fallen family members—father and mother and brothers and sisters— were captives of a different sort. They had rushed headlong into a desert that had been the home of Native peoples for centuries, even millennia. They went there in search of a "New Jerusalem" conjured up by a "Boy Prophet." They were captives, not of the Indians, but of a "vision" proclaimed by a white man. They were held in thrall by a

religious dream that rested on supernatural claims and accommo-
dated no other reality.

And what of the American people who so eagerly embraced the
anti-Indian posturing of Royal Stratton's *Captivity of the Oatman Girls,*
the curious audiences that thronged lecture halls to peer at the tattoos the "savages" had cut into Olive's face? Perhaps these people—
and the author-minister himself—were captives of yet another sort,
victims of a belief system according to which racial differences were
equated with cultural and spiritual worth and one people's nobility
could be affirmed only by denying that of others. Not all whites
shared these destructive beliefs, of course. Those who did, however,
contributed in no small measure to the climate of suspicion, distrust,
and antagonism that poisoned white and Indian relations through
much of the nineteenth century.

And what of the American Indians who regarded every white
intruder into their territory as an enemy or potential enemy? Most
Indians never subscribed to the notion that violent resistance to the
tide of white settlement would be effective in turning it aside. A few,
however, accepted that idea or something like it. A few assigned col-
lective guilt for atrocities committed by white individuals, or groups of
white individuals, to the whole white race; a few regarded the whole
white race as legitimate targets for their revenge. These Indians were
also captives—of ideas and beliefs that could not accommodate the
changing realities of a new life in a land that had to be shared with a
new people.

Beyond the Oatmans, Brewsters, Strattons, Fairchilds, the Yavapais,
Apaches, Pimas, Maricopas, Quechans, and Mohaves; beyond all of
the other people whose lives were personally touched by the desert
massacre and captivity; long after the religious rivalries that divided
the "Brewsterites" from the "Brighamites" had been forgotten and
the whites and the Indians of the desert had entered into a life of
nonviolent coexistence, the Oatman story continued to exert a powerful influence on white and Indian relations in the Southwest. And

not by any means for the good. Fed in large part by Royal Stratton's prose, the story of the Oatman tragedy attained the status of legend. Hardly any American who traveled along the Gila River in the half century that followed the attack on the Oatmans was ignorant of the story or failed, at some point in the journey, to reflect on the family's plight. As the story was told and retold, in books, newspapers, and magazines, and spread by word of mouth from wagon to wagon, in stagecoaches, and finally even in the safety and comfort of the first railroad trains that crossed the desert, travelers were reminded that the Indians of the region were a "treacherous," "brutal," even "diabolical" people. Again due to Stratton's influence, the Apaches were almost always blamed for the attack on the Oatmans. As it acquired legendary power, the story became more and more damaging, both to the Apaches and to the efforts of white men and women of good will to come to some accommodation with them. Before the great Apache warrior and shaman Geronimo was finally subdued by the U.S. Cavalry in 1886, long before Geronimo met his death as a prisoner of war in Oklahoma in 1909, the Oatman story—now the "Oatman Legend"— undermined efforts to bring peace to the southwestern desert.

The Oatman story was not the only source of anti-Apache propaganda, of course. A host of excited journalists posted stories about the cavalry's "Apache wars" of the 1870s and 1880s, thus helping to fan the fires of "Apache fever," a curious mixture of contempt, fear, outrage, and admiration. But the Oatman story, as the first and one of the most notable of the anti-Apache diatribes, still continued to exert its influence. The facts that the Apaches may have had nothing at all to do with the fate of the Oatmans, that the tragedy was misunderstood from the outset, and that it was misrepresented over and over again seemed to count for little. Perhaps this was yet another example of "captivity."

It is a truism that all good stories have a beginning, a middle, and an end. The story of the Oatman family began, as I have shown, in a wooded valley in southwestern Vermont, where Roys Oatman was born in 1809. The long middle of the story was played out in New York and Illinois, on the immigrant trail from Missouri to the desert Southwest, along the Gila River in what is now Arizona, in the nearby Mohave Valley, and in California, Oregon, New York (again), Illinois, Michigan, and Texas. But where does the story end? And *when* does it end? With Olive's departure from the Mohave Valley in 1856? With the publication of Royal Stratton's book in San Francisco in 1857? With Olive's marriage to John Fairchild in Michigan in 1865? With her death in Sherman, Texas, in 1903?

Perhaps the story has no end—at least not in the conventional sense. Perhaps there is no date on a calendar or place on a map that represents the last chapter in the tragic history. Perhaps it will end only when the truth is known and sober minds can reflect on it. Perhaps it will really be over only when all of the characters in the drama are released from the captivities—physical, intellectual, emotional, and spiritual—that so long and so forcefully held them in their grip.

Notes

Unless otherwise specified, all citations to "Stratton" are to the third (1858) edition of Royal B. Stratton, *Captivity of the Oatman Girls.* The following abbreviations are used in the notes:

AR	*Arizona Republican* (Phoenix)
BOM	*The Book of Mormon* (1830)
DAC	*Daily Alta California* (San Francisco)
DBHC	Deed Books, Hancock County Recorder's Office, Carthage, Illinois
DBWC	Deed Books, Whiteside County Recorder's Office, Morrison, Illinois
DC	*The Doctrine and Covenants of the Church of Jesus Christ of Latter-day Saints* (1981)
DEB	*Daily Evening Bulletin* (San Francisco)
LAS	*Los Angeles Star*
NYDT	*New York Daily Tribune*
NYT	*New York Times*
OB	*The Olive Branch* (Kirtland, Ohio, and Springfield, Illinois)
SDU	*San Diego Union*
SFH	*San Francisco Herald*
SFWC	*San Francisco Weekly Chronicle*
TS	*Times and Seasons* (Nauvoo, Illinois)

INTRODUCTION

1. Oatman's first name has been variously spelled as "Royce," "Royse," "Rois," "Roice," and "Roise." Since he consistently signed his own name "Roys," that spelling has been followed in this book. See, e.g., grant deed from Roys [sic] Oatman and Mary Ann Oatman to Louis C. Maynard, September 23, 1837, DBHC, book E, p. 30; warrantee deed from Roys Oatman and Mary Ann Oatman to Henry Bond, December 4, 1849, DBWC, book F, p. 450; Roys Oatman to Brevet Major Samuel P. Heintzelman, February 15, 1851, Documents Relating Mainly to Arizona, Bancroft Library, printed in Maloney, "Some Oatman Documents," 109.

2. The Indians who attacked the Oatmans and took Olive and Mary Ann captive have not been positively identified. Although Olive Oatman herself described the attackers as Tonto Apaches, the available evidence strongly suggests that they were Western Yavapais, or Tolkepayas. See discussion in chapter 4.

3. The Indian captivity narratives are so numerous that, according to a recent study, "the full corpus of texts has yet to be identified." The number is known, however, to exceed two thousand. See Derounian-Stodola and Levernier, *Indian Captivity Narrative*, 8. Now recognized as an American literary genre, the narratives have inspired a large body of secondary literature. In addition to the study by Derounian-Stodola and Levernier, this includes Namias, *White Captives*; Drimmer, *Scalps and Tomahawks*; Demos, *The Unredeemed Captive*; Castiglia, *Bound and Determined*.

4. OB 1 (1848): 82.

5. See, e.g., OB 1 (1848): 9, 11, 25, 26, 30, 48, 90; 1 (1849): 116–19, 179, 204, 205; 2 (1849): 44, 45, 78; 2 (1850): 111, 117, 134, 135, 136, 144, 152, 154, 182; 3 (1850): 17, 18, 38, 69, 70; 3 (1851) 124, 127, 137, 138, 150, 151, 162, 163, 164–68, 176, 178; 4 (1851): 1–3, 13, 14, 29, 30, 31, 63, 66, 69, 70.

6. Morgan, *Bibliography of Churches of the Dispersion*, 145.

7. All quotations have been transcribed from the original sources. Except as otherwise noted, idiosyncrasies of naming and spelling and errors of grammar and punctuation have been left intact.

CHAPTER 1

1. Chuck Oatman, Oatman Genealogy Page, http://www.sentex.net/~cdoatman/oatman.html (accessed June 12, 2004).

2. Hemenway, *Vermont Historical Gazeteer*, 3:835, 4:360.

3. "L. D. Oatman's Sudden Demise," *Red Cloud (Neb.) Nation* (Oct. 10, 1901), gives Lorenzo Dow Oatman's birth date as July 31, 1836; "Lorenzo Dow Oatman," *Red Cloud Chief* (Oct. 11, 1901), gives it as July 13, 1836.

4. U.S. Census, Population Schedule, Locke Township, Cayuga County, New York, 1820.

5. Moses Sperry to Sarah Abbott, May 17, 1858, Abbott Family Collection (private), Edward J. Abbott, Morrison, Ill.

6. L[orenzo] D[ow] Oatman to "Aunty" (Sarah S. Abbott), n.d., on letterhead of Holland House, Red Cloud, Neb[raska], Abbott Family Collection. Sarah Sperry Abbott to Elizabeth Sperry Hoyt, June 3, 1870, Donna Mae Palmer Spackman Collection, Latter-day Saints Archives, Salt Lake City, refers to a graveyard in Whiteside County, Illinois, in which "one of Roys and Mary Ann's twins" was buried. The surviving twin would have been Charity Ann or Roland, who were born after the family moved to Whiteside County, probably in 1846.

7. Sperry, "Life of Charles Sperry," 441.

8. DC, 21:1, 57; Launius, *Kirtland Temple*; BOM, 566–67; Allen and Leonard, *Latter-day Saints*, 69, 123–24, 140–45; McConkie, *Mormon Doctrine*, 305–307, 415–17, 531–33, 854.

9. Flanders, *Nauvoo*, 322. See Miller and Miller, *Nauvoo*, 5; J. Wellington Norris, *A Business Advertiser and General Directory of the City of Chicago, for 1845–6* (Chicago: J. Campbell & Co., 1845), 152.

10. TS 2, no. 10 (March 15, 1841), 349.

11. See Stratton, 28–29; DBHC, book L, p. 93.

12. See Compton, *In Sacred Loneliness*, 4–11.

13. McKiernan, *The Voice of One Crying*, 131, 136; Van Wagoner, *Sidney Rigdon*, 368–70.

14. Ibid., 379–91; G. M. Hinkle (West Buffalo, Iowa) to "Brother Robinson," Sept. 25, 1845, in *Messenger and Advocate of the Church of Christ* (Pittsburgh) 1, no. 23 (Oct. 15, 1845): 362.

15. "Six Years' Captivity among the Indians—Narrative of Miss Olive Oatman," NYT (May 4, 1858), 5, describes the house as a log cabin. On June 3, 1999, Edward Abbott of Morrison, Illinois, showed me the site of the cabin.

16. DC 124: 27–40; see McConkie, *Mormon Doctrine*, 116, 22, 257; Flanders, *Nauvoo*, 47, 209–210.

17. Sperry, "Life of Charles Sperry," 442–43.

18. Ibid., 443, 444; Carter, *Our Pioneer Heritage*, 421, 422 (referring to "Journal of Harrison Sperry, Sr.").

19. Sperry, "Life of Charles Sperry," 444.

20. Oatman land records are in DBWC, book F, pp. 29, 1150. For Abbott land records, see DBWC, book K, pp. 501, 513. Biographical references to the Abbotts can be found in *Portrait and Biographical Album of Whiteside County*, 464, and Davis, *History of Whiteside County*, 897.

21. *Portrait and Biographical Album of Whiteside County*, 464–69; Van Noord, *King of Beaver Island*, 82, 223–25; Hirshson, *Lion of the Lord*, 65; Van Wagoner, *Sidney Rigdon*, 370.

CHAPTER 2

1. OB 1 (1848): 33; 2 (1849): 61.

2. OB 1 (1848): 94.

3. Ibid, 33–34.

4. See OB 1 (1848): 9, 11, 25, 26, 30, 48, 90; 1 (1849) 116–19, 179, 204, 205; 2 (1849): 44, 45, 78; 2 (1850): 111, 117, 134, 135, 136, 144, 152, 154, 182; 3 (1850): 17, 18, 38, 69, 70; (1851); 124, 127, 137, 138, 150, 151, 162, 163, 164–68, 176, 178; 4 (1851): 1–3, 13, 14, 29, 30, 31, 63, 66, 69, 70.

5. OB 1 (1848): 35; 2 (1849): 63–64.

6. Brewster, *Words of Righteousness*, 15.

7. TS (Dec. 15, 1842), 32.

8. Ibid.; the original revelation is in DC, 28; see also Gregg, *History of Hancock County*, 368.

9. Faulring, *American Prophet's Record*, 265; see also Smith, *History of the Church*, 214.

10. Brewster, *A Warning to the Latter Day Saints*, 5; Vogel, "James Colin Brewster," 128–29.

11. OB 1 (1848): 91.

12. Vogel, "James Colin Brewster," 129.

13. OB 1 (1848): 82.

14. See Morgan, *Bibliography of the Churches of the Dispersion*, 113.

15. OB 1 (1849): 146; OB 2 (1849): 20.

16. Brewster, *Address to the Church of Christ*, 5–6.

17. Sage, *Letters and Papers*, 2: 103–104, quoted in OB 1 (1849): 105.

18. OB 2 (1850): 155.

19. Roys Oatman to Bro[ther] Hazen Aldrich, July 30, 1850, in OB 3 (1850): 38.

20. Ibid., 35, 38.

21. OB 4 (1851): 61

22. OB 3 (1850): 37.

23. Ibid. The U.S. Census, Population Schedule, Valencia County, New Mexico, 1850, lists some members of the party. Stratton, 37, says simply that the company numbered "more than fifty souls."

24. Because no diary or journal of this journey has been found, dates, places visited, events, and other particulars must be reconstructed from other sources. The date of departure given here is established by entries in OB 3 (1850): 127, and 4 (1851): 61.

25. Bigler and Bagley, *Army of Israel*, 22, 44–49.

26. BOM, 9, 28, 73, 144–45, 358, 363, 532.

27. Current editions of the *Book of Mormon* have changed the original "a white and a delightsome people" in this passage to "a pure and a delightsome people." See 2 Nephi 30:6.

28. Hill, *Joseph Smith*, 119–20; Stott, "New Jerusalem Abandoned," 71–85; Allen and Leonard, *Latter-day Saints*, 62–63, 115; BOM, 117.

29. Vogel, *Indian Origins*, 38–44; Roberts, *Studies of the Book of Mormon*, 67; OB 3 (1851): 139–41.

30. Stratton, 39.

31. OB 3 (1851): 141.

32. Greene, *Kanzas Region*, 58–59. Barry, *Beginning of the West*, 954–55, summarizes the few definitive references to Greene that have been found. Greene's own book does not identify the spot where he met the Brewster train, but Barry thinks it was near Pawnee Fork. Greene's description of Oatman as an "untameable Wisconsan," though in error as to his origin, suggests that Oatman had visited the Strang colony in Wisconsin before joining the Brewsterites at Independence.

33. OB 3 (1851): 119.

34. Ibid., 126.

35. Stratton, 47–48; OB 4 (1851): 62.

36. Greene, *Kanzas Region*, 59, suggests that the cattle were lost before the train reached New Mexico; other accounts clearly state that cattle were lost in New Mexico, though they do not rule out the possibility that there were also earlier losses.

37. OB 4 (1851): 39.

38. After the company divided, Ira Thompson, who went with the Oatmans, wrote Hazen Aldrich that the split occurred on October 9 and his party reached the Rio Grande on October 19. "We shall start in a few days,"

he added, "for the Colorado, which is about 700 miles. We will write more soon. Brethren, be faithful and fear not, for then you surely will overcome and wear the crown." See OB 3 (1851): 127. These are not the words of a man who had caught "gold fever," but of one who still believed in the quest for Bashan.

39. OB 3 (1851): 127. Ira Thompson said that the Brewsters and Goodales "started for Santa Fe, or Albuquerque, over the mountains."

40. Ibid., 127 (when Thompson's letter was typeset back in Kirtland, "La Joya" became "Lohoga").

41. OB 3 (1851): 151; OB 4 (1851): 17; Stratton, 51–52.

42. OB 4 (1851): 17.

CHAPTER 3

1. OB 4 (1851): 17.

2. Stratton, 50–51; OB 3 (1851): 148; 4 (1851): 17, 62.

3. Stratton, 52. The term "mountain fever" in the mid-nineteenth century described any of various febrile diseases occurring in mountainous regions, not a specific disease.

4. OB 4 (1851): 17.

5. Ibid., 17–18; Stratton, 54–55.

6. OB 4 (1851): 18.

7. Ibid.; Parrish, "Following the Pot of Gold," 4.

8. Stratton, 57.

9. Ibid., 58; OB 4 (1851): 18.

10. Parrish, "Following the Pot of Gold," 4.

11. Ibid.

12. Stratton, 59.

13. Ibid.

14. OB 4 (1851): 18.

15. Ibid.

16. On February 24 or 25, at Camp Yuma, Dr. Le Conte told Major Heintzelman that Mrs. Oatman "expected to be confined in a few days." See Heintzelman, *Transcription*, 13.

17. Stratton, 62. After explaining why Oatman decided to leave the Pima and Maricopa villages, Mrs. Wilder's letter (as printed in OB) reads: "So *we* started on the 10th of February" (emphasis added). But only three sentences later she writes, "The 18th of February, we started with the Kellys." It is thus

apparent that "so we started on the 10th of February" is a misprint and should have read "so *he* [i.e., Oatman] started on the 10th of February." OB 4 (1951): 18 (emphasis added).

18. Stratton, 67.

19. During the period covered by this book, whites habitually misidentified the Quechans, who lived at or near "Yuma," at the confluence of the Gila and Colorado rivers, as "Yumas." The terms "Yuman" and "Yumans," in contrast, refer to the large linguistic family that includes the Yavapais, Quechans, Mohaves, Havasupais, Hualapais, Maricopas, and Cocopas

20. Goodwin, *Western Apache*, 88–89; Braatz, "The Yavapais," 58.

21. Santiago, *Massacre at the Yuma Crossing*, 114–26, 146.

22. Pattie, Personal Narrative, 62–64; see Sherer, *Bitterness Road*, 23.

23. See Braatz, "The Yavapais," 203–204.

24. This letter was taken to Fort Yuma by Juan the Sonorian and later transported to Camp Grant, Arizona. In 1877 it was sent from Camp Grant to historian Hubert Howe Bancroft. The original is now preserved in Documents Relating Mainly to Arizona, Bancroft Library, University of California, Berkeley. It is printed in Maloney, "Some Oatman Documents," 109.

25. Heintzelman's journal for February 21, written after he had received the letter, reveals that Oatman had asked for four horses. See Heintzelman, *Transcription*, 11.

26. Stratton, 67–68.

27. Ibid, 69, 70. Juan's account, though differing materially from the account in Stratton (69–70), is more believable because it is more nearly contemporaneous. See note 28.

28. See "Statement of the Sonoranian Juan," in Documents Relating Mainly to Arizona, Bancroft Library, University of California, Berkeley, printed in Maloney, "Some Oatman Documents," 109 (estimating the distance at forty leagues); see also Heintzelman, *Transcription*, 11 (stating the distance to be sixty miles).

29. Stratton, 70–71.

30. After talking with Lorenzo and others who had visited the attack site, Heintzelman concluded that it was "within a mile or two [of] where Dr. Le Conte lost his horses." See Heintzelman, *Transcription*, 20 (entry for March 27, 1851). If this is correct, the Oatmans would not have gone far enough to see the note. Lorenzo said that they "missed" the note but speculated that his father might have seen it and concealed the fact from his children. Stratton, 71, 77.

31. Stratton, 71, gives this date as March 18, but contemporaneous letters, journals, and statements clearly establish that it was February 18. The erroneous date was copied from Stratton innumerable times and even used by Olive Oatman when she prepared her "Narrative" (see 17–24). Bancroft, who had access to some of the contemporaneous documents, correctly established the date as February 18. See Bancroft, *History of Arizona and New Mexico*, 485 n. 20.

32. See Stratton 76; Bartlett, *Personal Narrative*, 2:202–203.

33. "Lorenzo D. Oatman's and Others' Statements in Relation to the Murder and Robbery on the Mexican Side of the Gila in February 1851," in Documents Relating Mainly to Arizona, printed in Maloney, "Some Oatman Documents," 110–11. In 1856 Olive told a newspaper reporter that there were nineteen Indians in the band. See "Five Years Among the Indians: Story of Olive Oatman," DEB (June 24, 1856), 1. This, however, could have been no more than an estimate.

34. The facts of the attack described here are derived mainly from the statements given by Lorenzo Oatman and others after their arrival at Fort Yuma on March 27, 1851. See "Lorenzo D. Oatman's and Others' Statements." To the extent that the much longer account in Stratton, 81–89, differs from the earlier statements, it has been ignored. Plausible details found only in the Stratton account have been included (e.g., the story of the torn feather bed [88]). The statements given by Lorenzo and the others give Olive's age as "nearly thirteen" and little Mary Ann's as eight; after he spoke to Lorenzo, Heintzelman wrote in his journal that Olive was thirteen and Mary Ann eight. See Heintzelman, *Transcription*, 21.

CHAPTER 4

1. Stratton, 88–89, 115–16, 122.
2. Ibid., 132.
3. Ibid.
4. Oatman, "Narative," 30.
5. Stratton, 132, 135.
6. Ibid., 125.
7. Kroeber, "Olive Oatman's Return," 10, says that two hundred miles was "a fantastic exaggeration, of course." Stratton almost certainly consulted a map and supplied the number of miles necessary to account for a trip from the massacre site to a distant Tonto Apache village. If he did not believe

the attackers to be Tontos, he might have given much lower estimates of the distance covered.

8. Stratton, 145.

9. Ibid., 149.

10. Braatz, *Surviving Conquest,* 29.

11. Gifford, *Northeastern and Western Yavapai,* 254; Braatz, "The Yavapais," 46; Trimble, *The People,* 232; Braatz, *Surviving Conquest,* 30.

12. Braatz, *Surviving Conquest,* 36.

13. See Braatz, *Surviving Conquest,* 46 ("Yavapai and Western Apache oral traditions describe enduring violence and its role in society").

14. Ibid. ("Killing enemies was essential to avenging earlier defeats and casualties"); see also Braatz, "The Yavapais," 242 ("Yavapai tradition required vengeance for lost relatives").

15. See Brooks, *Captives and Cousins,* 258 (cycle of vengeance as a way of redressing wrongs, though it led to the commission of many more wrongs).

16. Brooks, *Captives and Cousins,* is a thoroughly documented and carefully reasoned analysis of southwestern captivity practices. It examines motives and effects in persuasive detail.

17. Stratton, 138; see Gifford, *Northeastern and Western Yavapai,* 254, referring to the Yavapais' "virtual neglect of agriculture."

18. Stratton, 151.

19. See "Statement of the Sonoranian Juan" and the discussion in chapter 3 of this book.

20. Kroeber, "Olive Oatman's Return," 6.

21. Braatz, *Surviving Conquest,* 253–54 n. 66, argues at some length that it is no more probable that the captors were Yavapais than Tontos. He allows that Olive's estimates of the distance traveled from the massacre site to the captors' village "must be considered suspect" because she was "under a great deal of stress" at the time but argues that her estimates should not be disregarded because "she had spent several weeks riding and walking with her family along the Santa Fe Trail and Southern Route and may have developed a keen sense of distance." He does not address the discrepancy between the different reckonings she gave or the geographic improbabilities they entail. Braatz argues that Olive's inability to understand the Mohaves' language when she first encountered them suggests that her captors were Apaches rather than Yavapais, since the Mohave language is related to Yavapai but not to Apache and Olive would presumably have understood the Mohaves if she had been living for a year among the Yavapais. But he

overlooks Olive's statement that the daughter of the Mohave chief was fluent in the language of the capturing Indians, a statement that suggests that the captors were Yavapai-speaking Tolkepayas. See Stratton, 156, and discussion in note 23 of this chapter.

Braatz does not consider Olive's declaration that "almost the only tribe with whom they [the captors] had any intercourse was the Mohaves" or explain how this could have been the case when the Mohave and Apache territories were separated by a wide expanse of Yavapai territory. See Stratton, 149. Nor does he explain why Apache captors would not simply have killed Olive and Mary Ann, as they did the other family members, rather than that take them captive, since Apaches would have known how far they were from their home territory and how difficult it would have been to transport the girls over such a long distance.

Braatz points to a poorly documented story about an unnamed Spanish woman who is supposed to have appeared in Tucson several days after the attack on the Oatman family, claiming she had escaped from a party of Tonto Apaches who had just brought an unspecified number of American captives into their camp. But the story of the Spanish woman was not corroborated by any independent evidence, and the first verified report of it was not made until more than five years after the Oatman attack. See [Wallace,] "Olive Oatman, the Apache Captive," 1. If, in fact, the Spanish woman escaped from Indian captivity, there is no verifiable evidence that her captors were Tontos (Tucson is even farther from Tonto territory than the site of the Oatman attack). If there was such a woman, and if she did in fact escape from an Indian camp to which American captives had just been brought, she could have been just as mistaken about the identify of the capturing Indians as Olive Oatman.

Braatz ignores the only direct testimony on the question, the statement made by the Mohave Tokwatha to A. L. Kroeber in 1903 that the capturing Indians were Yavapai. Among scholarly writers, A. L. Kroeber, Clifton B. Kroeber, Odie B. Faulk, Emmy E. Werner, Lynn Galvin, Katherine Zabelle Derounian-Stodola, and Albert Hurtado have all identified the captors as Yavapai (Kroeber says "they were certainly Yavapai"). See A. L. Kroeber, "Olive Oatman's Return," 1, 9, 10; A. L. Kroeber and Clifton B. Kroeber, "Olive Oatman's First Account of Her Captivity among the Mohave," 309, 315 n. 10; Faulk, *Destiny Road*, 74; Werner, *Pioneer Children on the Journey West*, 134; Galvin, "Cloudwoman," 10, 12, 13; Derounian-Stodola, "The Captive and Her Editor," 172; Hurtado, *Intimate Frontiers*, 68. Stewart,

"A Brief History of the Mohave Indians," 220, states that the captors were "probably Western Yavapai."

22. The modern town of Salome, Arizona, is located in the McMullen Valley between the Harquahala and Harcuvar Mountains at or near the site of Wiltaika, west of present-day Phoenix. Gifford, *Northeastern and Western Yavapai*, 250. Kroeber, "Olive Oatman's Return," 10, states that the village where the Oatman girls were held "was probably at a spot in or between the Harcuvar and Harquahala mountains"; Stewart, "A Brief History of the Mohave Indians," 220, states that the village "may have been located somewhere between the Harcuvar and Harquahala Mountains." *Harcuvar* ("cottonwood water") and *Harquahala* ("running water" or "always water") are Mohave words. See Barnes, *Arizona Place Names*, 196–97, 198. The Yavapai equivalents are *Ahakuwa* ("cottonwood trunk") and *Hakehela* ("running water"). Gifford, *Northeastern and Western Yavapais*, 250 n. 9. The Mohave who told Kroeber that Olive and Mary Ann were captured by Yavapais also told him that the place where the family was attacked was "Aha-ka-tamoha, west of Phoenix." Kroeber, "Olive Oatman's Return," 6, 17 n. 24. Kroeber was unable to identify this place. Although no place name listed by Gifford precisely corresponds to "Aha-ka-tamoha," the Yavapai name for Harcuvar ("Ahakuwa") resembles it.

23. Stratton, 156. It seems more likely that this Mohave woman would have been fluent in Tolkepaya, which is linguistically related to Mohave, than in Apache, which is not.

24. Ibid., 159.

25. Ibid., 160, 162.

26. Ibid., 162.

27. Ibid., 235.

28. For the Mohaves' appearance, see Foreman, Pathfinder, 237; Stewart, "A Brief History of the Mohave Indians," 223–24 (quoting Lorenzo Sitgreaves); Sherer, *Bitterness Road*, 34 (quoting Sitgreaves); Kroeber, *Handbook*, 728–29.

29. Stratton, 175.

30. Stratton, 177–79; Oatman, "Narative," 43–44. See Ives, *Report upon the Colorado River*, 75 (describing Avikwame and noting Olive's allusions to it). The mountain, which rises 5,639 feet above sea level in Nevada's Newberry Mountains, is referred to on modern maps as Spirit (sometimes Dead) Mountain.

31. Stratton, 177.

32. Ibid., 179.

33. Ibid., 218.

34. Stratton, 223–30. Kroeber thought the account of this "crucifixion" was "probably inaccurate" but "not made up of whole cloth." He thought it may have derived from a cruel Mohave practice (apparently learned from the Yavapai) of spread-eagling a male captive on a bed of coals. See Kroeber, "Olive Oatman's Return," 13.

35. Kroeber, *Handbook*, 752.

36. Ibid.

37. Munro, Brown, and Crawford, *Mojave Dictionary*, 20, defines *'ahwe* as "enemy."

38. Kroeber, *Handbook*, 753.

39. On June 22, 1903, a Mohave named Tokwatha (or "Musk Melon") shared his recollections of Olive and Mary Ann Oatman with A. L. Kroeber. He told Kroeber that the girls were kept on the west side of the river, two or three hundred yards north of the place where his (Tokwatha's) house stood in 1903; this was a little north of the "Pump House," or Needles City Water Works, near the Colorado River. Between the time the girls lived in the valley and 1903, the river had moved to the west, washing away the site of the house where the girls were kept; in Olive and Mary Ann's time, there was much more farmland on the California side. See Kroeber, "Olive Oatman's Return," 1, 2.

40. Stratton, 164–65. Olive's description of the house comports well with descriptions of Mohave dwellings given by other travelers in the mid-nineteenth century. See Foreman, *Pathfinder*, 239–40 (journal of A. W. Whipple); Kroeber, *Handbook*, 731–34.

41. Stratton, 156, 175, 235; "Five Years among the Indians," 1; Rice, *Los Angeles Star*, 281.

42. When U.S. Army Lieutenant A. W. Whipple (1818–1863) led a party of government surveyors through the Mohave Valley early in 1854, the Mohaves introduced their "five great chiefs" as Manuel, Francisco, Joachin, Oré, and José Maria. Foreman, *Pathfinder*, 244. All of these names are Spanish, but the chiefs also had Mohave names, which they seem not to have disclosed to Whipple. Kroeber, *Handbook*, 749, states that the Mohaves "are bashful about their names before strangers."

43. Pettid, "The Oatman Family" (manuscript), 81, states: "The name of this Chief was Hiss-spahn-ah-say, Pussard Vagina." Pettid was a sloppy writer who frequently made startling assertions without documentation or even

explanation. However, the Mohave word for vagina is "ispan" (Munro, Brown, and Crawford, *Mojave Dictionary*, 299), and it is possible that this Mohave word is the root of Stratton's "Espaniola," "Aespaniola," "Espaniole," "Espanesay," and "Aspenosay" as well as Pettid's "Hiss-spahn-ah-say."

44. Kroeber, *Handbook*, 749.

45. Stratton, 165.

46. The spelling of Mohave words and names varies, even among the Mohaves. The spelling given here is from Sherer, "Great Chieftains," 2. Munro, Brown, and Crawford, *Mojave Dictionary*, 73, gives *Hamakhav* and *'Am'akhav* as correct spellings. "Ahamakav" is the spelling adopted by the Ahamakav Cultural Society in Mohave Valley, Arizona.

47. Stewart, "Mohave," 57.

48. Sherer, "Great Chieftains," 2. Kroeber, *Handbook*, 745, states that the hereditary chiefs were called *hanidhala*. This was not a Mohave word, however, but an imitation of the Spanish *general*. "Pipatahon" is also spelled "pi'pataahan" and "hanidhala" is also spelled "hanidal." See Munro, Brown, and Crawford, *Mojave Dictionary*, 75, 154.

49. Sherer, *Clan System*, 16, 45–46; Kroeber, *Handbook*, 741.

50. Kroeber, "Olive Oatman's Return," 6, 17 n. 25. This name was also spelled "Oach," "Och," "O-cha," "'Ooch," and "Owitš." See Kroeber, *Handbook*, 742; Sherer, *Clan System*, 15, 42–43, 45; Munro, Brown, and Crawford, *Mojave Dictionary*, 222.

51. Sherer, "Great Chieftains," 3; Sherer, *Clan System*, 14, 45; Munro, Brown, and Crawford, *Mojave Dictionary*, 131.

52. Kroeber, *Handbook*, 745–47, setting forth a Mohave narrative relating to about 1855.

53. "Spantsa" is the name Olive was given in a handwritten "pass" issued Jan. 27, 1856, to a Quechan named Francisco by Lieutenant Colonel Martin Burke, commander of Fort Yuma. For the text of the pass, see the end of chapter 5. Kroeber, "Olive Oatman's Return," 1, says that the Mohaves called Olive "Aliutman" in 1903. This, however, was certainly not a Mohave name but a phonetic spelling of the Mohave pronunciation of "Olive Oatman" (or the diminutive "Ollie Oatman"). Pettid, "The Oatman Story" (manuscript), 94, asserts that "Spantsa" meant "rotwomb." As usual, Pettid offers neither documentation nor explanation for this provocative assertion. However, since "ispan" is the Mojave word for "vagina" (see Munro, Brown, and Crawford, *Mojave Dictionary*, 299, and discussion at note 43 above) and since familiar Mojave names were often sexually explicit, the assertion is plausible.

CHAPTER 5

1. Stratton, 182–83, describes the process of tattooing the girls' chins but does not mention any arm tattoos. When the editor of the LAS visited Olive at the Monte in 1856, however, he observed and described the tattoos on her arms. See [Wallace,] "Olive Oatman, the Apache Captive," 1. In later years Olive concealed the tattoos on her arms with long sleeves.

2. Stratton, 231; see also 285–86.

3. See, e.g., "Arrival of Miss Oatman," LAS, April 12, 1856, 2.

4. See *Reese River Reveille (Austin, Nev.)* (May 23, 1863), 4; Fish, "History of Arizona," 210; "Tribal Atrocities Alleged in Divorce Suit against Wealthy Mohave Indian Outdoes Fiction," AR (April 30, 1922), 5. Putzi, "'Tattooed still,'" 166, suggests that Olive's tattoos may be taken as evidence that she and Mary Ann were adopted into the Mohave tribe and that Olive was married to a Mohave.

5. Kroeber, *Handbook*, 752. The Quechans, who were culturally and linguistically related to the Mohaves, believed that captives were spiritually unclean and that sexual relations with them would lead to insanity. See Forbes, *Warriors of the Colorado*, 204 n. 43.

6. Kroeber, *Handbook*, 747.

7. Stratton, 230, quotes Olive as saying: "I saw but little reason to expect anything else than the spending of my years among them, and I had no anxiety that they should be many. I saw around me none but savages, and (dreadful as was the thought) among whom I must spend my days. There were some with whom I had become intimately acquainted, and from whom I had received humane and friendly treatment, exhibiting real kindness. . . . There were some few for whom I began to feel a degree of attachment."

8. Derounian-Stodola in, "The Captive and Her Editor," 176–77, argues that Whipple's failure to discover Olive in the Mohave Valley suggests that she may have had no wish to be discovered and that, by this time at least, her acceptance of Mohave culture (her Mohave "transculturation") "must have been close to complete."

9. Stratton, 197–98.

10. Ibid., 200.

11. Stratton, 95, states that Lorenzo was not sure whether he was thrown or had fallen from the cliff. In the statement he gave after reaching Yuma, however, he asserted clearly that, after the Indians dragged him across the top of the cliff, they went back to the wagon; he then crept on his hands and

knees to the edge of the cliff and rolled down the slope to the bottom. "Lorenzo D. Oatman's and Others' Statements."

12. After he arrived at Yuma, Lorenzo stated that he did not go up to the top of the cliff and view the bodies before leaving the scene. See "Lorenzo D. Oatman's and Others' Statements." Stratton, 98–99, states that Lorenzo crawled to the top of the cliff, where he saw the wrecked wagon and fallen bodies from a distance but could not bring himself to look into their lifeless faces. Stratton's version seems calculated to shield Lorenzo from criticism for not approaching the bodies and positively determining whether they were alive or dead.

13. Stratton, 104.

14. Ibid., 105–108; "Lorenzo D. Oatman's and Others' Statements"; OB 4 (1851): 18. Although Stratton suggests that Lorenzo traveled alone in the desert for three or four days and nights, he encountered the Kellys and Wilders on the second day after the attack and was actually alone only two days and one night.

15. Stratton, 108; OB 4 (1851): 19 (Mrs. Wilder's letter dated May 16, 1851).

16. Letter of Willard Wilder, quoted in Pettid, "The Oatman Story," (manuscript), 54.

17. OB 4 (1851): 20.

18. Heintzelman, *Transcription*, 15.

19. Ibid., 17.

20. Ibid., 23.

21. Ibid., 79.

22. Ibid.

23. See Stratton, 112–13.

24. Heintzelman, *Transcription*, 35.

25. Stratton, 240.

26. See Lorenzo D. Oatman to Asa M. Abbott, May 19, 1854, Abbott Family Collection.

27. Ronstadt's original letter is now preserved in Documents Relating Mainly to Arizona, printed in Maloney, "Some Oatman Documents," 111. The Indian Ronstadt referred to as Francisco might in fact have been Mohave, although it seems much more likely that he was the same Quechan named Francisco who later played a key role in bringing Olive out of the Mohave Valley. Born in Hanover early in the nineteenth century, Ronstadt came to America, probably in the early 1850s, married into a Mexican family,

Hispanicized his given names, and became a prominent citizen of the Mexican state of Sonora. About 1886 he moved with his family to Tucson, Arizona, where he died in 1889. See Ronstadt, *Borderman.*

28. J[oseph] A. F[ort] to editor of SFH, March 9, 1856, in LAS (March 29, 1856), 2.

29. J. Neely Johnson to Lorenzo D. Oatman, January 29, 1856, printed in Stratton, 247. The California State Archives do not contain this letter, which has probably been lost or destroyed.

30. Brevet Lieutenant Colonel Martin Burke to editor, LAS (March 15, 1856), 2.

31. A photographic copy of this pass is in the Olive Anna Oatman Papers. The location of the original is unknown. Stratton, 261, sets forth a verbatim copy of the pass in which the name "SPANTSA" has been changed to "OLIVIA." Olive probably informed Stratton that the Indian name was sexually provocative, and he or she probably decided to conceal it on the ground that readers would find it offensive. For discussion, see chapter 4, note 53.

CHAPTER 6

1. Stratton, 234, 263. Following the usual practice among whites, Stratton referred to the Quechan as a "Yuma."

2. Ibid., 236.

3. Oatman, "Narative," 50.

4. Ibid., 48–51; Stratton, 252–63.

5. Kroeber, "Olive Oatman's Return," 2.

6. Ibid., 3.

7. Ibid.

8. See Stratton, 265; Oatman, "Narative," 51.

9. Stratton, 264–65.

10. See Parrish, "Following the Pot of Gold," 8, stating that after the famine that killed Mary Ann, "Olive became the wife of the chief's son."

11. [Wallace,] "Olive Oatman, the Apache Captive," 1.

12. Kroeber, "Olive Oatman's Return," 5.

13. Ibid., 5, 17 n. 20.

14. See J[oseph] A. F[ort] to editor of SFH, March 9, 1856, 2; Kroeber, "Olive Oatman's Return," 5.

15. Bvt. Lt. Col. Martin Burke to editor, LAS (March 15, 1856), 2; Bvt. Lt. Col. George Nauman to Maj. Gen. John Ellis Wool, Feb. 27, 1856, LAS (March 29, 1856), 2; Oatman, "Narative," 53.

16. The men were Charles D. Poston (1825–1902) and Edward D. Tuttle (1834–1928), both Arizona pioneers. See Edward D. Tuttle to Mary Webb, September 25, 1927, Huntington Library, San Marino California, p. 11; Poston, "Oatman Family," 2; Sandwich, *The Great Western*, 51 at n. 20; Elliott, "The Great Western," 18–19; Parrish, "Following the Pot of Gold," 7. Poston is often called the "Father of Arizona." Although Tuttle did not come to Yuma until 1863 (and thus could have had no personal knowledge of affairs there in 1856), he lived and worked in Yuma, in the Mohave Valley, and on the Gila River in later years and became intimately acquainted with men and women who were in Yuma and the Mohave Valley when Olive Oatman was there. In their last years both Poston and Tuttle established themselves as authorities on Arizona history.

17. Stratton, 275.

18. "Five Years Among the Indians," 1.

19. Bvt. Lt. Col. Martin Burke to editor, 2.

20. Beattie, "Diary of a Ferryman," 101.

21. See J[oseph] A. F[ort] to editor, LAS, March 29, 1856, 2.

22. Oatman, "Narative," 54–55.

23. Kroeber, "Olive Oatman's Return," 5.

24. Parrish, "Following the Pot of Gold," 4.

25. [Wallace,] "Olive Oatman, the Apache Captive," 1.

26. "The Rescue of Miss Olive Oatman from the Mohave Indians," LAS (March 29, 1856), 2 (reprinting article from SFH).

27. "Miss Olive Oatman," LAS (April 5, 1856), 2.

28. *Journal of the Seventh Session of the Assembly of the State of California* (Sacramento: James Allen, State Printer, 1856), 518, 578, 582–83, 603, 722; *Journal of the Seventh Session of the Senate of the State of California* (Sacramento: James Allen, State Printer, 1856), 656, 731–32; "California Legislature," DAC (March 25, 1856), 3; "California Legislature," DEB, April 5, 1856, 1; "California Legislature," DAC (April 5, 1856), 2; "Miss Olive Oatman," 2. It is not clear whether the bill died because Governor Johnson vetoed it or because his signature was essential to its approval and he did not sign it. See "Miss Oatman," LAS (June 21, 1856), 2 (bill vetoed); but see "The Olive Oatman Bill," LAS (May 3, 1856), 2 ("bill became a law, the ten days' grace

having passed, without the Governor returning it"). Although the bill passed both houses of the legislature, it does not appear in the official record of statutes for 1856.

29. *Journal of the House of Representatives of the United States: Being the Third Session of the Thirty-fourth Congress* (Washington, D.C.: Cornelius Wendell, Printer, 1856), 204; U.S. House of Representatives, Report no. 55, 34th Cong., 3d sess., Jan. 10, 1857.

30. "Five Years Among the Indians," 1.

31. Bill Wright, "Tales & Details," SDU (Aug. 27, 1934), 2nd news sec., 1.

32. Schwartz, *Rogue River Indian War*, 135, 136, 148–49, 154, 161.

33. Gilfillan, "An Interesting Letter,"117.

34. Stearns, *Reminiscences*, 38.

35. Gilfillan, "An Interesting Letter," 118.

CHAPTER 7

1. Anthony, *Fifty Years of Methodism*, 91, 130.

2. Wells, *History of Siskiyou County*, 32.

3. Although there is no direct evidence that Stratton read captivity narratives, the works were so widely read in the mid-nineteenth century that the chance that an educated man with some literary interests would not have encountered them is slight. See Derounian-Stodola and Levernier, *Indian Captivity Narratives*, 14: "From the late seventeenth through to the end of the nineteenth centuries, captivity narratives about hundreds of captives among every major American Indian tribe were published, distributed, and read in virtually all sections of the country." The author of one of the most popular of the Indian narratives (reissued more than thirty times after its first publication in 1824) wrote: "It is presumed that at this time there are but few native Americans that have arrived to middle age, who cannot distinctly recollect of sitting in the chimney corner when children, all contracted with fear, and there listening to their parents or visitors, while they related stories of Indian conquests, and murders, that would make their flaxen hair nearly stand erect, and almost destroy the power of motion." James E. Seaver, ed., *A Narrative of the Life of Mrs. Mary Jemison* (Norman: University of Oklahoma Press, 1992), 53.

4. Stratton, 285.

5. Ibid., 65, 74, 92, 98, 129, 279, 280, 283; Stratton, *A Sermon Delivered on Thanksgiving Day*, passim, 33.

6. See Hurtado, *Intimate Frontiers*, 72.

7. Stratton, 285–86. See Derounian-Stodola and Levernier, *Indian Captivity Narrative*, 3 (most female captives remained silent about sexual abuse or explicitly stated that their captors respected their chastity); Washburn, introduction to *Narratives of North American Indian Captivity*, xlv (female captives rarely acknowledged rape, perhaps to avoid the stigma such an acknowledgment would subject them to on their return to "polite society").

8. Stratton, 283.

9. "New Book," DEB, April 3, 1857, 3.

10. "Olive Oatman's Captivity," SFH, April 11, 1857, 2.

11. Bancroft, *History of Arizona and New Mexico*, 486 n. 22.

12. It might be supposed that white notions of racial superiority would be implicit but not explicit in Stratton's writings. In fact, the minister's racial prejudices were articulated in very definite and often vehement language. Thus he gave thanks "to Almighty God for the blessings of civilization" and the "superior social life" that the whites enjoyed, while at the same time condemning "the degradation, the barbarity, the superstition, the squalidness" of the Indians' life. He described the Indians' homeland as "an unvisited savageness" and their lifestyle as "filth and superstition." Language of this kind flowed freely from Stratton's pen. See, for example, Stratton 283, 285.

13. "Second Edition of a California Work," DEB, July 29, 1857, 3.

14. Stratton, 290.

15. "11,000! Second Edition of the Captivity and Rescue of Olive Oatman," (advertisement), DEB, July 29, 1857, 2.

16. *Minutes of the California Annual Conference* (1856), 5, 11; *Minutes of the California Annual Conference* (1857), 4, 6, 10; *Catalogue of the University of the Pacific*, 4.

17. "Arrival of the Moses Taylor and St. Louis," NYT (March 27, 1858), 1; "Passengers Arrived," NYT (March 27, 1858), 8; Stratton, 278.

18. See Pilkington, *Methodist Publishing House*, 347–428.

19. Stratton, 14–16.

20. Lorenzo D. Oatman to Asa and Sarah Abbott, April 4, 1858, Abbott Family Collection.

21. One print of a Powelson *carte-de-visite* photograph of Olive Oatman is preserved in the Donna Mae Palmer Spackman Collection; another is in the Edward J. Pettid Papers, Department of Special Collections, Library of the University of Arizona, Tucson; and a third is in the Arizona Historical Society in Tucson. Derounian-Stodola, "The Captive and Her Editor," 188 n. 4,

suggests that Olive, like the nineteenth-century abolitionist Sojourner Truth, may have signed and sold photographs of herself when she lectured.

22. "List of New Works," *American Publishers' Circular and Literary Gazette* [New York] (May 15, 1858), 235. In his preface to the third edition, Stratton notes that those who urged a New York edition thought the book "would meet with a large and ready sale if it could be put into the market *at prices ruling on this side of the continent*," thus suggesting that the price of the two California editions was higher. Stratton, 13 (emphasis added).

23. "Six Years' Captivity among the Indians—Narrative of Miss Olive Oatman," NYT, May 4, 1858, 5.

24. "Indian Lectures: 'Lo! The Poor Captive!'" (advertisement), *New York Tribune* (May 10, 1858), 1.

25. 1 Cor. 14:34.

26. See Braude, *Radical Spirits*, 96–97.

27. "Miss Oatman, the Mohave Captive," *Rochester Union and Advertiser* (March 26, 1860), 2.

28. Sarah Sperry to Elizabeth Hoyt, May 25, 1858 [1859?], Donna Mae Palmer Spackman Collection. In her lecture script, Olive noted that Lorenzo suffered "at times from the effect of the terrible blow inflicted upon *him.*" Oatman, "Narative," 55–56 (emphasis in original).

29. "The Apachee Captive," *Rochester Daily Union and Advertiser* (April 28, 1865), 2.

30. Although Olive's "Narative" is not dated, it refers on pp. 56–57 to her meeting with a Mohave chief who was visiting New York "last February." Newspaper reports date the chief's New York visit to February 1864. Thus the "Narative" must have been completed sometime after February of 1864.

31. Oatman, "Narative," 44.

32. Putzi, "'Tattooed still,'" 169, argues that Olive's tattoos "allowed her to manipulate her audience, drawing attention to the mark at the same time that she spurned it."

33. Oatman, "Narative," 57.

34. Oatman, "Narative," 56–58 (emphasis in original).

35. See "The Apachee Captive," 2 (reporting on lecture given April 27 for the benefit of the Cornhill S[unday] School).

36. Sarah Abbott to her family in Utah, August 9, 1863, Donna Mae Palmer Spackman Collection.

37. The names given here were found in a short search of the Internet in June 2001.

38. Bogdan, *Freak Show*, 297.

CHAPTER 8

1. Olive Oatman to Sarah Abbott, July 15, 1866, Donna Mae Palmer Spackman Collection.

2. See *Morrison & Fourmy's General Directory of the City of Sherman 1887–88* (Galveston: Morrison & Fourmy, 1887), 69; *Morrison & Fourmy's General Directory of the City of Sherman, 1891–92* (Galveston: Morrison & Fourmy, 1890), 73; *Denison-Sherman City Directory . . . 1893–94* (Atlanta, Ga.: Maloney Directory Co., n.d.), 49; *City Directory of Sherman-Denison, Texas, 1896–1897* (Atlanta, Ga.: Maloney Directory Co., 1895), 120 ("retired capitalist").

3. Marriage license and certificate, Whiteside County Clerk, Morrison, Illinois.

4. The U.S. Census, Population Schedule, Beaver Township, Fillmore County, Minnesota, 1870, shows Denver Oatman, age 4, born in Minnesota, living with his parents, Lorenzo and Edna Oatman. This enumeration was made on June 17, 1870.

5. Edna Canfield Oatman to Sarah Abbott, Sept. 17, 1882, Donna Mae Palmer Spackman Collection.

6. Sarah Abbott to Elizabeth (Betsey) Hoyt, Aug. 5, 1866, ibid.

7. Putzi, "'Tattooed still,'" 171–72, suggests that a body mark on a woman may be the basis for a powerful sexual tie between the woman and a man and that it allows the woman and man to "come together as two experienced, mature individuals, without illusions or misgivings."

8. See R. B. Stratton to Asa M. Abbott, August 29 and September 6, 1866, Abbott Family Collection.

9. Olive Oatman Fairchild to Sarah Abbott, March 24, 1879, ibid.

10. J. B. Fairchild to A. M. Abbott, Aug. 2, 1881, ibid.

11. Stratton was enrolled as chaplain of the 16th Regiment of New York Infantry Volunteers on June 24, 1861. However, he made only two visits to the unit and delivered only two sermons before resigning on October 31, 1861. Curtis, *From Bull Run to Chancellorsville*, 29, 83, 323.

12. Stratton, *Church Government*, 6.

13. *The Albany Directory for the Year Commencing June 1, 1862* (Albany, N.Y.: Adams, Sampson & Co., 1862), 135, 163, 200.

14. Conn, *First Congregational Church*, 35.

15. Van Ausdall, "The Eighth Minister."

16. "Died" and "Death of Rev. R. B. Stratton," *Worcester Evening Gazette* (Jan. 25, 1875), 2; "Brevities," DAC, Feb. 14, 1875, 1.

17. Conklin, *Picturesque Arizona*, 196.

18. John B. Fairchild to Mrs. John T. Dennis, December 21, 1905, Oatman Papers, Sharlot Hall Museum/Archives, Prescott, Arizona.

19. Olive Oatman Fairchild, note inscribed on back of envelope addressed to Mrs. Asa M Abbott, postmarked November [illegible], 1882, Abbott Family Collection.

20. Pettid, "The Oatman Story" (manuscript), 191, 194.

21. See recollections of Katherine Collier (erroneously identified as "Katherine Collie") in Pettid, "The Oatman Story," 199.

22. Ibid., 198, 199.

23. See page titled "Death of Olive Ann" in handwriting of Edward J. Pettid, interleaved between two pages of his "Oatman Story" (manuscript).

24. "Apache Hank," *Reese River Reveille (Austin, Nev.)*, (May 23, 1863), 4.

25. "A Captive's Son," AR (March 26, 1893), 5.

26. Fish, "History of Arizona," 210.

27. See Hall, "Olive A. Oatman."

28. See "Tribal Atrocities Alleged in Divorce Suit against Wealthy Mohave Indian Outdoes Fiction," AR (April 30, 1922), 5.

29. Frank W. Jordan to Mr. Sidney T. Fritsche, December 14, 1952, Oatman Papers, Sharlot Hall Museum/Archives.

30. See *Statutes at Large of the United States of America from December, 1925, to March, 1927* (Washington, D.C., Government Printing Office, 1927), vol. 44, pt. 3, 1507 (chap. 5904, "An Act To grant certain lands situated in the State of Arizona to the National Society of the Daughters of the American Revolution," approved June 15, 1926).

31. OB 4 (1851): 32, 39, 65.

32. At least as late as July 1852, Brewster was still in New Mexico. See SFH (July 30, 1852), 2, quoted in Morgan, *A Bibliography of the Churches of the Dispersion*, 114. Vogel, "James Colin Brewster," 133, however, states that Brewster "apparently returned to the United States, having never reached California."

33. SFH (July 30, 1852), 2, quoted in Morgan, *A Bibliography of the Churches of the Dispersion*, 114. See Vogel, "James Colin Brewster," 133 n. 87.

34. U.S. Census, Population Schedule, City of Litchfield, Montgomery County, Illinois, 1870.

35. Derounian-Stodola and Levernier, *Indian Captivity Narrative*, 2.

Bibliography

ARCHIVES AND MANUSCRIPT COLLECTIONS

Abbott Family Collection (private). Edward J. Abbott, Morrison, Ill.

Deed Books. Hancock County Recorder's Office. Carthage, Ill.

Deed Books. Whiteside County Recorder's Office. Morrison, Ill.

Documents Relating Mainly to Arizona. Bancroft Library. University of California, Berkeley.

Donna Mae Palmer Spackman Collection. Latter-day Saints Archives. Salt Lake City.

Pettid, Edward J., Papers. Department of Special Collections. Library of the University of Arizona. Tucson.

Oatman Papers. Sharlot Hall Museum/Archives. Prescott, Ariz.

Oatman, Olive Ann, Papers. Center for Archival Collections. Jerome Library. Bowling Green State University. Bowling Green, Ohio.

INDIVIDUAL MANUSCRIPTS

Braatz, Timothy. "The Yavapais: A History of Indians in North-Central Arizona to 1910." Ph.D. diss., Arizona State University, 1997.

Burke, Martin. "Memorandum of Questions put to Miss Oatman rescued from 'Mohave' Indians, & her answers," Fort Yuma, Calif., March 1, 1856. With a covering letter, Burke to Captain D. R. Jones, Assistant Adjutant General, Benicia, Calif., March 1, 1856. Letter B 1856, Division and Department of the Pacific, Letters Received (entry 3584). Record Group 393. Records of U.S. Army Continental Commands. National Archives. Washington, D.C.

Collier, Katherine. "Mohave Tattoo: The Captivity of Olive Oatman." Arizona Historical Society, Tucson.

Fish, Joseph. "History of Arizona" (preface dated Aug. 1, 1906). Arizona State Archives. Phoenix.

Hawthorne, Barbara D. "The Oatmans" (microfiche copy). Family History Library. Salt Lake City.

Hunter, Carolyn. "Olive Oatman's Stories." Arizona Historical Society, Tucson.

Oatman, Olive. "A Narative." Photographic copy in Olive Ann Oatman Papers, Center for Archival Collections, Jerome Library, Bowling Green State University, Bowling Green, Ohio. Published as "Olive Ann Oatman's Lecture Notes and Oatman Bibliography." Edited by Edward J. Pettid. *San Bernardino County Museum Association Quarterly* 16, no. 2 (1968): ii, 1–39. Location of original unknown.

[Parrish, Susan Thompson Lewis.] "Following the Pot of Gold at the Rainbow's End in the Days of 1850: The Life of Mrs. Susan Thompson Lewis Parrish of El Monte, California. By Virginia V. Root." Huntington Library. San Marino, Calif.

————. "Westward in 1850." Huntington Library. San Marino, Calif.

Pettid, Edward J., S. J. "The Oatman Story" (photocopy of unpublished manuscript). Edward J. Pettid Papers. Department of Special Collections. Library of the University of Arizona, Tucson. Location of original manuscript unknown.

Van Ausdall, Rev. Charles G. "The Eighth Minister, Rev. Royal Byron Stratton, 1864–1866." First Congregational Church. Great Barrington, Mass.

VIDEO

Fredricks, Kathy, producer and director. *The Yavapai Story*. VHS. Falls Church, Virginia: Landmark Films, 1992.

GOVERNMENT DOCUMENTS

Heintzelman, Samuel P., Bvt. Maj. Report dated July 15, 1853, to Maj. E. D. Townsend, in "Indian Affairs on the Pacific." 4th Cong., 3rd sess., 1857. H. Exec. Doc. 76, pp. 34–58.

Ives, Joseph C. *Report upon the Colorado River of the West*. Washington, D.C.: Government Printing Office, 1861.

BOOKS AND ARTICLES

Albers, Jan. *Hands on the Land: A History of the Vermont Landscape.* Cambridge, Mass.: MIT Press, 2000.

Allen, James B., and Glen M. Leonard. *The Story of the Latter-day Saints.* 2nd ed. Salt Lake City: Deseret Book, 1992.

Anderson, Dorothy Daniels. *Arizona Legends and Lore: Tales of Southwestern Pioneers.* Phoenix: Golden West, 1991.

Anthony, C. V. *Fifty Years of Methodism: A History of the Methodist Episcopal Church within the Bounds of the California Annual Conference from 1847 to 1897.* San Francisco: Methodist Book Concern, 1901.

Arnold, Oren. "Slave Girl of the Mohaves." *Desert Magazine* 3, no. 5 (March 1940): 3–8.

———. *Thunder in the Southwest: Echoes from the Wild Frontier.* Norman: University of Oklahoma Press, 1952.

Arrington, Leonard J. *Brigham Young: An American Moses.* New York: Alfred A. Knopf, 1985.

Bancroft, Hubert Howe. *History of Arizona and New Mexico, 1530–1888.* San Francisco: History Company, 1889.

Banks, Leo. W. *Stalwart Women: Frontier Stories of Indomitable Spirit.* Wild West Collection 6. Phoenix: Arizona Highways Books, 1999.

Barnes, Will C. *Arizona Place Names.* Introduction by Bernard L. Fontana. Tucson: University of Arizona Press, 1988.

Barney, James M. "The Oatman Massacre" (parts 1, 2, 3). *The Sheriff* 7, no. 11 (November 1948): 11–13, 24–25; 7, no. 12 (December 1948): 13, 24–25; 8, no. 1 (January 1949): 6, 18–19.

Barry, Louise. *The Beginning of the West: Annals of the Kansas Gateway to the American West, 1540–1854.* Topeka: Kansas State Historical Society, 1972.

Bartlett, John Russell. *Personal Narrative of Explorations and Incidents in Texas, New Mexico, California, Sonora, and Chihuahua.* 2 vols. New York: D. Appleton, 1854.

Basso, Keith H. "Western Apache." In Ortiz, *Handbook of North American Indians,* Vol. 10, *Southwest,* 462–88.

Batman, Richard. *American Ecclesiastes: The Story of James Pattie.* New York: Harcourt Brace Jovanovich, 1984.

Beattie, George William, ed. "Diary of a Ferryman and Trader at Fort Yuma, 1855–1857." *Annual Publications of the Historical Society of Southern California* 19 (1928): 89–128.

Beckham, Stephen Dow. *Requiem for a People: The Rogue Indians and the Frontiersmen.* Norman: University of Oklahoma Press, 1971.

Bee, Robert L. "Quechan." In Ortiz, *Handbook of North American Indians,* Vol. 10, *Southwest,* 86–98.

Bell, James G. "A Log of the California Texas-California Cattle Trail, 1854," edited by J. Evetts Haley. *Southwestern Historical Quarterly* 35 (1932): 290–316.

Bennett, John C. *The History of the Saints: or, an Exposé of Joe Smith and Mormonism.* Boston: Leland and Whiting, 1842.

Biffle, Kent. "Old West Tale, Secrets Hidden behind a Veil." *Dallas Morning News,* August 7, 1994, 45A, 47A.

Bigler, David L., and Will Bagley. *Army of Israel: Mormon Battalion Narratives.* Spokane: Arthur H. Clark, 2000.

Bogdan, Robert. *Freak Show: Presenting Human Oddities for Amusement and Profit.* Chicago: University of Chicago Press, 1988.

The Book of Mormon: An Account Written by the Hand of Mormon, upon Plates Taken from the Plates of Nephi. Palmyra, N.Y.: E. B. Grandin, 1830.

Boyd, James P. *Recent Indians Wars.* Philadelphia: Publishers Union, 1891.

Braatz, Timothy. *Surviving Conquest: A History of the Yavapai Peoples.* Lincoln: University of Nebraska Press, 2003.

Braude, Ann. *Radical Spirits: Spiritualism and Women's Rights in Nineteenth-Century America.* Boston: Beacon Press, 1989.

Brewster, James Colin. *An Address to the Church of Christ, and Latter Day Saints.* Springfield, Ill., 1848.

———. *A Warning to the Latter Day Saints, Generally Called Mormons: An Abridgement of the Ninth Book of Esdras.* Springfield, Ill., 1845.

———. *The Words of Righteousness to All Men, Written from One of the Books of Esaras* [sic], *Which was Written by the Five Ready Writers, In the Forty Days, Which was Spoken of by Esaras, in His Second Book, Fourteenth Chapter of the Apocrypha, Being One of the Books Which Was Lost and Has Now come Forth, by the Gift of God, In the Last Days.* Springfield, Ill.: Ballard and Roberts, 1842.

Brodie, Fawn M. *No Man Knows My History: The Life of Joseph Smith, the Mormon Prophet.* New York: Alfred A. Knopf, 1945.

Brooks, James F. *Captives and Cousins: Slavery, Kinship, and Community in the Southwest Borderlands.* Chapel Hill: University of North Carolina Press, 2002.

Brown, James A. "Mound Builders." In *Encyclopedia of North American Indians,* edited by Frederick E. Hoxie, 398–401. Boston: Houghton Mifflin, 1996.

Browne, J. Ross. *Adventures in the Apache Country: A Tour through Arizona and Sonora, with Notes on the Silver Regions of Nevada.* New York: Harper and Bros., 1869.

———. "A Tour through Arizona." *Harper's New Monthly Magazine* 29 (1864): 689–711.

Bucke, Emory Stevens, ed. *The History of American Methodism.* Vol. 1. New York and Nashville: Abingdon Press, 1964.

Burt, Olive W. *Young Wayfarers of the Early West.* New York: Hawthorne Books, 1968.

Bushman, Richard L. *Joseph Smith and the Beginnings of Mormonism.* Urbana: University of Illinois Press, 1984.

Bynum, Lindley. Introduction to *Life among the Indians,* by Royal B. Stratton. San Francisco: Grabhorn Press, 1935. Reprinted in Lorenzo D. and Olive A. Oatman. *The Captivity of the Oatman Girls among the Apache and Mohave Indians.* New York: Dover, 1994.

Carmony, Neil B., and David F. Brown, eds. *Tough Times in Rough Places: Personal Narratives of Adventure, Death and Survival on the Western Frontier.* Silver City, N.M.: High-Lonesome Books, 1992.

Carter, Kate B. *Our Pioneer Heritage,* Vol. 16. Salt Lake City: Daughters of Utah Pioneers, 1973.

Castiglia, Christopher. *Bound and Determined: Captivity, Culture-Crossing, and White Womanhood from Mary Rowlandson to Patty Hearst.* Chicago: University of Chicago Press, 1996.

Catalogue of the University of the Pacific for the Academical Year 1857–'58, Santa Clara, California. San Francisco: Commercial Book and Job Steam Printing Establishment, 1858.

Clifford, Josephine. "A Romance of Gila Bend." *Overland Monthly and Out West Magazine* 9 (1872): 447–52.

Clark, Hal and Doris. *The Oatman Story.* Las Vegas, Nev.: H. and D. Clark's Quest, 2002.

Clohisy, Matt. "Olive Oatman: An Apache Captive." *The Westerners New York Posse Brand Book* 16, no. 2 (1969): 37–40.

Compton, Todd. *In Sacred Loneliness: The Plural Wives of Joseph Smith.* Salt Lake City: Signature Books, 1998.

Conklin, E[noch]. *Picturesque Arizona, Being the Result of Travels and Observations in Arizona during the Fall and Winter of 1877.* New York: Mining Record, 1878.

Conn, Howard J. *The First Congregational Church of Great Barrington 1743–1943.* Great Barrington, Mass.: Anniversary Year Committee, 1943.

Conner, Daniel Ellis. *Joseph Reddeford Walker and the Arizona Adventure.* Edited by Donald J. Berthrong and Odessa Davenport. Norman: University of Oklahoma Press, 1956.

Conrad, David E. "The Whipple Expedition in Arizona, 1853–1854." *Arizona and the West* 11 (1969): 147–78.

Corbusier, William F. "The Apache-Yumas and Apache-Mojaves." *American Antiquarian* 8 (1886): 276–339.

Corle, Edwin. *The Gila: River of the Southwest.* Rivers of America Series. New York: Rhinehart, 1951.

Cozzens, Samuel Woodworth. *The Marvellous Country; or, Three Years in Arizona and New Mexico, the Apaches' Home.* Boston: Lee and Shepard, 1867.

Cremony, John C. *Life among the Apaches.* San Francisco: A. Roman and Co., 1868.

Crutchfield, James A. *It Happened in Arizona.* Helena, Mont.: Falcon Press, 1994.

Crocheron, Augusta Joyce. *The Children's Book, a Collection of Short Stories and Poems: A Mormon Book for Mormon Children.* Bountiful, Utah: privately printed, 1890.

Curtis, Newton Martin. *From Bull Run to Chancellorsville: The Story of the Sixteenth New York Infantry Together with Personal Reminiscences.* New York: G. P. Putnam's Sons, 1906.

Davis, William W. *History of Whiteside County, Illinois from Its Earliest Settlement to 1908.* Vol. 2. Chicago: Pioneer, 1908.

Demos, John. *The Unredeemed Captive: A Family Story from Early America.* New York: Alfred A. Knopf, 1994.

Derounian-Stodola, Kathryn Zabelle. "The Captive and Her Editor: The Ciphering of Olive Oatman and Royal B. Stratton." *Prospects: An Annual of American Cultural Studies* 23 (1998): 171–92.

———. "The Indian Captivity Narratives of Mary Rowlandson and Olive Oatman: Case Studies in the Continuity, Evolution, and Exploitation of Literary Discourse." *Studies in the Literary Imagination* 27, no. 1 (Spring 1994): 33–46.

Derounian-Stodola, Kathryn Zabelle, and James Arthur Levernier. *The Indian Captivity Narrative, 1550–1900.* New York: Twayne, 1993.

Dillehay, Thomas D. *The Settlement of the Americas: A New Prehistory.* New York: Basic Books, 2000.

Dillon, Richard H. "Bound for Bashan." *Papers of the Bibliographical Society of America* 57 (1963): 449–53.

————. "The Ordeal of Olive Oatman." *American History* 30, no. 4 (1995): 30–32, 70–72.

————. The Search: An Apache Capture and the Filial Devotion of Lorenzo Oatman." *Montana The Magazine of Western History* 19, no. 2 (1969): 92–93.

————. "Tragedy at Oatman Flat: Massacre, Captivity, Mystery." *American West* 18, no. 2 (1981): 46–59.

The Doctrine and Covenants of the Church of Jesus Christ of Latter-day Saints. Salt Lake City: Church of Jesus Christ of Latter-day Saints, 1981.

Drannan, William F. *Thirty-one Years on the Plains and in the Mountains or, the Last Voice from the Plains: An Authentic Record of a Life Time of Hunting, Trapping, Scouting and Indian Fighting in the Far West by Capt. William F. Drannan, Who Went on to the Plains When Fifteen Years Old.* Chicago: Rhodes and McClure, 1900.

Drimmer, Frederick, ed. *Scalps and Tomahawks: Narratives of Indian Captivity.* New York: Coward-McCann, 1961. Reprinted as *Captured by the Indians: 15 Firsthand Accounts, 1750–1870.* New York: Dover, 1985.

Dunn, J. P. *Massacres of the Mountains: A History of the Indian Wars of the Far West.* New York: Harper and Bros., 1886.

Elliott, J. F. "The Great Western: Sarah Bowman, Mother and Mistress to the U.S. Army." *Journal of Arizona History* 30 (1989): 1–26.

Etter, Patricia A. *To California on the Southern Route, 1849: A History and Annotated Bibliography.* Spokane: Arthur H. Clark, 1998.

"An Excursion to the Coco-Maricopa Indians Upon the River Gila." *The Ladies' Repository (Cincinnati)* 15 (1855): 15–16.

Ezell, Paul H. "History of the Pima." In Ortiz, *Handbook of North American Indians,* Vol. 10, *Southwest,* 149–60.

Farish, Thomas Edwin. *History of Arizona.* 8 vols. Phoenix: Filmer Bros. Electrotype, 1915–18.

Faulk, Odie B. *Destiny Road: The Gila Trail and the Opening of the Southwest.* New York: Oxford University Press, 1973.

Faulring, Scott H., ed. *An American Prophet's Record: The Diaries and Journals of Joseph Smith.* Salt Lake City: Signature Books in association with Smith Research Associates, 1989.

The First Church Old South of Worcester, Massachusetts, Founded A. D. Seventeen Hundred and Sixteen: Bi-centennial Celebration, May Twenty-one to Twenty-eight Nineteen Hundred and Sixteen. Worcester, 1916.

Fisher, Lillian M. *Feathers in the Wind: The Story of Olive Oatman.* Alpine, Calif.: Two Bears, 1992. Reprinted, Unionville, N.Y.: Royal Fireworks Press, 2001.

Five Years among Wild Savages: The Renowned Apachee Captive, Miss Olive Oatman (broadside). Toledo, Ohio: Blade Print, n.d.

Flanders, Robert Bruce. *Nauvoo: Kingdom on the Mississippi*. Urbana: University of Illinois Press, 1965.

Forbes, Jack D. *Warriors of the Colorado: The Yumas of the Quechan Nation and Their Neighbors*. Norman: University of Oklahoma Press, 1965.

Foreman, Grant, ed. *A Pathfinder in the Southwest: The Itinerary of Lieutenant A. W. Whipple during His Explorations for a Railway Route from Fort Smith to Los Angeles in the Years 1853 & 1854*. Norman: University of Oklahoma Press, 1941.

Frisbie, Barnes. *History of Middletown, Vermont*. Bicentennial ed. Middletown, Vt.: Middletown Springs Historical Society, 1975.

Galvin, Lynn. "Cloudwoman: The Life of Olive Oatman, an Old California Indian Captive." *The Californians* 13, no. 2 (1996): 10–19.

Gifford, Edward W. *Northeastern and Western Yavapai*. Berkeley: University of California Press, 1936.

Gilfillan, Mrs. R. H. "An Interesting Letter about Olive Oatman." In R. B. Stratton, *Captivity of the Oatman Girls: A True Story of Early Emigration to the West*. Revised and abridged by Chas. H. Jones. Salem, Ore.: Oregon Teachers Monthly, 1909.

Goodwin, Grenville. *The Social Organization of the Western Apache*. Chicago: University of Chicago Press, 1942.

Granger, Byrd Howell. *Arizona's Names (X Marks the Place)*. Tucson: Falconer, distributed by Treasure Chest Publications, 1983.

Grayson County Frontier Village. *The History of Grayson County, Texas*. Winston-Salem, N.C.: Grayson County Frontier Village and Hunter Publishing, 1979.

Greene, Max. *The Kanzas Region: Forest, Prairie, Desert, Mountain, Vale, and River*. New York: Fowler and Wells, 1856.

Gregg, Thomas. *History of Hancock County, Illinois*. Chicago: Chas. C. Chapman and Co., 1880.

Hafen, LeRoy R., and Ann W. Hafen. Introduction to *Rufus B. Sage, His Letters and Papers, 1836–1847, with an Annotated Reprint of his "Scenes in the Rocky Mountains and in Oregon, California, New Mexico, Texas, and the Grand Prairies,"* edited by LeRoy R. Hafen and Ann W. Haven, 1:13–27. 2 vols. Glendale, Calif.: Arthur H. Clark Co., 1956.

Haley, J. Evetts. *The Diary of Michael Erskine Describing His Cattle Drive from Texas to California, Together with Correspondence from the Gold Fields 1854–1859*. Midland, Tex.: Nita Stewart Haley Memorial Library, 1979.

Hall, Sharlot M. "Olive A. Oatman—Her Captivity with the Apache Indians, and Her Later Life." *Out West* 29, no. 3 (1908): 216–27.

Hansen, Klaus J. *Quest for Empire: The Political Kingdom of God and the Council of Fifty in Mormon History*. East Lansing: Michigan State University Press, 1967.

Hardman, Keith J. *Charles Grandison Finney, 1792–1875, Revivalist and Reformer*. Syracuse, N.Y.: Syracuse University Press, 1987.

Harwell, Henry O., and Marsha C. S. Kelly. "Maricopa." In Ortiz, *Handbook of North American Indians*, Vol. 10, *Southwest*, 71–85. Washington, D.C., Smithsonian Institution, 1983.

Heard, J. Norman. *White into Red: A Study of the Assimilation of White Persons Captured by Indians*. Metuchen, N.J.: Scarecrow Press, 1973.

Heintzelman, Samuel P. *A Transcription of Major Samuel P. Heintzelman's Journal, 1 January 1851–31 December 1853*. Transcribed by Creola Blackwell. Yuma, Ariz.: Yuma County Historical Society, 1989.

Heizer, R. F. Review of "Life among the Indians: Being an Interesting Narrative of the Captivity of the Oatman Girls among the Apache and Mohave Indians. Royal B. Stratton." *Journal of California Anthropology* 5, no. 1 (summer 1978): 133–34.

Hemenway, Abby Maria, ed. *The Vermont Historical Gazetteer: A Magazine*. Claremont, N.H., 1877.

Hill, Donna. *Joseph Smith, the First Mormon*. Garden City, N.Y.: Doubleday, 1977.

Hirshson, Stanley P. *The Lion of the Lord: A Biography of Brigham Young*. New York: Alfred A. Knopf, 1969.

History of the Pacific Northwest: Oregon and Washington. Portland: North Pacific History Co., 1889.

The History of the Reorganized Church of Jesus Christ of Latter Day Saints. Vol. 3. Independence, Mo.: Herald House, 1987.

History of Southern Oregon. Portland: A. G. Walling, 1884.

Hoxie, Frederick E., ed. *Encyclopedia of North American Indians*. Boston: Houghton Mifflin, 1996.

Hubbard, Freeman H. "Wife of the Chief." *True West* 6, no. 2 (November–December, 1958): 16–17, 37–39.

Hughes, Samuel. "The Murder at Oatman's Flat." *The Arizona Graphic* (October 28, 1899): 4, 7. Reprinted in *Tucson Citizen*, September 26, 1913, 4; and *Arizona Sheriff* 30, no. 2 (May 1977): 4–8, 38–40. Also reprinted in Joseph Miller. *The Arizona Story, Compiled and Edited from Original Newspaper Sources*, 14–21. New York: Hastings House, 1952.

Hurtado, Albert L. *Intimate Frontiers: Sex, Gender, and Culture in Old California.* Albuquerque: University of New Mexico Press, 1999.

Iverson, Peter. *Carlos Montezuma and the Changing World of the American Indians.* Albuquerque: University of New Mexico Press, 1982.

Jackson, Earl. *Tumacacori's Yesterdays.* 2nd printing, revised. Globe, Ariz.: Southwest Parks and Monuments Association, 1973.

Kessell, John L. *Friars, Soldiers, and Reformers: Hispanic Arizona and the Sonora Mission Frontier, 1767–1856.* Tucson: University of Arizona Press, 1976.

Kestler, Frances Roe, comp. *The Indian Captivity Narrative: A Woman's View.* New York: Garland, 1990.

Khera, Sigrid, and Patricia S. Mariella. "Yavapai." In Ortiz, *Handbook of North American Indians,* vol. 10, *Southwest,* 38–54.

Kimball, Stanley B. *Historic Sites and Markers along the Mormon and Other Great Western Trails.* Urbana: University of Illinois Press, 1999.

King, Frank M. *Pioneer Western Empire Builders: A True Story of the Men and Women of Pioneer Days.* N.p.: privately printed: 1946. Reprinted Pasadena, Calif.: Trail's End, n.d.

Koch, Harry A. "The Oatman Massacre (1850)." *Arizona Sheriff* 30, no. 2 (May 1977): between pp. 36 and 37.

Kroeber, A. L. *Handbook of the Indians of California.* Bulletin 78 of the Bureau of American Ethnology of the Smithsonian Institution. Washington, D.C., Government Printing Office, 1925. Reprint: New York: Dover, 1976.

———. "Olive Oatman's Return." *Kroeber Anthropological Society Papers* 4 (1951): 1–18.

———. "The Route of James O. Pattie on the Colorado in 1826: A Reappraisal by A. L. Kroeber [with comments by R. C. Euler and A. H. Schroder]." Edited by Clifton B. Kroeber. *Arizona and the West* 6 (1964): 119–36.

Kroeber, A. L., and Clifton B. Kroeber. *A Mohave War Reminiscence, 1854–1880.* University of California Publications in Anthropology, vol. 10. Berkeley and Los Angeles: University of California Press, 1973. Reprinted, New York: Dover, 1994.

———. "Olive Oatman's First Account of Her Captivity among the Mohave." *California Historical Society Quarterly* 41 (1962): 309–17.

Kroeber, Clifton B., and Bernard L. Fontana. *Massacre on the Gila: An Account of the Last Major Battle between American Indians, with Reflections on the Origin of War.* Tucson: University of Arizona Press, 1986.

Krythe, Maymie R. "The Oatman Family." *Ranch Romances,* April 29, 1949, 42–45.

Lampman, Evelyn Sibley. *White Captives.* New York: Atheneum, 1975.

Lankford, Kelly I. "Olive Oatman." In *Encyclopedia of the American West,* edited by Charles Phillips and Alan Axelrod. 3:1211–12. New York: Macmillan Reference USA, 1996.

Launius, Roger D. *The Kirtland Temple: A Historical Narrative.* Independence, Mo.: Herald House, 1986.

Lawton, Wendy. *Ransom's Mark: A Story Based on the Life of the Pioneer Olive Oatman.* Daughters of the Faith Series. Chicago: Moody, 2003.

Lewis, Oscar. *The Autobiography of the West: Personal Narratives of the Discovery and Settlement of the American West.* New York: Henry Holt, 1958.

Locher, Frederick. "When Death Stalked Santa Fe Trail." *California Highway Patrolman* 16, no. 2 (March 1952): 13, 79–83.

"'Lo! The Indian' Captive!" (broadside). Rome, N.Y.: A. Sandford, Printer, February 3, 1859. Copy in the Sophia Smith Collection. Smith College. Northampton, Mass.

Love, Frank. *Hell's Outpost: A History of Old Fort Yuma.* Yuma, Ariz.: Yuma Crossing, 1992.

Lyman, Edward Leo. *San Bernardino: The Rise and Fall of a California Community.* Salt Lake City: Signature Books, 1996.

Maloney, Alice Bay, ed. "Some Oatman Documents." *California Historical Society Quarterly* 21 (1941): 107–12.

Manual and Catalogue of the (First Church) Old South, Worcester, Mass., July 1, 1877. Worcester: Noyes, Snow and Co., 1877.

Marquardt, H. Michael, and Wesley P. Walters. *Inventing Mormonism: Tradition and the Historical Record.* Salt Lake City: Smith Research Associates, distributed by Signature Books, 1994.

Martin, Douglas D. *Yuma Crossing.* Albuquerque: University of New Mexico Press, 1954.

Matthews, Glenna. *The Rise of Public Woman: Woman's Power and Woman's Place in the United States, 1630–1970.* New York: Oxford University Press, 1992.

McClintock, James H. *Arizona: Prehistoric—Aboriginal, Pioneer—Modern: The Nation's Youngest Commonwealth within a Land of Ancient Culture.* 3 vols. Chicago: S. J. Clarke, 1916.

McConkie, Bruce R. *Mormon Doctrine.* 2nd ed. Salt Lake City: Bookcraft, 1966.

McKiernan, F. Mark. *The Voice of One Crying in the Wilderness: Sidney Rigdon, Religious Reformer 1793–1876.* Independence, Mo.: Herald House, 1979.

McLeRoy, Sherrie W. "Olive Ann Oatman Fairchild." In *The New Handbook of Texas*, 2:934. Austin: Texas State Historical Association, 1996.

McNamee, Gregory. *Gila: The Life and Death of an American River.* Library of the American West, edited by Herman J. Viola. New York: Orion Books, 1994.

Miller, David E., and Della S. Miller. *Nauvoo: The City of Joseph.* Santa Barbara and Salt Lake City: Peregrine Smith, 1974.

Miller, Joseph. *The Arizona Story, Compiled from Original Newspaper Sources.* New York: Hastings House, 1952.

Minutes of the California Annual Conference, M. E. Church, Fourth Session, Held in San Jose, California, Aug. 27th–Sept. 3d, 1856. San Francisco: Sterett and Co., 1856.

Minutes of the California Annual Conference, of the Methodist Episcopal Church, Fifth Session, Held in San Francisco, California, Sept. 17th to 24th, 1857. San Francisco: B. F. Sterett, 1857.

Minutes of the California Annual Conference of the Methodist Episcopal Church Seventh Session, Held at Petaluma, September 15th to 20th, A. D. 1859. San Francisco: Commercial Book and Job Steam Presses, 1859.

Minutes of the California Annual Conference of the Methodist Episcopal Church, Eighth Session, Held at Santa Clara, September 12th to 18th, 1860. San Francisco: B. F. Sterett, 1860.

Möllhausen, Balduin. *Diary of a Journey from the Mississippi to the Coasts of the Pacific with a United States Government Expedition.* Translated by Mrs. Percy Sinnett. 2 vols. London: Longman, Brown, Green, Longmans, and Roberts, 1858.

Morgan, Dale L. "A Bibliography of the Church of Jesus Christ of Latter Day Saints [Strangite]." *Western Humanities Review* 5 (1950–51) 43–114.

———. *A Bibliography of the Churches of the Dispersion.* No pub., n.d. (introduction reprinted from *Western Humanities Review* 7 (1953): 255–66).

Munro, Pamela, Nellie Brown, and Judith G. Crawford. *A Mojave Dictionary.* Los Angeles: Department of Linguistics, University of California, Los Angeles, 1992.

Murray, Iain H. *Revival and Revivalism: The Making and Marring of American Evangelicalism, 1750–1858.* Edinburgh, Scotland, and Carlisle, Penn.: Banner of Truth Trust, 1994.

Namias, June. *White Captives: Gender and Ethnicity on Successive American Frontiers.* Chapel Hill: University of North Carolina Press, 1993.

Nichols, Johanna. "Linguistic Diversity and the First Settlement of the New World." *Language* 66 (1990): 475–521.

Oaks, George Washington. *Man of the West: Reminiscences of George Washington Oaks, 1840–1917.* Recorded by Ben Jaastad. Edited by Arthur Woodward. Tucson: Arizona Pioneers' Historical Society, 1956.

Oatman, Olive. "Olive Ann Oatman's Lecture Notes and Oatman Bibliography." Edited by Edward J. Pettid. *San Bernardino County Museum Association Quarterly* 16, no. 2 (1968): ii, 1–39.

Odens, Peter. *Fire over Yuma: Tales from the Lower Colorado.* Yuma, Ariz.: Southwest Printers, 1966.

Oettermann, Stephan. "On Display: Tattooed Entertainers in America and Germany." In *Written on the Body: The Tattoo in European and American History,* edited by Jane Caplan, 193–211. Princeton: Princeton University Press, 2000.

The Olive Branch, or Herald of Peace and Truth to all Saints. 4 vols. Kirtland, Ohio, and Springfield, Ill.: 1848–1850.

Ormsby, Waterman L. *The Butterfield Overland Mail by Waterman L. Ormsby, Only Through Passenger on the First Westbound Stage,* Edited by Lyle H. Wright and Josephine M. Bynum. San Marino, Calif.: Huntington Library, 1954.

Ortiz, Alfonso, ed. *Handbook of North American Indians.* Vol. 10, *Southwest.* Washington, D.C.: Smithsonian Institution, 1983.

Parrish, Susan Thompson Lewis. *Following the Pot of Gold at the Rainbow's End in the Days of 1850, by Virginia V. Root.* Edited by Leonore Rowland. Downey, Calif.: Elena Quinn, 1960.

Pattie, James O. *Personal Narrative of James O. Pattie.* Edited by Richard Batman. Missoula, Mont.: Mountain Press, 1988.

Peckham, Howard H. *Captured by Indians: True Tales of Pioneer Survivors.* New Brunswick, N.J.: Rutgers University Press, 1954.

Peplow, Edward H., Jr. *History of Arizona.* 3 vols. New York: Lewis Historical, 1958.

———. "Women of the Old West." *Outdoor Arizona* 46, no. 7 (1973): 23–26, 43–46.

Pettid, Edward J., S. J. "Henry Stuart Hewit, M. D." *Arizona Medicine* 26, no. 1 (1969): 62–70.

———. Introduction to "Olive Ann Oatman's Lecture Notes and Oatman Bibliography." Edited by Edward J. Pettid. *San Bernardino County Museum Association Quarterly* 16, no. 2 (1968): ii.

———. "John Lawrence Le Conte, M. D." (parts 1 and 2). *Arizona Medicine* 23, no. 10 (1976): 843–45; no. 11 (1976): 956–59.

———. "Listen, Mohaves!" *Smoke Signals (Parker, Ariz.)* 13, no. 3 (September 15, 1968): 1–2.

———. "The Oatman Story: A Frontier Tragedy." *Arizona Highways* 44, no. 11 (1968): 4–9.

Pilkington, James Penn. *The Methodist Publishing House: A History.* Vol. 1, *Beginnings to 1870.* New York: Abingdon Press, 1968.

Portrait and Biographical Album of Whiteside County, Illinois. Chicago: Chapman Bros., 1885.

Poston, Charles D. "The Oatman Family." *Phoenix Daily Herald,* June 6, 1891, 1.

Putzi, Jennifer. "'Tattooed still': The Inscription of Female Agency in Elizabeth Stoddard's *The Morgesons.*" *Legacy* 17 (2000): 165–73.

Rasmussen, Cecilia. "Tale of Kindness Didn't Fit Notion of Savage Indian." *Los Angeles Times,* July 17, 2000, B8.

Rau, Margaret. *The Ordeal of Olive Oatman: A True Story of the American West.* Greensboro, N.C.: Morgan Reynolds, 1997.

Rice, William B. "The Captivity of Olive Oatman—A Newspaper Account." *California Historical Society Quarterly* 21 (1941): 97–106.

———. *The Los Angeles Star, 1851–1864: The Beginnings of Journalism in Southern California.* Edited by John Walton Caughey. Berkeley and Los Angeles: University of California Press, 1947.

Roberts, B. H. *A Comprehensive History of the Church of Jesus Christ of Latter-day Saints, Century I.* Vol. 2. Salt Lake City: Church Deseret News Press, 1930.

———. *Studies of the Book of Mormon.* Edited by Brigham D. Madsen. Urbana: University of Illinois Press, 1985.

Ronstadt, Federico José María. *Borderman: Memoirs of Federico José María Ronstadt.* Edited by Edward F. Ronstadt. Foreword by Bernard L. Fontana. Albuquerque: University of New Mexico Press, 1993.

Ruffner, Budge. *All Hell Needs Is Water.* Illustrations by Helen Shackelford. Tucson: University of Arizona Press, 1972.

Ruland-Thorne, Kate. *Yavapai: The People of the Red Rocks, the People of the Sun.* Edited by Aliza Caillou. Sedona, Ariz.: Thorne Enterprises, 1993.

"Sacramento Theater! . . . Second Night Of the new original play, dramatized by Mr. C. E. Bingham. . . . The Captivity and Massacre of the Oatman Family! By the Apache & Mohave Indians!" (broadside). Sacramento: Daily Bee Print, [1857]. Newberry Library. Chicago.

Sage, Rufus B. *Rufus B. Sage, His Letters and Papers, 1836–1847, with an Annotated Reprint of his "Scenes in the Rocky Mountains and in Oregon, California, New*

Mexico, Texas, and the Grand Prairies. "Edited by LeRoy R. Hafen and Ann W. Haven. 2 vols. Glendale, Calif.: Arthur H. Clark Co., 1956.

Sandwich, Brian. *The Great Western: Legendary Lady of the Southwest.* Southwestern Studies 94. Texas Western Press, University of Texas at El Paso, 1991.

Santiago, Mark. *Massacre at the Yuma Crossing: Spanish Relations with the Quechans, 1779–1782.* Tucson: University of Arizona Press, 1998.

"Saved from a Life of Indian Slavery!" *Butterfield Express* 1, no. 12 (October 1963): 1, 5–6.

Schroeder, Albert H. *A Study of Yavapai History.* Santa Fe: National Park Service, 1954.

Schwartz, E. A. *The Rogue River Indian War and Its Aftermath, 1850–1980.* Norman: University of Oklahoma Press, 1997.

Scott, H. W., ed. *History of Portland, Oregon.* Syracuse, N.Y.: D. Mason and Co., 1890.

Scott, Peter Dale. "Olive Oatman." *Critical Quarterly (Oxford and Cambridge, UK)* 37 (1995): 91–93.

Sheldon, Francis E. "Pioneer Illustration in California." *Overland Monthly* (2d series) 11 (1888): 337–52.

Sherer, Lorraine. *Bitterness Road: The Mojave, 1604 to 1860.* Ballena Press Anthropological Papers 41, edited by Sylvia Brakke Vane. Menlo Park, Calif.: Ballena Press, 1994.

———. *The Clan System of the Fort Mojave Indians.* Los Angeles: Historical Society of Southern California, 1965.

———. "Great Chieftains of the Mojave Indians." *Southern California Quarterly* 48 (1966): 1–35.

Sheridan, Thomas E. *Arizona: A History.* Tucson: University of Arizona Press, 1995.

Shipps, Jan. *Mormonism: The Story of a New Religious Tradition.* Urbana: University of Illinois Press, 1985.

Shoumatoff, Alex. *Legends of the American Desert: Sojourns in the Greater Southwest.* New York: Alfred A. Knopf, 1997.

Smith, Dean. "A Desert Massacre." *Arizona Trend* 3, no. 6 (1989): 71–73.

Smith, Ethan. *View of the Hebrews: or the Tribes of Israel in America.* Poultney, Vt.: Smith and Shute, 1825.

Smith, Joseph, Jr. *The History of the Church of Jesus Christ of Latter-day Saints.* Vol. 5. Edited by B. H. Roberts. Salt Lake City: Deseret Book Co., 1964.

Smith, Robert Benjamin. "Apache Captives' Ordeal." *Wild West* 6, no. 1 (June 1993): 42–48, 80.

Smythe, William E. *History of San Diego, 1542–1907.* San Diego: History Co., 1907.

Sorensen, Cloyd, Jr. "The Oatman Massacre Site." *The Wrangler of the San Diego Corral, the Westerners* 4, no. 2 (1971): 1, 4–5.

Sperry, Charles. "Life of Charles Sperry." In *Our Pioneer Heritage,* Vol. 9. Edited by Kate B. Carter. Salt Lake City: Daughters of Utah Pioneers, 1966.

Spicer, Edward H. *Cycles of Conquest: The Impact of Spain, Mexico, and the United States on the Indians of the Southwest, 1533–1960.* Tucson: University of Arizona Press, 1962.

Spier, Leslie. *Yuman Tribes of the Gila River.* Chicago: University of Chicago Press, 1933. Reprinted, New York: Dover, 1978.

Stearns, Orsen Avery. *Reminiscences of Pioneer Days and Early Settlers of Phoenix and Vicinity (and) a Brief Sketch of the Life and Character of Samuel Colver.* Ashland, Ore., 1921–1922.

Stewart, Kenneth M. "A Brief History of the Mohave Indians since 1850." *The Kiva* 34 (1969): 219–36.

———. "Mohave." In Ortiz, *Handbook of North American Indians,* Vol. 10, *Southwest,* 55–70.

Stockton, Charles W., and Gordon C. Jacoby, Jr. *Long-term Surface Water-Supply and Streamflow Trends in the Upper Colorado River Basin.* Lake Powell Research Project Bulletin 18. Institute of Geophysics and Planetary Physics, University of California, Los Angeles, 1976.

Stott, G. St. John. "New Jerusalem Abandoned: The Failure to Carry Mormonism to the Delaware." *Journal of American Studies* 21 (1987): 71–85.

Stratton, Royal B. *Captivity of the Oatman Girls: Being an Interesting Narrative of Life Among the Apache and Mohave Indians: Containing also An interesting account of the Massacre of the Oatman Family, by the Apache Indians, in 1851; the narrow escape of Lorenzo D. Oatman; the Capture of Olive A. and Mary A. Oatman; the Death by Starvation of the latter; the Five Years Suffering and Captivity of Olive A. Oatman; also, her singular recapture in 1856; as given by Lorenzo D. and Olive A. Oatman, the only surviving members of the family, to the author, R. B. Stratton.* San Francisco: Whitton, Towne and Co.; Chicago: Charles Scott and Co., 1857.

———. *Captivity of the Oatman Girls: Being an Interesting Narrative of Life among the Apache and Mohave Indians, containing an Interesting Account of the Massacre of the Oatman Family, by the Apache Indians, in 1851; the Narrow Escape of Lorenzo D. Oatman; the Capture of Olive A. and Mary A. Oatman; the*

Death, by Starvation, of the Latter; the Five Years' Suffering and Captivity of Olive A. Oatman; also, Her Singular Recapture in 1856; as Given by Lorenzo D. and Olive A. Oatman, the Only Surviving Members of the Family, to the Author, R. B. Stratton. New York: Carlton and Porter, 1858.

———. *Captivity of the Oatman Girls, a True Story of Early Emigration to the West.* Revised and abridged by Charles H. Jones. Salem, Ore.: Oregon Teachers Monthly, 1909.

———. *Captivity of the Oatman Girls.* Upper Saddle River, N.J.: Literature House / Gregg Press, 1970.

———. *Captivity of the Oatman Girls.* Lincoln: University of Nebraska Press, 1983.

———. *The Captivity of the Oatman Girls among the Apache and Mohave Indians.* Illustrations by Mallette Dean. New York: Dover, 1994.

———. *Church Government: A Sermon Preached in the Arbor Hill M. E. Church, March 2, 1862, by Rev. R. B. Stratton on Church Government, Its True Place and Use.* Albany, New York: Weed, Parsons and Co., 1862.

———. *Life Among the Indians: Being an Interesting Narrative of the Captivity of the Oatman Girls, Among the Apache and Mohave Indians, containing also An interesting account of the Massacre of the Oatman Family, by the Apache Indians, in 1851; the narrow escape of Lorenzo D. Oatman; the Capture of Olive A. and Mary A. Oatman; the Death by Starvation of the latter; the Five Years Suffering and Captivity of Olive A. Oatman; also, her singular recapture in 1856; as given by Lorenzo D. and Olive A. Oatman, the only surviving members of the family, to the author, R. B. Stratton.* San Francisco: Whitton, Towne and Co., 1857.

———. *Life Among the Indians, or: The Captivity of the Oatman Girls among the Apache & Mohave Indians; Containing also: An interesting account of the Massacre of the Oatman Family, by the Apache Indians in 1851; the narrow escape of Lorenzo D. Oatman; the Death by Starvation of the latter; the Five Years' Suffering and Captivity of Olive A. Oatman; also, her singular recapture in 1856; as given by Lorenzo D. & Olive A. Oatman, the only surviving members of the family, to the author, R. B. Stratton.* Introduction by Lindley Bynum. Illustrations by Mallette Dean. Rare Americana, 3rd ser., no. 2. San Francisco: Grabhorn Press, 1935.

———. *Life among the Indians: Captivity of the Oatman Girls.* New York: Garland, 1977.

———. *Captivity of the Oatman Girls: Being an Interesting Narrative of Life among the Apache and Mohave Indians, containing an Interesting Account of the Massacre of the Oatman Family, by the Apache Indians, in 1851; the Narrow*

Escape of Lorenzo D. Oatman; the Capture of Olive A. and Mary A. Oatman; the Death, by Starvation, of the Latter; the Five Years' Suffering and Captivity of Olive A. Oatman; also, Her Singular Recapture in 1856; as Given by Lorenzo D. and Olive A. Oatman, the Only Surviving Members of the Family, to the Author, R. B. Stratton. Alexandria, Va.: Time-Life Books, 1982.

———. *A Sermon Delivered on Thanksgiving Day, November 24th, 1864, in the First Congregational Church, Great Barrington, Mass., by Rev. R. B. Stratton.* Lee, Mass.: Josiah A. Royce, 1865.

Sullivan, Freyda. "Ordeal of the Oatmans: Family Massacred, Olive Oatman Was Captured, Sold as Slave, Rescued." *National Tombstone Epitaph,* May 1982, 1, 6–10.

Taylor, Edith S., and William J. Wallace. *Mohave Tattooing and Face-Painting.* Southwest Museum Leaflets 20. Los Angeles: Southwest Museum, 1947.

Taylor, Paul. "Oatman Massacre Causes National Furor." *Indian Trader (Gallup, N.M.)* 9, no. 10 (1985): 15–16, 21.

Thrapp, Dan L. *The Conquest of Apacheria.* Norman: University of Oklahoma Press, 1967.

———. *Encyclopedia of Frontier Biography.* 3 vols. Lincoln and Spokane: University of Nebraska Press in association with Arthur H. Clarke Co., 1988.

Tramp, John C. *Prairie and Rocky Mountain Adventures.* Columbus, Ohio: Segner and Condit, 1870.

Trimble, Stephen. *The People: Indians of the American Southwest.* Santa Fe: School of American Research, 1993.

Utley, Robert M. *The Indian Frontier of the American West, 1846–1890.* Albuquerque: University of New Mexico Press, 1984.

Van Dyke, T. S. *The City and County of San Diego.* San Diego: Leberthon and Taylor, 1888.

Van Noord, Roger. *King of Beaver Island: The Life and Assassination of James Jesse Strang.* Urbana: University of Illinois Press, 1988.

Van Wagoner, Richard S. *Sidney Rigdon: A Portrait of Religious Excess.* Salt Lake City: Signature Books, 1994.

Vogel, Dan. *Indian Origins and the Book of Mormon: Religious Solutions from Columbus to Joseph Smith.* Salt Lake City: Signature Books, 1986.

———. "James Colin Brewster: The Boy Prophet Who Challenged Mormon Authority." In *Differing Visions: Dissenters in Mormon History,* edited by Roger D. Launius and Linda Thatcher. Urbana: University of Illinois Press, 1994.

[Wallace, William A.] "Olive Oatman, the Apache Captive." *Los Angeles Star,* April 19, 1856, 1.

[Walling, A. G.] *History of Southern Oregon.* Portland: A. G. Walling, 1884.

Washburn, Wilcomb E. Foreword to *Captivity of the Oatman Girls,* by Royal B. Stratton, v–xv. Lincoln: University of Nebraska Press, 1983.

———. Introduction to *Narratives of North American Indian Captivity: A Selective Bibliography.* Edited by Alden T. Vaughan. New York: Garland, 1983.

Weber, David J. *The Taos Trappers: The Fur Trade in the Far Southwest, 1540–1846.* Norman: University of Oklahoma Press, 1968.

Wells, Edmund. *Argonaut Tales: Stories of the Gold Seekers and the Indian Scouts of Early Arizona.* New York: Frederick H. Hitchcock, 1927.

Wells, Harry L. *History of Siskiyou County, California.* Oakland: D. J. Stewart and Co., 1881.

Whipple, Amiel Weeks. *A Pathfinder in the Southwest: The Itinerary of Lieutenant A. W. Whipple during His Explorations for a Railway Route from Fort Smith to Los Angeles in the Years 1843 and 1854.* Edited by Grant Foreman. Norman: University of Oklahoma Press, 1941.

Werner, Emmy E. *Pioneer Children on the Journey West.* Boulder, Colo.; Westview Press, 1995.

Widstoe, John A. *Joseph Smith: Seeker after Truth, Prophet of God.* Salt Lake City: Bookcraft, 1951.

Williams, Anita Alvarez de. "Cocopa." In Ortiz, *Handbook of North American Indians,* Vol. 10, *Southwest,* 99–112.

Willson, Roscoe G. "Chapter One in the Tragedy of the Oatman Family," "Concluding Chapter in the Tragedy of the Oatman Family, and "Did Olive Marry a Mohave Chief?" *Arizona Days and Ways* (magazine section of the *Arizona Republic*), June 13, 1954, 6; June 20, 1954, 6; June 27, 1954, 9.

Yount, George C. *George C. Yount and his Chronicles of the West.* Edited by Charles L. Camp. Denver: Old West, 1956.

Index